Studies in Christian Philosophy

A Virtue Ethical View of Trinitarian Sanctification, Ronald M. Rothenberg
Omniscience, Foreknowledge, and the Problem of Divine Freedom, Graham Floyd

A Virtue Ethical View of
Trinitarian Sanctification

A Virtue Ethical View of
Trinitarian Sanctification

Jesus' Roles as Teacher, Example, and Priest

Ronald M. Rothenberg

Fontes

A Virtue Ethical View of Trinitarian Sanctification:
Jesus' Roles as Teacher, Example, and Priest

Copyright © 2019 by Ronald M. Rothenberg

ISBNs:
978-1-948048-08-8 (hardback)
978-1-948048-09-5 (paperback)

All rights reserved. No part of this publication may be reproduced, stored in a retrieval system, or transmitted in any form or by any means—electronic, mechanical, photocopy, recording, or any other—except for brief quotations in printed reviews, without the prior permission of the publisher.

Unless otherwise noted, all translations are by the author. Scriptures cited or translated from Novum Testamentum Graece, 28th Edition, Stuttgart: Deutsche Bibelgesellschaft, 2012 and Biblia Hebraica Stuttgartensia, Logos Bible Software, 2006.

FONTES PRESS
DALLAS, TX
www.fontespress.com

To Jesus Christ,
our beloved Lord and Savior,
be honor and glory forever,
and to
Joanna,
beloved wife
and
precious gift from God.

Contents

Abbreviations xiii
Preface xvii
Introduction 1
   Problem and Background 2
   Thesis 7
   Argument and Overview 8
   Methodology 8

1. Three Historic Backgrounds: Trinitarianism, Virtue Ethics, and
   Sanctification 13
   The Impact of Trinitarian Proponents on Sanctification 13
      A Selective History of the Trinity 14
      Critical Appropriation of Trinitarian Sanctification 17
   The Impact of the Eclipse and Resurgence of Virtue Ethics on
   Sanctification 20
      A Selective History of Virtue Ethics 21
      Critical Appropriation of Virtue Ethical Sanctification 23
   The Historical Development of the Doctrine of Sanctification 26
      A Selective History of Sanctification 27
      The Definition of Sanctification: Positional and Progressive 38
      Assessment of the Position-only View 39
   Conclusion 46

2. Defining Virtue Ethics in Sanctification: Nature and Function 51
   Toward a Definition of Virtue Ethics: Contemporary Issues in Ethics 52
      Three Types of Virtue Ethics 57
      Metaphysical Realism is Biblically Consistent—Nominalism is Not 62
   Three Historic Sources of Virtue Ethics: Aristotle, Augustine, Aquinas 71
      Aristotle's Virtue Ethics 71
      Augustine's Virtue Ethics 72
      Aquinas' Virtue Ethics 74
   Definition by Biblical-Theological Historical Synthesis 75
   Conclusion 76

3. Jesus' Roles as Teacher and Example 79
   The Existence of the Theological Virtues in the Teaching of Jesus 81
   Jesus' Teaching as Moral Motivation 85
      Faith as a Motive in Luke 18:1–8 85
      Love as a Motive in John 14:15, 23 86
      Endurance as a Motive in Luke 8:1–15 87
      An Objection and Conclusion 88
      Motivational Internalism 89
      Objections and Responses 91

    Application: The Process of Sanctification (Virtues as Cognition and Motivation) ... 93
    Jesus' Example: Imitation of Virtue by Habituation and Reciprocity ... 95
        Imitating Christ's Example ... 96
        Imitation by Habituation ... 97
        Imitation by Reciprocity ... 100
        Objections (Sola fide) and Responses ... 106
    Application: The Believer's Responsibility in Sanctification as a Process ... 110
    Jesus' Active Sanctification through the Word: Ephesians 5:25–33; Hebrews 4:12 ... 112
        Ephesians 5:25–33 ... 112
        Hebrews 4:12 ... 117
    Statement of Virtue Ethical Trinitarian Sanctification Ordered by the Triune Premise ... 119
    Conclusion ... 120

4. Jesus' Role as Priest ... 123
    An Introduction to the Doctrine of Christ's Heavenly Intercession ... 123
        Four Historic Interpretations of the Intercession ... 125
    Linguistic and Thematic Connection of Intercession Passages ... 129
    Virtue Ethical Trinitarian Sanctification in Romans 8:14–16, 26–28, 34 ... 130
        Romans 8:34: The Son's Intercession ... 130
        Romans 8:14–16, 26–27: The Spirit's Intercession ... 131
        Romans 8:27–28, 33: The Father and the Intercession ... 135
    The Canonical Context: Brief Consideration of Supplementary Intercession Passages ... 136
        Hebrews 2:14–18; 4:14–16 ... 136
        John 17:17, 19 ... 139
        Zechariah 3:1–2 ... 141
    Jesus' Active Intercessory Sanctification ... 142
    Statement of Virtue Ethical Trinitarian Sanctification Ordered by the Triune Premise ... 144
    Application: The Believer's Experience of Prayer("Father Primarily" Prayer) ... 145
    Conclusion ... 148

Conclusion ... 149
    Summary of Conclusions ... 150
    Contribution ... 151
    Continued Research ... 153
    A Final Exhortation to the Church ... 154

Appendix 1 Table A1: Overview of the History of Sanctification ... 156

Appendix 2 Table A2: Theological and Associated Virtues in the Epistles ... 158

Appendix 3 Table A3: Theological and Associated Virtues in the Gospels ... 160

Appendix 4 Table A4: Four Views of the Intercession of Christ 166
Appendix 5 Table A 5: Linguistic and Thematic Connection of
Intercession Passages 168
Appendix 6: The Issue of John 16:26–27 and the Two Intercessions 170
Bibliography 173

Abbreviations

APQ	*American Philosophical Quarterly*
ACC	*Ancient Christian Commentary*
AO	*Aristotelis Opera*
BDAG	*Greek-English Lexicon of the New Testament and Other Early Christian Literature*, 3rd ed.
BDB	*Enhanced Brown-Driver-Briggs Hebrew and English Lexicon*
BECNT	Baker Exegetical Commentary on the New Testament
BKC	*The Bible Knowledge Commentary*
BNTC	Black's New Testament Commentary
BoT	*Banner of Truth*
BST	The Bible Speaks Today
CC	Calvin's Commentaries
CD	*Church Dogmatics*
CCSG	Corpus Christianorum Series Graeca
CCSL	Corpus Christianorum Series Latina
CR	Corpus Reformatorum
CREP	*Concise Routledge Encyclopedia of Philosophy*
CSEL	Corpus Scriptorum Ecclesiasticorum Latinorum
CTJ	*Calvin Theological Journal*
CW	*Collected Works of John Stuart Mill*

DSE	*Dictionary of Scripture and Ethics*
DTIB	*Dictionary for Theological Interpretation of the Bible*
EDBT	*Evangelical Dictionary of Biblical Theology*
EBC	*The Expositor's Bible Commentary*
EKKNT	Evangelisch-katholischer Kommentar zum Neuen Testament
GCS	Die Griechischen christlichen Schriftsteller der ersten Jahrhunderte
GNO	*Gregorii Nysseni Opera*
HAL	*The Hebrew and Aramaic Lexicon of the Old Testament*
HTR	*Harvard Theological Review*
ISBE	*International Standard Bible Encyclopedia*
IVPBBCNT	*The IVP Bible Background Commentary: New Testament*
IVPNTC	IVP New Testament Commentary Series
JBL	*Journal of Biblical Literature*
JETS	*Journal of the Evangelical Theological Society*
JGES	*Journal of the Grace Evangelical Society*
JRESR	Journal of Religious Ethics Studies in Religion
KGS	*Kant's Gesammelte Schriften*
Louw-Nida	*Lexicon of the New Testament: Based on Semantic Domains*
LCL	Loeb Classical Library
LW	*Luther's Works*
MSJ	*Master's Seminary Journal*
MW	*Melanchthons Werke in Auswahl*
MEP	*Macmillan Encyclopedia of Philosophy*
NAC	New American Commentary
NBD	*New Bible Dictionary*
NCBC	New Cambridge Bible Commentary
NDT	*New Dictionary of Theology*
NICNT	The New International Commentary on the New Testament

NIDNTT	The New International Dictionary of New Testament Theology
NIGCT	New International Greek Testament Commentary
NTS	New Testament Studies
NSBT	New Studies in Biblical Theology
OHST	The Oxford Handbook of Systematic Theology
OOII	Opera Omnia Iussu Impensaque,
PAO	Patrum Apostolicorum Opera: Textum Ad Fidem Codicum et Graecorum Et Latinorum
PCNT	Paideia Commentaries on the New Testament
PNTC	Pillar New Testament Commentary
RevExp	Review and Expositor
SBLMS	Society of Biblical Literature Monograph Series
SC	Sources chrétiennes
SWJT	Southwestern Journal of Theology
SNTSMS	Society for New Testament Studies Monograph Series
RelSRev	Religious Studies Review
REP	Routledge Encyclopedia of Philosophy
RTR	Reformed Theological Review
TM	Tabletalk Magazine
TS	Theological Studies
TynBul	Tyndale Bulletin
WA	D. Martin Luthers Werke: Kritische Gesamtausgabe
WBC	Word Biblical Commentary
WMANT	Wissenschaftliche Monographien zum Alten und Neuen Testament
WUNT	Wissenschaftliche Untersuchungen zum Neuen Testament
Works	The Works of John Bunyan
Works	The Complete Works of Stephen Charnock
Works	The Works of Jonathan Edwards
Works	The Works of John Owen

Preface

Almost a decade of research and study went into this work. The topic of sanctification was chosen in part because of a deep recognition of personal deficiencies and the shared desire with other believers to grow in this area. As Ryle warns, reading or writing in this case on the topic of sanctification does not make one any more sanctified, but it may be used by God to stimulate further the desire to seek holiness from Him.

While all the inadequacies of this work belong to the author, several people have greatly improved the quality of this book and made it possible. It is with deep appreciation that the following people are acknowledged in this regard. Kevin Kennedy, serving as major advisor for the doctoral and dissertation process and through his expertise in the structure and art of argument, has been of invaluable help in formulating objections and improving the overall logic and readability of the argument. Craig Mitchell, serving as minor advisor, opened the author's eyes to the importance of virtue ethics, the role of philosophy with respect to Christian theology, and the general panoramic of the history of ideas, all of which undergird the synthesis of philosophy, ethics, and theology represented by this work. Robert Caldwell, serving as dissertation reader, offered many helpful suggestions. George Klein, dean for the doctoral program, has provided much appreciated pastoral support. Joanna Rothenberg, with years of loving support and many hours of editing has made this book possible. Finally, the author's accountability partners encouraged much holiness.

Ronald M. Rothenberg
Grand Prairie, TX, 2014

Introduction

In his work *De Sancta Trinitate*, Gregory of Nyssa warned, "And let no one take out from the whole the power of sanctification to assign (it) to the operation of the Spirit, hearing the Savior in the Gospel saying to the Father concerning the disciples, 'Father, sanctify them in your name.'"[1] Since the time of Gregory's writing, theologians such as L. Berkhof have become accustomed to speaking about "a division of labor in the Trinity" such that individual persons of the Trinity are described by those like W. Marshall as being "the immediate principal agent" of a particular divine act.[2] While such characterizations of the Trinity's work are not incorrect and along with other factors, these theologians have tended historically toward emphasizing the Spirit "as the primary divine agent for progressive sanctification," as expressed by W. Barrick, with the result that the roles of Christ, the Father, and the mutual cooperation of all three persons of the Trinity in sanctification are neglected.[3]

---

1 "Καὶ μηδεὶς κατ᾽ ἐξαίρετον ἀπονεμέτω τῇ ἐνεργείᾳ τοῦ Πνεύματος τὴν ἁγιαστικὴν ἐξουσίαν, ἀκούσας τοῦ Σωτῆρος ἐν τῷ Εὐαγγελίῳ περὶ τῶν μαθητῶν πρὸς τὸν Πατέρα λέγοντος· «Πάτερ, ἁγίασον αὐτοὺς ἐν τῷ ὀνόματί σου»." Gregory of Nyssa *Ad Eustathium de sancta trinitate* 7 (*GNO* 3 pt. 1:11). All translations by the author unless otherwise noted.

2 Louis Berkhof, *Systematic Theology* (Eerdmans, 1938), 266; Walter Marshall, *The Gospel-Mystery of Sanctification* (Southwick and Peluse, 1811), 277–278. For claims similar to Berkhof's see: Rick Brannan, ed. *Historic Creeds and Confessions*, Electronic ed. (Logos Research Systems, 1997), HC Q 24; John Owen, *Πνευματολογια· or, a Discourse Concerning the Holy Spirit*, Works 3:93; Augustus Hopkins Strong, *Systematic Theology*, (American Baptist Publication Society, 1907), 1:343. For claims similar to Marshall's see: John Murray, *Redemption: Accomplished and Applied* (Eerdmans, 1954), Kindle edition, s.v. "II.2.The Pattern.2; II.3; II.6.4; II.7. The Agent of Sanctification"; Arthur Walkington Pink, *The Doctrine of Sanctification* (Logos Research Systems, 2005), 89.

3 William D. Barrick, "Sanctification: The Work of the Holy Spirit and Scripture," *MSJ* 21, no. 2 (2010): 183. For similar claims see: Stanley M. Horton, "The Pentecostal Perspective," in *Five Views on Sanctification*, ed. Stanley N. Gundry (Zondervan, 1987), 118; J. Robertson Mc-

In such a theological atmosphere, Gregory's warning still stands as a cogent reminder not to forget that sanctification is a Trinitarian act in Scripture.[4] Although some recent theologians have given a more Trinitarian account of sanctification, much work is still needed to describe the cooperative nature of the Trinity's activity in sanctification. This book contributes to that work by arguing for the thesis that virtue ethics is key to understanding Trinitarian progressive sanctification.

Problem and Background

Three trends in the current field of sanctification include: viewing sanctification as a Trinitarian act (Trinitarian sanctification), finding links between virtue ethics and sanctification (virtue ethical sanctification), and defining sanctification as "position-only," or denying that the present progressive and future perfective aspects are properly part of sanctification (the position-only view), contrary to traditional views of sanctification. This book combines some of the insights of Trinitarian sanctification and virtue ethical sanctification in order to develop the idea of a virtue ethical view of Trinitarian sanctification, which provides a richer expression of the biblical doctrine of sanctification and draws more broadly on the whole of the Christian tradition of interpretation compared to current accounts of sanctification. Since acceptance or rejection of the position-only view is determinative of the nature of sanctification and not a primary focus, then this trend is briefly addressed.[5] This book rejects the position-only view and primarily deals with the progressive aspect of sanctification.[6]

Quilkin, "The Keswick Perspective," in *Five Views on Sanctification*, ed. Gundry, 155; Murray, *Redemption*, pt. 2, ch. 7, "Sanctification: The Agent of Sanctification"; J. C. Ryle, *Holiness: Its Nature, Hindrances, Difficulties and Roots* (William Hunt and Company, 1889), 309–310, 444, 448; John F. Walvoord, *The Holy Spirit: A Comprehensive Study of the Person and Work of the Holy Spirit* (Zondervan, 2010), ch. 23.

    4 For a similar judgment see: James Leo Garrett, *Systematic Theology: Biblical, Historical, and Evangelical*, 2nd ed., vol. 2 (Ages Digital Library, 2006), s.v. "2.8.66.4.C.1."

    5 Some proponents of the Position-Only view include: William G. Coberly, "An Exegetical Argument for the Position-Only View of Sanctification" (M.T. thesis, The Master's Seminary, 2004), 1–4; Clarence Tucker Craig, "Paradox of Holiness," *Interpretation* 6 (1952): 151, 153, 160–161; Victor Paul Furnish, *Theology and Ethics in Paul*, The New Testament Library (1968; repr. Westminster John Knox, 2009), 123, 155, 239–241; David G. Peterson, *Possessed by God: A New Testament Theology of Sanctification and Holiness*, NSBT 1 (InterVarsity, 1995), 13, 24–25, 103, 115–116, 123, 125, 133–137. The Position-Only view is addressed in chapter 2.

    6 Assertions in this book might still be understood under the new terms or categories into which the Position-Only view has proposed transferring the concept of progressive sanctification, such as transformation, growth, walking-worthily, etc.

Although the first two aforementioned trends are the focus, this book does not deny that there may be other important contemporary trends in the field. In fact, another circumstance in the current field of sanctification is the ongoing debates among the traditional views of sanctification (Reformed, Lutheran, Wesleyan, etc.). As in the past, these debates involve such issues as the role of the law, monergism versus synergism, the relationship of sanctification to justification, legalism versus antinomianism/libertinism, transformation by a continuous process versus a post-conversion instantaneous crisis-event, and the two nature conflict versus perfectionism. While any discussion of sanctification can hardly avoid touching on these issues of the traditional debates, they are not the primary concern of this book.[7] Furthermore, a virtue ethical view of Trinitarian sanctification is not intended to be an additional view of sanctification alongside or a defense of any one of the traditional views, but rather a supplement to those views.

Since this book combines and develops the trends of Trinitarian sanctification and virtue ethical sanctification, it is important to understand what these trends are and how they emerged. This introduction provides a brief overview of these trends in order to orient readers to the subject of a virtue ethical view of Trinitarian sanctification, while chapter 2 offers a more detailed analysis and history.

The contemporary trend of Trinitarian sanctification emanated from the history of the Trinity, which has at least two major contemporary narratives. In the earlier historiography, the doctrine of the Trinity suffered eclipse (decline and eventual neglect) due to a complex of historical, doctrinal, and cultural factors in which it waned from the time after Aquinas to full eclipse with F. D. E. Schleiermacher and was revived in the second half of the twentieth century.[8] In the more recent revisionist retelling of the history of the Trinity, the doctrine was never eclipsed, and the recent flurry of interest in the Trinity stirred up by K. Barth, K. Rahner, and John Zizioulas is viewed as part of

---

7 The traditional views are listed in chapter 2, which briefly introduces the controversies most relevant to this book and provides an extensive list of excellent sources that define these views and the issues that they debate.

8 Stanley J. Grenz, *Rediscovering the Triune God: The Trinity in Contemporary Theology* (Fortress Press, 2004), 4–5, 12–13; Veli-Matti Kärkkäinen, *The Trinity: Global Perspectives* (WJK Press, 2007), xii, xvi–xvii, xx, 89–90; Christoph Schwöbel, "Introduction," in *Trinitarian Theology Today: Essays on Divine Being and Act*, ed. Christoph Schwöbel (T&T Clark, 1995), 2, 5; Claude Welch, *In This Name: The Doctrine of the Trinity in Contemporary Theology* (Scribner, 1952), vii–viii, 4–5; John Zizioulas, "The Doctrine of God the Trinity Today: Suggestions for an Ecumenical Study," in *The Forgotten Trinity*, ed. Alasdair I. C. Heron, vol. 3 of A Selection of Papers Presented to the BCC Study Commission on Trinitarian Doctrine Today (BCC/CCBI Inter-Church House, 1991), 19–21.

a continuing dialogue with Schleiermacher, G. W. F. Hegel, and I. A. Dorner.[9] Regardless of which narrative is taken, proponents of both accounts agree that the founders of contemporary Trinitarianism "did in fact stir up enthusiasm for the doctrine" of the Trinity.[10] As a result of this enthusiasm over the last several decades, scholars have begun (re)applying Trinitarianism to the doctrine of sanctification in order to view sanctification as an act not merely of the Spirit, but one in which all three persons of the Trinity participate.[11]

From the contemporary trend of Trinitarian enthusiasm, this book critically appropriates the general insight of viewing sanctification as a Trinitarian act and also critically appropriates some of the particular insights from S. S. Wilson's formulation of Trinitarian sanctification.[12] Specifically, some insights critically appropriated from Wilson include focusing on Trinitarian sanctification from a Christological perspective and the "Triune premise," or the idea that generally, but not absolutely, "the inseparable working of God has been 'appropriated' to the persons of the Godhead according to a certain order or 'taxis,'" which is defined as "'from' the Father 'through' the Son and 'by' the Spirit."[13] The "Triune premise" is used to provide Trinitarian descriptions of sanctification.

---

9 Gilles Emery and Matthew Levering, "Introduction," in *The Oxford Handbook of the Trinity*, ed. Gilles Emery and Matthew Levering (Oxford University Press, 2011), 1; Christine Helmer, "Between History and Speculation: Christian Trinitarian Thinking after the Reformation," in *The Cambridge Companion to the Trinity*, ed. Peter C. Phan (Cambridge University Press, 2011), 149–151; Richard A. Muller, *The Triunity of God*, vol. 4, *Post-Reformation Reformed Dogmatics: The Rise and Development of Reformed Orthodoxy*, ca. 1520 to ca. 1725 (Baker Academic, 2003), 22–23, 414–415. In Holmes' revisionist account, Zizioulas rather than Lossky is credited with being one of the founders of contemporary Trinitarianism. Stephen R. Holmes, *The Quest for the Trinity: The Doctrine of God in Scripture, History and Modernity* (IVP Academic, 2012), ch 9.

10 Samuel M. Powell, "Nineteenth-Century Protestant Doctrines of the Trinity," in *The Oxford Handbook of the Trinity*, ed. Gilles Emery and Matthew Levering (Oxford University Press, 2011), 267; cf. Emery and Levering, "Introduction," 1.

11 Anthony A. Hoekema, "The Reformed Perspective," in *Five Views on Sanctification*, ed. Gundry, 59–90; Luis M. Bermejo, *The Spirit of Life: The Holy Spirit in the Life of the Christian* (Loyola University Press, 1989), 10–16; Bruce A. Ware, *Father, Son, and Holy Spirit: Relationships, Roles, and Relevance* (Crossway, 2005); John Webster, *Holiness* (Eerdmans, 2003); R. N. Frost, "Sin and Grace," in *Trinitarian Soundings in Systematic Theology*, ed. Paul Louis Metzger (T&T Clark, 2006), 101–112; Scott Sparling Wilson, "Trinity and Sanctification: A Proposal for Understanding the Doctrine of Sanctification According to a Triune Ordering" (PhD. diss., Southeastern Baptist Theological Seminary, 2009).

12 Wilson, "Trinity and Sanctification." Wilson's dissertation is important because it is possibly the longest discussion of Trinitarian sanctification to date.

13 Wilson, "Trinity and Sanctification," 16, 33. Emphasis original. In his suggestions for further research, Wilson proposed that instead of treating "the working of all three divine persons" as he did, that a "series of three full monograph-length treatments of the sanctifying work of the Father, the Son, and the Spirit," each from a Trinitarian perspective, is needed (p. 253).

Particularly in the late nineteenth and early twentieth centuries and sometimes later, sanctification was frequently attributed *primarily*, if not almost exclusively, to the Spirit rather than presented as Trinitarian as it often was in earlier periods.[14] Furthermore, in many of the historic works and in those of the contemporary Trinitarian proponents previously cited, Christ's role in progressive sanctification is primarily and in many instances exclusively passive. In these writings, one way Christ's work in progressive sanctification is described as passive is that Christ's death on the cross accomplishes positional sanctification which serves as the passive basis for the Spirit to apply progressive sanctification.[15] This book combines and develops the tradition and the ideas from the contemporary Trinitarian proponents by highlighting a more active role for Christ in progressive sanctification than generally has been emphasized previously in order to describe progressive sanctification in a Trinitarian manner that more fully includes Christ.[16]

The recent trend of virtue ethical sanctification, or of finding links between virtue ethics and sanctification, arises out of the history of philosophy and ethics. Before giving a preliminary introduction to the history, it is important to define virtue ethics. In the fields of philosophy and ethics, there does not seem to be an agreed upon definition of virtue ethics other than generally to characterize it as a teleological ethical theory involving character and virtue in contrast to deontological ethical systems involving

---

14 Chapter 2 explores some of the reasons offered by the older history and the revisionists for why sanctification is preceived as being less Trinitarian in some periods. However, this book is not primarily concerned with *why* many scholars began to attribute sanctification primarily to the Spirit, but rather with responding to this historic occurrence by emphasizing the role of Christ in order to describe sanctification as a more Trinitarian process. Chapter 2 provides examples of and exceptions to scholars who appropriate sanctification primarily or almost exclusively to the Spirit.

15 Another way that Christ's work in progressive sanctification is described as passive is the historical tendency of making union with Christ the passive basis upon which the Spirit actively applies progressive sanctification. Union does not have to result in a passive description of progressive sanctification, but historically this has been the tendency. Since union is such a broad issue, it is passed over in this argument in favor of pursuing its impact on sanctification as an area for future research.

16 If someone objects that the attempt to highlight the active work of Christ in the Trinity makes this work Christological rather than Trinitarian, then there are at least three responses to this objection. First, Emery and Levering explain that "Trinitarian theology is intrinsically connected to Christology. Contemporary reflection seeks to avoid the dichotomy that separated what is 'Trinitarian' from what is 'Christological'" ("Introduction," 2). Second, the whole purpose of highlighting the active work of Christ in sanctification in this book is to have a role (or a more adequate description of that role) for Christ that can be connected to that of the Father and the Spirit. Third and in the following explanation of the exegetical argument of this book, the concluding Trinitarian statements of each analysis that incorporate the active role of the Son into the Triune premise indicate that the main focus of this work is Trinitarian and not merely Christological.

duty and rules.[17] This book argues for a definition of Christian virtue ethics which broadly follows the Aristotelian-Augustinian-Thomistic tradition, and in which virtue ethics and Trinitarian progressive sanctification are taken as *partial* synonyms. Consequently, virtue ethical Trinitarian sanctification is defined as the teleological (character oriented) process based on natural law and requiring metaphysical realism in which believers actualize their positional holiness by imitating the nature/character of the Father as expressed in the creation and the Son by habitually acting in accordance with created purposes through the power of the Holy Spirit, prayer-help of Christ, and motivation of Spirit-empowered virtues, to be transformed into the *telos* or "end" of the good, the image of Christ.[18]

Turning to the history of virtue ethics, currently there seems to be a general consensus in the fields of philosophy and ethics over the historical narrative that following a golden age up until at least Aquinas, virtue ethics waned until it was eclipsed by I. Kant and was revived by G. E. M. Anscombe.[19] Similar to the history of the Trinity, there have been some revisionist efforts, but the consensus narrative of an eclipse and resurgence of virtue ethics seems to be prevailing for now.[20] With the resurgence of interest in virtue ethics over

---

17 For example, Hursthouse, Louden, and Statman define virtue ethics by this contrast. Some authors such as Hursthouse and Statman define specific characteristics common to various authors' descriptions of virtue ethical systems. This book discussess such common characteristics in chapter 2. Rosalind Hursthouse, *On Virtue Ethics* (Oxford University Press, 2001), 1, 8–17; Robert B. Louden, "Virtue Ethics," in *MEP*, ed. Donald M. Borchert (Macmillan, 2006), 9:687; Daniel Statman, "Introduction to Virtue Ethics," in *Virtue Ethics*, ed. Daniel Statman (Georgetown University Press, 1997), 7–11.

18 Alston claims that "'metaphysical realism' is used in various ways, ... historically, the most prominent such positions are the medieval: commitment to the objective reality of universals and the opposition to one or another metaphysical *idealism*." Emphasis original. William P. Alston, "What Metaphysical Realism is Not," in *Realism and Antirealism*, ed. William P. Alston (Cornell University Press, 2002), 97. Geisler and Feinberg claim that natual law refers to "the view that there are innate or natural moral laws known by all men." Norman L. Geisler and Paul D. Feinberg, *Introduction to Philosophy: A Christian Perspective* (Baker, 1980), 432. This definition of virtue ethics is not comprehensive and does not entail all that is involved with this term. The technical terms involved in this defintion such as teleology, deontology, and metaphysical realism are explained further in chapter 3. Kotva and Smith have also argued for the dependence of teleology on realism and for realism's biblical consistency. Joseph J. Kotva, *The Christian Case for Virtue Ethics* (Georgetown University Press, 1996), 153–155; R. Scott Smith, *Virtue Ethics and Moral Knowledge: Philosophy of Language after Macintyre and Hauerwas*, Ashgate New Critical Thinking in Philosophy (Ashgate, 2003), 5, 8, 219.

19 Hursthouse, *Virtue Ethics*, 1–3; Kotva, *Case for Virtue*, 5; Michael A. Slote, *From Morality to Virtue* (Oxford University Press, 1992), xiii; Servais Pinckaers, *The Sources of Christian Ethics*, trans. Mary Thomas Noble (Catholic University of America Press, 1995), 220, 233, 241–242, 245–247, 253.

20 For example, an exception to the standard narrative seems to be Keenan's historiography in which "the tradition seesaws back and forth between" duty/law and virtue. Keenan may be characterized as an exception because Downs, Gill, Louden, Tousley and Kallenberg,

nearly the last forty years, a number of scholars began to make links between virtue ethics and sanctification.[21]

From the contemporary trend of virtue ethical sanctification, this book critically appropriates the general idea that sanctification and virtue ethics are somehow related and also critically appropriates some of the specific insights of S. Hauerwas and J. Kotva, two important figures in the contemporary resurgence of virtue ethics. The general idea of a link between virtue ethics and sanctification is developed, in part, by demonstrating through the history of sanctification that traditional descriptions of sanctification involve Christian virtue ethics. Hauerwas' concept of character is used to explain how Aristotle's principle of reciprocity (the idea that doing leads to being and being leads to doing) is *similar* to Jesus' teaching and can be described in terms that do not violate the Reformation dictum of *sola fide* or salvation by grace through faith alone (Eph 2:8–10). Several of Kotva's biblical observations serve as the basis for this book's exegetical arguments, and his claim that virtue ethics and sanctification are linked because both are teleological is more fully developed by this book in establishing the nature of virtue ethics generally as being biblically consistent. As Kotva points out, traditional conceptions of virtue ethics do need some modification in order to strive for complete biblical consistency, but such a harmonization is possible so that a form of virtue ethics can be construed that is biblically consistent.[22]

Thesis

The thesis of this book is that virtue ethics is key to understanding Trinitarian progressive sanctification. The book argues that while some have overemphasized the role of the Spirit and others have depicted Christ as having a primarily passive role in progressive sanctification, the emphasis on the active role

---

and Wilson affirm the consensus narrative of an eclipse. James F. Keenan, "Moral Theological Reflections," in *Jesus and Virtue Ethics: Building Bridges between New Testament Studies and Moral Theology* (Sheed & Ward, 2002), 1–2, 7–8; David J. Downs, "Vices and Virtues, Lists Of," in *DSE*, ed. Joel B. Green (Baker Academic, 2011); Christopher Gill, "Cynicism and Stoicism," in *The Oxford Handbook of the History of Ethics*, ed. Roger Crisp (Oxford University Press, 2013), Kindle edition, s.v. "Cynicism and Stoicism: 5.2 Stoicism"; Louden, "Virtue Ethics," 9:687; Nikki Coffey Tousley and Brad J. Kallenberg, "Virtue Ethics," in *DSE*, ed. Green; Jonathan R. Wilson, "Virtue(s)," in *DSE*, ed. Green. Revisions of Plato, Aristotle, and Kant are treated in footnotes in chapter 3.

21 Brian S. Borgman, *Feelings and Faith: Cultivating Godly Emotions in the Christian Life* (Crossway, 2009); Stanley Hauerwas, *Character and the Christian Life: A Study in Theological Ethics* (Trinity University Press, 1975); Kotva, *Case for Virtue*; Gilbert C. Meilaender, *The Theory and Practice of Virtue* (University of Notre Dame Press, 1984); Joseph Woodill, *The Fellowship of Life: Virtue Ethics and Orthodox Christianity* (Georgetown University Press, 1998).

22 Kotva, *Case for Virtue*, 61.

of Christ in conjunction with a recovery of virtue ethics demonstrates how a virtue ethical view of Trinitarian sanctification functions.

This book seeks to recover the pre-Reformation virtue ethical emphasis of the tradition's biblical interpretation of sanctification in a way compatible with Reformation and post-Reformation evangelical sensibilities concerning salvation by grace though faith alone apart from works (Eph 2:8–10), while at the same time employing an emphasis on the Trinity similar to that of the contemporary Trinitarian proponents. The primary concern of this book is not merely to retrieve virtue ethics, but rather to argue that progressive sanctification functions biblically in a virtue ethical and Trinitarian manner actively involving Christ and not only the Spirit.

Argument and Overview

By combining some of the critically appropriated insights of the contemporary trends of Trinitarian sanctification and virtue ethical sanctification, this book argues from the history of doctrine, philosophical compatibility of virtue ethics with the Bible, and detailed exegesis of texts which emphasize Christ's active roles as teacher, example, and priest that virtue ethics is key to understanding how Trinitarian progressive sanctification functions.

The thesis is supported with four reasons why virtue ethics is key to understanding Trinitarian progressive sanctification: (1) the Trinity, virtue ethics, and sanctification are historically and conceptually interconnected in the tradition and Scripture, (2) virtue ethics based on metaphysical realism is the most biblically consistent ethical framework for Trinitarian progressive sanctification, (3) Jesus' active roles as a teacher and example of virtue play an important part in Trinitarian sanctification, and (4) Jesus' priestly heavenly intercession aimed at manifesting virtue in believers is crucial to understanding how the Trinity progressively sanctifies believers.

Methodology

The method used in this work involves historical, philosophical, exegetical, and theological components. Historically, in keeping with J. Pelikan's "primary motivation" for historical theology, this book is a work of systematic theology that has a historical basis; it is not a piece of historical theology.[23]

---

23 Jaroslav Pelikan, *Historical Theology: Continuity and Change in Christian Doctrine*, Theological Resources (Westminster, 1971), 100. See also: Alister E. McGrath, *Historical Theology: An Introduction to the History of Christian Thought*, 2nd ed. (Wiley-Blackwell, 2013), 9, 14.

As a result, the strategy used in this work is to give a historical argument to establish that recent views of sanctification are myopic and leave a lacuna of virtue ethical Trinitarian sanctification, which this book attempts to fill by critically retrieving these emphases (virtue ethics and Trinitarian sanctification) from the tradition. The brief historical sections are selective and use the following three methods: (1) Pelikan's "historical study of discrete doctrines" rather than the method of "comparison of ... doctrinal systems *in toto*"; (2) G. Garraghan's "comparative method" by which the development of a single doctrine is noted over time through agreement and difference; and (3) the "motif-research" method of the Lundensian school in the sense that the mere presence or absence of a doctrinal formulation is not assumed to verify the existence or non-existence of a doctrine.[24] Lastly, due to the limited scope of the historical sections, the doctrines are treated in the restricted historical contexts of ecclesiastical history and the history of ideas according to standard periodization schemes.[25]

Philosophically, possibly the main issue is the relationship between philosophy and theology. The relationship between these fields of study is important for this book because its method is to use philosophical concepts and categories to retrieve and define virtue ethics in relation to sanctification. Concerning the relationship between philosophy/reason and theology/faith, N. Geisler argues that there are five logical positions: "(1) revelation only; (2) reason only; (3) revelation over reason; (4) reason over revelation; and (5) revelation and reason."[26] Geisler correctly dismisses the first and second positions on the basis that "those who hold strongly to a 'revelation only' view provide arguments or reasons of some kind to support it" and pure rationalism fails because "something is always presupposed or simply believed."[27] Both position four and position five (despite its apparent dominance in theology) seem to violate the doctrine of biblical sufficiency (2 Tim 3:16–17) by making reason equal to or superior to the authority of Scripture (Rom 13:1; 2 Thess 2:15; 2 Pet 1:18–21). As a result, position three (revelation over reason/philosophy) seems to conform best to the biblical teaching that all truth (John 14:6) and authority come from and are subordinated to God (Rom 13:1) and his Word (John 17:17).

Since it is realistically impossible and biblically inconsistent to "shun" philosophy, then theologians are better off determining which philosophies are

---

24 Pelikan, *Historical Theology*, 101–109; Gilbert J. Garraghan, *A Guide to Historical Method* (Fordham University Press, 1946), 410–412.
25 Pelikan, *Historical Theology*, 111–128.
26 Geisler and Feinberg, *Introduction to Philosophy*, 255–268.
27 Ibid., 268.

biblically consistent and which are not.²⁸ In addition to Geisler's refutation of position one above, it is realistically impossible to avoid philosophy in theology for at least three reasons: (1) almost all theological methods contain philosophical presuppositions at least in the form of common sense assumptions in their hermeneutics, (2) there is some overlap in content as well as method between the disciplines of philosophy and theology, and (3) philosophy and theology were one discipline until Ockham separated them, a situation exacerbated by the Enlightenment rationalists.²⁹ The fact that it is biblically inconsistent to shun philosophy is evident from the number of passages that support the use of philosophy (Acts 17:25, 28; 1 Cor 15:33; Col 2:8; 1 Tim 1:12).³⁰ The historical and conceptual interconnectedness as well as the practical inextricable nature of philosophy from theology make it necessary for theologians to discern which philosophies are biblically consistent and which are not. This work answers the call for interdisciplinary work in the *loci* of both theological method and the Trinity in part by its four component method, in part by its argument which reintegrates virtue ethics back into theology through the doctrines of sanctification and the Trinity, and in part through philosophical argument.³¹

Exegetically, this book shifts the methodological paradigm from building the doctrine of sanctification based on theological constructions, such as the so-called Triune premise, to grammatical-historical textual exegesis in order to argue that Christ has an active role in applying his finished work in cooperation with the Spirit and Father. For example, for most scholars mentioned

---

28 Yarnell argues that "the free churches shun ... philosophy." Malcolm B. Yarnell III, *The Formation of Christian Doctrine* (B&H Academic, 2007), 65.

29 Evans, *Pocket Dictionary*, 92; Bruce D. Marshall, "Philosophy and Theology," in *The Encyclopedia of Christianity*, ed. Erwin Fahlbusch and Geoffrey William Bromiley (Eerdmans; Brill, 2005), 4:197; W. R. Sorley, "The Beginnings of English Philosophy," in *The Cambridge History of English and American Literature*, ed. W. A. Ward and A. R. Waller (Cambridge University Press, 1909) 4:272.

30 In response to standard objections against using philosophy from Col 2:8, Geisler argues that the use of the definite article before the word philosophy qualifies that only the false philosophy of the Colossian heresy based on men is prohibited and so implies that true philosophy based on Christ is permitted. Norman L. Geisler, "Colossians," *BKC* (Victor Books, 1985), 2:667; Daniel Hill and Daniel J. Treier, "Philosophy," in *DTIB*, ed. Kevin J. Vanhoozer et al. (Baker Academic, 2005), 593.

31 Ronald Jay Feenstra and Cornelius Plantinga, "Introduction," in *Trinity, Incarnation, and Atonement: Philosophical and Theological Essays*, ed. Ronald Jay Feenstra and Cornelius Plantinga, vol. 1 of Library of Religious Philosophy (University of Notre Dame Press, 1989), 2; Fred Sanders, "The State of the Doctrine of the Trinity in Evangelical Theology," *SWJT* 47, no. 2 (2005): 170, 175; Francis Watson, *Text, Church and World: Biblical Interpretation in Theological Perspective* (Eerdmans, 1994), vii, 12; Stephen Williams, "The Theological Task and the Theological Method," in *Evangelical Futures: A Conversation on Theological Method*, ed. John J. Stackhouse (Baker, 2000), 163–164.

in the "problem statement" section, the Triune premise and the Reformation *sola fide* emphasis cause them to interpret passages such as Rom 8:26, 27, 34; Eph 5:25–27; Heb 2:14–18; 4:14–16; 7:23–28; 9:23–28 and others as indicating that Christ passively provides the basis for sanctification through the foundation of his finished work. While affirming the Triune premise and *sola fide* but carefully examining the text on its own terms, the exegesis of this book will demonstrate that Christ has an active role in sanctification in cooperation with the Father and Spirit.

Theologically, this book makes use of the author's own concept of the "unity of all doctrine" and J. Webster's "theology of retrieval." The concept of the "unity of all doctrine" stands opposed to the doctrine of the contemporary Trinitarian proponents which holds that Trinitarian theology is defined in part by making the Trinity the center or organizing principle of all theology.[32] Instead, the "unity of all doctrine" holds biblically that since God's law reflects his character (Lev 19:2; Ps 19:7–10) and since God's law is a unity (Gal 5:3; James 2:10), then God's character or attributes must have a unity (Jer 10:10; 23:6; 1 John 1:5; 4:8). By way of theological analogy, since God's character has a unity and since the doctrines about God reflect his character, then the doctrines about God must have a unity or harmony. If one follows the invention of the biblically inconsistent idealistic philosophy of the German Enlightenment and tries to impose a central organizing principle on biblical doctrines, then the unity of all doctrines is broken or warped and one's system of theology will be distorted.[33]

To illustrate, suppose that one's system of theology is like a tapestry and that it is possible that there is a red thread (such as Christ or the Trinity) that runs through the whole (Matt 22:34–40). If the red thread is woven too tight in knitting the textile together (overemphasized in constructing one's system, perhaps by making it the central organizing principle), then the whole picture (system of doctrine) on the tapestry will be distorted. Conversely, if the red thread is woven too loosely (underemphasized, perhaps by eclipse), then the whole tapestry may unravel (heterodox theology in the extreme). Since all the threads (doctrines) in the tapestry (system) must be related to each other with the right tension (emphasis), then two or more threads (doctrines) in the tapestry (system) can be compared or related together. Rather than the

---

32 Barth, *CD*, 1, pt. 1:154; Rahner, *Trinity*, 18.
33 For the origin of the idea of a central organizing principle see: Letham, *Union with Christ*, 135–136. Whereas realism consists of the two claims that "there are facts of a certain kind" and that these facts "are in some way mind-independent or independent of human thought" or "independent of our evidence for them," nihilism is a denial of realism's first claim and idealism is denial of realism's second claim. Brink, *Moral Realism*, 14–16.

Trinitarian resurgence's central organizing principle, this book is using the unity of all doctrine to relate virtue ethics, the Trinity, and the doctrine of sanctification harmoniously.

This book also makes use of Webster's "theology of retrieval." The term "theology of retrieval," is a relatively new designation coined by Webster to refer to "a mode of theology, an attitude of mind ... a cluster of theologies which reach a broadly similar set of judgments about the nature of systematic theology," including the primary judgment "that mainstream theological ... critiques of the Christian religion ... distanced theology ... from the legacies of its past."[34] The term "theology of retrieval" includes such more familiar theological designations as "post-liberal, post-critical, restorationist, palaeo-orthodox, intratextual [, and] even postmodern."[35] This work is a theology of retrieval in the sense that it does not seek to negatively critique or correct the tradition, but rather seeks to add to the insights of the past by retrieving virtue ethics and filling the lacuna of virtue ethical Trinitarian sanctification.

---

34 John Webster, "Theologies of Retrieval," in *OHST*, ed. Kathryn Tanner John Webster, and Iain Torrance (Oxford University Press, 2007), 584.

35 Ibid., 584.

CHAPTER 1

THREE HISTORIC BACKGROUNDS: TRINITARIANISM, VIRTUE ETHICS, AND SANCTIFICATION

The main claim of this chapter is that virtue ethics is key to understanding Trinitarian progressive sanctification because the Trinity, virtue ethics, and sanctification are historically and conceptually interconnected in the tradition of interpretation and Scripture. Since the systematic principle of the unity of all doctrine introduced earlier indicates that all doctrines are interconnected, this principle suggests that developments in the doctrines of the Trinity and virtue ethics have impacted the doctrine of sanctification. This chapter's exposition of the histories of the Trinity, virtue ethics, and sanctification demonstrates the historical veracity of the unity of all doctrine and the key role of virtue ethics in this interconnectedness in part by depicting the impact of virtue ethics on Trinitarian sanctification. The three histories also provide an important background which explains the emergence and significance of the three trends introduced in chapter one of Trinitarian sanctification, virtue ethical sanctification, and the position-only view. Additionally, this chapter provides further explanation of how some of the insights of these trends are being critically appropriated by this book in order to develop the idea of a virtue ethical view of Trinitarian sanctification.

THE IMPACT OF TRINITARIAN PROPONENTS ON SANCTIFICATION

The current trend of applying Trinitarianism to the doctrine of sanctification, or of viewing sanctification as an act not merely of the Spirit, but one in which all three persons of the Trinity participate has emerged from the history of Trinitarianism, which has at least two major contemporary narratives. Since the transition from one telling of the history of the Trinity to another retelling is itself part of the doctrine's history, then it is important to understand both historiographies.

A Selective History of the Trinity

According to the earlier historical narrative, there has been an eclipse (a period of neglect or overshadowing by other doctrines) and a resurgence of interest.[1] This history of the eclipse and resurgence of Trinitarianism was so accepted in theology that the historical narrative explaining it was called "the standard story."[2]

In the standard story, although the doctrine of the Trinity is not explicitly or formally stated in the Bible, it is implied so that the doctrine developed through a centuries-long process.[3] In the Patristic period, the doctrine of the Trinity was developed through the Christological and pneumatological debates, which resulted in the definitive doctrinal definitions of the councils of Nicaea 325, Constantinople 381, and Chalcedon 451.[4] From the age of the church fathers, such as Augustine (354–430), up until the time of Aquinas (1225–1274) in the Middle Ages, the Trinity was central in emphasis and function in Christian doctrine.[5] However, according to K. Rahner, Aquinas restructured and reformulated the doctrine of the Trinity into an abstract philosophical theory isolated from the rest of doctrine, church practice, and practical daily living, with the result that its importance and function began

---

[1] For complete histories of the Trinity according to the earlier narrative of eclipse and resurgence see: Edmund J. Fortman, *The Triune God: A Historical Study of the Doctrine of the Trinity*, Theological Resources (Westminster, 1972); Bertrand de Margerie, *The Christian Trinity in History*, trans. Edmund J. Fortman, SHT 1 (Bede's Publications, 1982).

[2] Daniel J. Treier and David Lauber, "Introduction," in *Trinitarian Theology for the Church: Scripture, Community, Worship*, ed. Daniel J. Treier and David Lauber (IVP Academic, 2009), 7. Even revisionists such as Helmer and Holmes recognize that there was a "standard narrative" or a "received story." Christine Helmer, "Between History and Speculation: Christian Trinitarian Thinking after the Reformation," in *The Cambridge Companion to the Trinity*, ed. Peter C. Phan (Cambridge University Press, 2011), 149–151; Stephen R. Holmes, *The Quest for the Trinity: The Doctrine of God in Scripture, History and Modernity* (IVP Academic, 2012), ch. 9.

[3] Fortman, *Triune God*, 35, 257–258, 291.

[4] John Baillie, John T. McNeill, and Henry P. Van Dusen, eds., *Christology of the Later Fathers*, The Library of Christian Classics (Westminster John Knox Press, 2006), 15; Philip Schaff and David Schley Schaff, *History of the Christian Church*, 3rd rev. and Electronic ed. (Charles Scribner's Sons, 1910), 3.9.117, 120, 122.

[5] Stanley J. Grenz, *Rediscovering the Triune God: The Trinity in Contemporary Theology* (Fortress Press, 2004), 7–16; Veli-Matti Kärkkäinen, *The Trinity: Global Perspectives* (Westminster John Knox Press, 2007), 19–64; Claude Welch, *In This Name: The Doctrine of the Trinity in Contemporary Theology* (Scribner, 1952), vii.

to wane.⁶ After the time of Aquinas in the Middle Ages into the eighteenth century Enlightenment, the Trinity was slowly eclipsed and at times even denied.⁷ The standard story, presumably following the critiques of K. Barth, E. Brunner, and C. Welch, generally recognizes the total eclipse of the Trinity to have occurred by the time of F. D. E. Schleiermacher (1768–1834), who infamously placed the Trinity at the end of his systematic theology and is charged with having denied its importance for Christian belief and practice.⁸ In the mid-twentieth century, Barth, Rahner, and Vladimir Lossky inspired a resurgence of interest in the Trinity.⁹

---

6 Karl Rahner, *The Trinity*, trans. Joseph Donceel (The Crossroad Publishing Company, 1970), 9–10, 16–18. While most in the resurgence seem to follow Rahner's view, Grenz points out that Cobb blames Augustine and LaCunga charges both the eastern and western traditions for the demise of Trinitarianism. Grenz, *Rediscovering the Triune God*, 13; John B. Jr. Cobb, "The Relativization of the Trinity," in *Trinity in Process: A Relational Theology of God* (Continuum, 1997), 5–7; Catherine Mowry LaCugna, *God for Us: The Trinity and Christian Life* (Harper SanFrancisco, 1991), 12.

7 Fortman has the Middle Ages as a time of stagnation and the Reformation as a time of concern with other doctrines. Although the reformers affirmed the doctrine of the Trinity, even during the Reformation there were those who began to deny it altogether such as Calvin's opponent Michael Servetus (1511–1553) and the forerunners of the Unitarians, including Faustus Socinus (1539–1604) and the Polish Brethren. F. L. Cross and Elizabeth A. Livingstone, eds., *The Oxford Dictionary of the Christian Church*, 3ʳᵈ Rev. ed. (Oxford University Press, 2005), 1506, 1531–1532; Fortman, *The Triune God*, 243–246; Timothy George, "Introduction," in *God the Holy Trinity: Reflections on Christian Faith and Practice*, ed. Timothy George (Baker Academic, 2006), 10; John Hunt, *From the Reformation to the End of the Last Century*, vol. 2 of *Religious Thought in England: A Contribution to the History of Theology* (AMS Press, 1973), 194–212. For example, in the Enlightenment, Voltaire (1694–1778) and Immanuel Kant (1771–1804) are infamous for having denied the Trinity. Immanuel Kant, "The Conflict of the Faculties," in *Religion and Rational Theology*, ed. Allen W. Wood and George Di Giovanni of The Cambridge Edition of the Works of Immanuel Kant (Cambridge University Press, 1996), 264; Voltaire, "Foi ou Foy," in *Dictionnaire philosophique* (Cosse et Gaultier-Laguionie, 1838), 506.

8 Fredrich Schleiermacher, *The Christian Faith*, ed. H.R. Mackintosh; and J. S. Stewart, 1ˢᵗ ed. (T&T Clark, 1999), 738–739, 749–750. Earlier critiques of Schleiermacher include: Barth, *CD* 1.1:303; Karl Barth, *The Theology of Schleiermacher: Lectures at Göttingen, Winter Semester of 1923–1924*, trans. Geoffrey W. Bromiley (Eerdmans, 1982), 192; Emil Brunner, *Erlebnis, Erkenntnis und Glaube*, 4ᵗʰ and 5ᵗʰ ed. (Zwingli-Verlag, 1923); Emil Brunner, *Die Mystik und Das Wort: Der Gegensatz zwischen moderner Religionsauffassung und christlichem Glauben dargestellt an der Theologie Schleiermachers*, 2ⁿᵈ, stark veränderte ed. (J. C. B. Mohr (Paul Siebeck), 1928). Welch, *In This Name*, vii, 4–9. Mackintosh made his influential critique before Welch, but Welch's critique seems to be the one popularly followed: H. R. Mackintosh, *Types of Modern Theology: Schleiermacher to Barth* (Nisbet and Co. Ltd., 1937), 78–79. Examples of Trinitarians referring to these critiques include: Grenz, *Rediscovering the Triune God*, 17; Fred Sanders, "Trinity," in *OHST*, ed. J. B. Webster, Kathryn Tanner, and Iain R. Torrance of Oxford Handbooks (Oxford University Press, 2007), 37–38; Christoph Schwöbel, "Introduction," in *Trinitarian Theology Today: Essays on Divine Being and Act*, ed. Christoph Schwöbel (T&T Clark, 1995), 2.

9 G. L. Bray, "Trinity," in *NDT*, ed. Sinclair B. Ferguson and J. I. Packer (InterVarsity Press, 2000), 694; Grenz, *Rediscovering the Triune God*, 4–5, 12–13; James M. Houston, "The Nature and Purpose of Spiritual Theology," *Evangelical Review of Theology* 16, no. 1 (1992): 132; Kärkkäinen, *The Trinity*, xii, xvi–xvii, xx, 89–90; Schwöbel, "Introduction," 2, 5; Welch, *In This Name*, vii–viii,

In the more recent revisionist retelling of the history of the Trinity, the doctrine was never eclipsed and the recent flurry of interest in the Trinity stirred up by Barth, Rahner, and John Zizioulas is viewed as part of a continuing dialogue with Schleiermacher, G. W. F. Hegel, and I. A. Dorner.[10] The revisionists base their retelling in part on a rejection of three important turning points in the standard story: (1) the revisionists reject Rahner's interpretation of Aquinas, (2) they dismiss the critiques of Schleiermacher's doctrine of the Trinity, and (3) they repudiate the claim that the Trinity was eclipsed.[11] The revisionist historical narrative of the Trinity likely already is or is fast becoming the accepted history of the Trinity in scholarship. Regardless of which narrative is taken, proponents of both accounts agree that the founders of contemporary Trinitarianism "did in fact stir up enthusiasm for the doctrine" of the Trinity.[12]

According to S. Grenz, this stirring of enthusiasm for the Trinity took place in two main phases.[13] The first phase ran from Barth's (1886–1968) *Ro-*

4–5; Zizioulas, "The Doctrine of God the Trinity Today: Suggestions for an Ecumenical Study," in *A Selection of Papers Presented to the BCC Study Commission on Trinitarian Doctrine Today*, ed. Alasdair I. C. Heron, The Forgotten Trinity 3 (BCC/CCBI Inter-Church House, 1991), 19–21. On evangelical participation in the recent Trinitarian enthuasism see: Fred Sanders, "The State of the Doctrine of the Trinity in Evangelical Theology," *SWJT* 47, no. 2 (2005): 153–175.

10   Gilles Emery and Matthew Levering, "Introduction," in *The Oxford Handbook of the Trinity*, ed. Gilles Emery and Matthew Levering (Oxford University Press, 2011), 1; Helmer, "Between History and Speculation," 149–151. In Holmes' revisionist account, Zizioulas rather than Lossky is credited with being one of the founders of contemporary Trinitarianism. Holmes, *Quest for the Trinity*, s.v. "Introduction"; ch. 9; Richard A. Muller, *The Triunity of God*, vol. 4 of *Post-Reformation Reformed Dogmatics: The Rise and Development of Reformed Orthodoxy*, ca. 1520 to ca. 1725 (Baker Academics, 2003), 22–23, 414–415.

11   For the revisionist reinterpretation of Aquinas see: Gilles Emery, *Trinity in Aquinas* (Sapientia Press of Ave Maria College, 2003); Gilles Emery, *The Trinitarian Theology of Saint Thomas Aquinas* (Oxford University Press, 2007); Holmes, *Quest for the Trinity*, s.v. "Chapter 1: Karl Rahner and John Zizioulas: Economy and Personhood; Chapter 7: Thomas Aquinas"; Karen Kilby, "Aquinas, the Trinity and the Limits of Understanding," *International Journal of Systematic Theology* 7, no. 4 (Oct 2005): 414–427; Matthew Levering, *Scripture and Metaphysics: Aquinas and the Renewal of Trinitarian Theology* (Blackwell, 2004); Jean-Pierre Torrell, *The Person and His Work*, vol. 1 of *Saint Thomas Aquinas* trans. Robert Royal, Rev. ed. (Catholic University of America Press, 2005). For the revisionist's rehabilitation of Schleiermacher see: Holmes, *Quest for the Trinity*, ch. 9; Richard R. Niebuhr, *Schleiermacher on Christ and Religion: a New Introduction* (Scribner, 1964), 6–13, 155–156; Samuel M. Powell, *The Trinity in German Thought* (Cambridge University Press, 2001); Robert R. Williams, *Schleiermacher the Theologian: The Construction of the Doctrine of God* (Fortress, 1978). For the revisionist's rejection of an eclipse see footnote 10. For other important points of revision see: Holmes, *Quest for the Trinity*, ch. 6, 7, 9; Bruce D. Marshall, "Trinity," in *The Blackwell Companion to Modern Theology*, ed. Gareth Jones of Blackwell Companions to Religion (Blackwell, 2004), 183–203.

12   Emery and Levering, "Introduction," 1; Samuel M. Powell, "Nineteenth-Century Protestant Doctrines of the Trinity," in *The Oxford Handbook of the Trinity*, ed. Gilles Emery and Matthew Levering (Oxford University Press, 2011), 267.

13   Grenz, *Rediscovering the Triune God*, 2–3.

mans Commentary (1919) to T. F. Torrance's (1913–2007) *The Christian Doctrine of God* (1996) and involved reformulating the doctrine of the Trinity.[14] The second phase runs from C. Gunton's (1941–2003) *The Doctrine of Creation* (1997) to the present and involves applying the doctrine of the Trinity to other doctrines and issues.[15] Therefore, as a part of the second phase of this Trinitarian enthusiasm, scholars have begun applying Trinitarianism to the doctrine of sanctification with the impact that sanctification is being increasingly viewed as an act not merely of the Spirit, but one in which all three persons of the Trinity participate.

Critical Appropriation of Trinitarian Sanctification

This section turns from establishing the impact of the contemporary Trinitarian proponents' emphasis on the Trinitarian nature of sanctification to how this insight is critically appropriated. Over the last several decades, a number of second phase scholars have applied the Trinity to the doctrine of sanctification. Some of these scholars include: A. W. Pink, A. Hoekema, L. Bermejo, J. L. Garrett, J. Webster, B. Ware, R. N. Frost, and S. S. Wilson.[16] Wilson is a grad-

---

14 Karl Barth, *The Epistle to the Romans*, trans. Edwyn C. Hoskyns (Oxford University Press, 1933); Grenz, *Rediscovering the Triune God*, 2–3; Thomas F. Torrance, *The Christian Doctrine of God: One Being Three Persons* (T&T Clark, 1996).

15 Grenz, *Rediscovering the Triune God*, 2–3; Colin E. Gunton, ed. *The Doctrine of Creation: Essays in Dogmatics, History and Philosophy* (T&T Clark, 1997). Whereas Grenz, Kärkkäinen, and Welch have focused on the first phase, Sexton has focused on the second: Jason S. Sexton, "The State of the Evangelical Trinitarian Resurgance," *JETS* 54, no. 4 (2001). For reasons for the enthuasism (resurgence) see: Ray Sherman Anderson, *Historical Transcendence and the Reality of God: A Christological Critique*, 1st American ed. (Eerdmans, 1975), 132; Zizioulas, "Doctrine of God," 20; Kärkkäinen, *The Trinity*, xxi, 154; Jason S. Sexton, "Stanley Grenz's Relatedness and Relevancy to British Evangelicalism," *Scottish Bulletin of Evangelical Theology* 28, no. 1 (Spr 2010): 68; Schwöbel, Introduction, 4–11. The revisionists have defined three classifications of Trinitarian works that roughly fit into Grenz's two phases of development: (1) one classification is works focusing on "the mystery of the Trinity" (first phase), (2) another category is works that "placed the consideration of the Trinitarian mystery at the center [sic.] of their dogmatic proposals" (second phase), and (3) a further grouping includes works that "treated particular aspects of Trinitarian doctrine ... or particular periods of the history of Trinitarian doctrines" (second phase). Emery and Levering, "Introduction," 3.

16 Arthur Walkington Pink, *The Doctrine of Sanctification* (Logos Research Systems, Inc., 2005), 61, 69, 74, 87–140; Anthony A. Hoekema, "The Reformed Perspective," in *Five Views on Sanctification*, ed. Stanley N. Gundry, Zondervan Counterpoints Collection (Zondervan, 1987), 59–90; Luis M. Bermejo, *The Spirit of Life: The Holy Spirit in the Life of the Christian* (Loyola University Press, 1989), 10–16; James Leo Garrett, *Systematic Theology: Biblical, Historical, and Evangelical*, 2nd ed. (Ages Digital Library, 2006), s.v. "2:2.8.66.4.C.1"; John Webster, *Holiness* (Eerdmans, 2003); Bruce A. Ware, *Father, Son, and Holy Spirit: Relationships, Roles, and Relevance* (Crossway Books, 2005); R. N. Frost, "Sin and Grace," in *Trinitarian Soundings in Systematic Theology*, ed. Paul Louis Metzger (T&T Clark International, 2006), 101–112; Scott Sparling Wil-

uate of Southeastern Baptist Theological Seminary, and his work is the most significant for this book in part because he has the longest and most detailed sustained discussion focusing exclusively on Trinitarian sanctification.

In the unpublished dissertation, "Trinity and Sanctification," Wilson's thesis is "that Scripture presents the sanctification of believers as the work of the triune God, accomplished according to a particular triune order."[17] Wilson claims that two of his aims are to correct "Spirit-only tendencies prevalent in modern writing and thinking on" sanctification and "to demonstrate the practical relevance of a trinitarian approach to sanctification."[18] By a "Triune order," Wilson means T. Oden's "Triune premise." In his systematic theology, Oden introduced the term "Triune premise" to describe the biblical and historic Trinitarian concept, based on the prepositions in 1 Cor 8:6–7; Rom 11:36; Eph 2:18, that "[t]he sequence of salvation proceeds *from* the benevolence of God the Father toward humanity, *through* the atoning death of the Son in offering redemption, *toward* the grace of the Spirit in applying and enabling redemption."[19] For Wilson, the "Triune premise" means that "the inseparable working of God has been 'appropriated' to the members of the Godhead according to a certain order or *'taxis,'*" which is defined as "'from' the Father 'through' the Son and 'by' the Spirit."[20] The term "appropriation" refers to the "doctrine of appropriations" expressed by Augustine's claim that "indeed the works of the Trinity are not separable; ... and can it be that when one of the three is named with regard to some work, the whole Trinity is understood to work?"[21]

---

son, "Trinity and Sanctification: A Proposal for Understanding the Doctrine of Sanctification According to a Triune Ordering" (PhD. diss., Southeastern Baptist Theological Seminary, 2009).

17 Wilson, "Trinity and Sanctification," 10.

18 Ibid., 10.

19 Emphasis original. Thomas C. Oden, *Life in the Spirit*, vol. 3 of *Systematic Theology* (HarperSanFrancisco, 1992), 25.

20 Oden, *Life in the Spirit*, 23; Wilson, "Trinity and Sanctification," 16, 33.

21 "*neque enim separabilia sunt opera trinitatis— ... An et quando unus trium in aliquo opera nominatur, uniuersa operari trinitas intelligitur?*" Augustine, *Enchir.* 12.38 (CCSL 46:71). See also: Augustine, *Trin.* 1.9.19 (CCSL 50:55–56). Mostert aptly summarizes Augustine's doctrine of appropriations: "[a]ccording to this doctrine, the divine acts *ad extra* are the acts of the *one* God, although they are attributed to one Person of the Trinity in particular." Christiaan Mostert, *God and the Future: Wolfhart Pannenberg's Eschatological Doctrine of God* (T&T Clark, 2002), 197. Although Augustine's doctrine of appropriations means that all three persons of the Trinity are involved in every divine act, it does not mandate that they are involved equally or that one person cannot be the primary agent as in the case of creation where many theologians take the Father to be primary or in the case of progressive sanctification where the Bible emphasizes the Spirit. However, since the contemporary Trinitarian proponents cited above have adequately demonstrated that biblically sanctification is a Trinitarian process and since the tradition, at least at some points, has generally neglected the work of the other Trinitarian persons in sanctification by overemphasizing the role of the Spirit, then this book seeks to

Three Historic Backgrounds: Trinitarianism, Virtue Ethics, and Sanctification 19

Wilson defends his thesis by outlining in successive chapters the appropriated or "individual" roles of the Father, the Son, and the Spirit in sanctification and how the three persons work together in sanctification.[22] Similar to other contemporary Trinitarian proponents, Wilson demonstrates that the Bible appropriates sanctification not only to the Spirit, (Rom 15:16; Eph 3:16; 2 Thess 2:13; 1 Pet 1:2), but also to the Father (John 17:17; Heb 12:10), the Son (John 17:19; 1 Cor 1:2, 30; Eph 5:25–27; Heb 2:11; 10:10; 13:12), and the whole Trinity (1 Cor 6:11; 1 Thess 5:23).[23] The Triune premise is used to provide Trinitarian descriptions or explanations of how the three persons work together in various aspects of sanctification.[24] Part of the significance of Wilson's work is that he extensively explains and explicitly applies Oden's Triune premise to sanctification, whereas other contemporary Trinitarian proponents such as Bermejo, Pink, Ware, and Webster seem to use the premise in a more limited and implicit manner.[25]

This book critically appropriates four aspects of Wilson's work. First, it unconditionally accepts that Wilson and the contemporary Trinitarian proponents have made the case that biblical sanctification is a Trinitarian act. Second, Wilson's point of a need for correcting the "error" of "Spirit-only tendencies prevalent in modern writing and thinking on" sanctification is conditionally accepted.[26] The presentations of authors who overemphasize the role of the Spirit and neglect the Trinity are strictly speaking not incorrect, but incomplete. Charity demands that their works be viewed as containing an overemphasis to be mitigated rather than error to be dismissed. Third, Wilson and the contemporary Trinitarian proponents' goal of demonstrating "the practical relevance of a trinitarian approach to sanctification" is accepted.[27]

Fourth, Wilson's use of the Triune premise is conditionally accepted. Although Oden has demonstrated that the Triune premise has a solid biblical and historical basis, at least two factors, which Wilson recognizes but dismisses, indicate that it should not be rigidly applied.[28] A careful study of the use of the biblical prepositions with respect to the Trinitarian persons indi-

---

highlight the work of primarily the Son as he actively cooperates with the Spirit and the Father in a virtue ethical view of Trinitarian sanctification.

22 Wilson, "Trinity and Sanctification," 68–217.

23 Wilson, "Trinity and Sanctification," 68–100, 109–147, 153–209. Among the others listed above, see also Hoekema's bibilical support for Trinitarian sanctification: Hoekema, "Reformed Perspective," 68–70.

24 Wilson, "Trinity and Sanctification," 100–108, 147–152, 209–217.

25 Pink, *Sanctification*, 89, 91, 118, 121; Bermejo, *Spirit of Life*, 15–16; Webster, *Holiness*, 78–84; Ware, *Father, Son, and Holy Spirit*, 173–182.

26 Wilson, "Trinity and Sanctification," 2–4, 10.

27 Ibid., 10.

28 Wilson, "Trinity and Sanctification," 16–18, 38–40; Oden, *Life in the Spirit*, 23–28.

cates that the Bible does not rigidly ascribe only one preposition to each person.[29] Moreover, Ambrose and Basil argued for variation in the application of the prepositions to the Trinitarian persons on the basis of their interpretation of Rom 11:36 and 1 Cor 8:6–7.[30] An overly rigid application of the Triune premise may contribute to a passive role of the Son in sanctification, as evidenced through Wilson's omission of the Son's active high priestly role and his passive interpretation of Eph 5:25–27.[31] Therefore, by affirming the Triune premise but not rigidly applying it, the doctrine of sanctification will be reframed by this book in virtue ethical Trinitarian terms to include an active role for the Son.

The Impact of the Eclipse and Resurgence of Virtue Ethics on Sanctification

Similar to Trinitarianism in theology, the current trend of finding links between virtue ethics and the doctrine of sanctification has emerged from the history of philosophy and ethics, in which there has been an eclipse followed by a resurgence of interest in virtue ethics.[32] As in the history of the Trinity, there have been some revisionist efforts, but the consensus narrative of an eclipse and resurgence of virtue ethics seems to be prevailing for now.[33] As indicated in chapter 1, at this point in the argument it is sufficient to understand virtue ethics as referring to ethics that focus on character in opposition to ethical systems that are focused on duty, obligation, and rules. Unlike the history of the Trinity, there is no standard story for the eclipse and resurgence

---

29 Acts 11:28; Rom 3:24; 8:2; 1 Cor 2:10, 14; Gal 3:14; 6:8.

30 Ambrose and Basil also offer more biblical examples of prepositional diversity. Ambrose, *Spir.* 2.9 (CSEL 79:120–125); Basil, *Spir.* 4.6–8.21, (SC 17:268–320).

31 Wilson only "designates the Spirit as the *active agent* of sanctification." Emphasis added. Wilson, "Trinity and Sanctification," esp. 146, also see: 109–152.

32 Rosalind Hursthouse, *On Virtue Ethics* (Oxford University Press, 2001), 1–3; Joseph J. Kotva, Jr., *The Christian Case for Virtue Ethics* (Georgetown University Press, 1996), 5; Michael A. Slote, *From Morality to Virtue* (Oxford University Press, 1992), xiii; Servais Pinckaers, *The Sources of Christian Ethics*, trans. Mary Thomas Noble (Catholic University of America Press, 1995), 220, 233, 241–242, 245–247, 253.

33 For example, an exception to the standard narrative seems to be Keenan's historiography in which "the tradition seesaws back and forth between" duty/law and virtue. Keenan may be characterized as an exception because Downs, Gill, Louden, Tousley and Kallenberg, and Wilson affirm the consensus narrative of an eclipse. James F. Keenan, "Moral Theological Reflections," in *Jesus and Virtue Ethics: Building Bridges between New Testament Studies and Moral Theology* (Sheed & Ward, 2002), 1–2, 7–8; David J. Downs, "Vices and Virtues, Lists Of"; Christopher Gill, "Cynicism and Stoicism," in *The Oxford Handbook of the History of Ethics*, ed. Roger Crisp (Oxford University Press, 2013); Robert B. Louden, "Virtue Ethics," in *MEP*, ed. Donald M. Borchert (Macmillan, 2006), 9:687; Nikki Coffey Tousley and Brad J. Kallenberg, "Virtue Ethics," in *DSE*, ed. Green; Jonathan R. Wilson, "Virtue(s)," in *DSE*, ed. Green.

of virtue ethics, but there is a basic historical outline and a dominant position.[34]

A Selective History of Virtue Ethics

The history of virtue ethics roughly divides into three periods widely recognized in philosophy: (1) pre-modernity (recorded history to 1600), (2) modernity (1600–1950), and (3) post-modernity (1950 to the present). In the early pre-modern period, it was widely recognized until recent revisionist efforts that the ethics from Aristotle (384–322 BC) to Aquinas (1225–1274) are virtue ethics.[35] The virtue ethics of Augustine, Aquinas, and others are closely tied to their view of sanctification.[36]

The eclipse of virtue ethics began after Aquinas with Ockham (1280–1349). The dominant position of the resurgence seems to be that G. E. M. Anscombe is correct in her claim that "Christianity, with its law conception of ethics," is responsible for the eclipse of virtue ethics by shifting the concepts of ethics from virtue and character to obligation and rules through the idea of "divine law."[37] However, S. Pinckaers is almost certainly correct that with William of Ockham's (1280–1349) philosophy rather than with his Christianity, "a chasm was fixed between ... the era of the Fathers and great scholastics," which marked the beginning of the eclipse of virtue as ethics shifted toward obligation.[38] The Reformers, particularly Luther, followed Ockham's approach and so set evangelical ethics on the course of a morality of obligation.[39]

---

34 Hursthouse, *On Virtue Ethics*, 2.

35 The following sources take a revisionist view of the virtue ethics in Plato and/or Aristotle and find duty ethic elements in them. John McDowell, "Deliberation and Moral Development in Aristotle's Ethics," in *Aristotle, Kant, and the Stoics: Rethinking Happiness and Duty*, ed. Stephen Engstrom and Jennifer Whiting (Cambridge University Press, 1996), 19; Gerasimos X. Santas, "Does Aristotle Have a Virtue Ethics?," in *Virtue Ethics*, ed. Daniel Statman (Georgetown University Press, 1997), 281; Michael A. Slote, "Virtue Ethics and Democratic Values," *Journal of Social Philosophy* 24, no. 2 (1993): 5–6; Gregory Velazco y Trianosky, "What Is Virtue Ethics All About?," *APQ* 27 (1990): 338.

36 Augustine. *Mor. Eccl.* 13.22; 13.23; 19.36; 25.46 (CSEL 90:26–28, 40–41, 51); Aquinas, *STh.*, III q.79 a.4 ad.1; III q.79 a.6 (*OOII* 12:223, 225).

37 G. E. M. Anscombe, "Modern Moral Philosophy," *Philosophy* 33, no. 124 (1958): 5–6.

38 Pinckaers, *Sources of Ethics*, 241, 253. For a similar judgment see: Henry Sidgwick, *Outlines of the History of Ethics* (Macmillan, 1886), 145. At least four historical facts militate against Anscombe's charge that Christian "divine law" introduced obligation: (1) Aristotle's non-Christian virtue ethics depended on the divine, (2) Augustine and Aquinas' Christian virtue ethics were compatible with "divine law," (3) Scotus' divine command theory was still compatible with virtue theory, and (4) none of these resulted in an ethics of obligation. Only Ockham's un-Christian or biblically inconsistent nominalism resulted in the idea of "obligation."

39 Alister E. McGrath, *The Intellectual Origins of the European Reformation*, 2nd ed. (Blackwell, 2004), 72, 80–82, 99, 101; Stephen J. Pope, "Natural Law and Christian Ethics," in *The Cam-*

In the modern period, the eclipse of virtue ethics occurred with the duty ethics of I. Kant (1724–1804) and J. S. Mill (1806–1873), which dominated modern ethics.[40] Contemporary evangelical ethics seem to be dominated by three rule-based Kantian-type ethical positions identified in N. Geisler's response to J. Fletcher's situation ethics: the lesser of the two evils (conflicting absolutism), the third option (unqualified absolutism), and the greater good (graded absolutism).[41]

Written at the dawn of post-modernity, G. E. M. Anscombe's (1919–2001) famous article "Modern Moral Philosophy" has been recognized for inciting the resurgence of interest in virtue ethics through her critique of Kant and Mill's ethics and her call to return to Aristotelian virtue ethics as a solution for the deficiencies of modern moral philosophy.[42] In 1981, the first edition of Alasdair MacIntyre's *After Virtue* contributed to the popularization of virtue ethics.[43] Following Anscombe's call, secular resurgence ethicists have re-

---

bridge Companion to Christian Ethics, 2nd ed., ed. Robin Gill of Cambridge Companions to Religion (Cambridge University Press, 2012), 72–73; Dietmar Lage, *Martin Luther's Christology and Ethics*, TSR 45 (Edwin Mellen, 1990), 17, 28; James B. Sauer, *Faithful Ethics According to John Calvin: The Teachability of the Heart*, TST 74 (Edwin Mellen, 1997), 152. Luther's position is vividly illustrated by his contrasting attitudes toward Aristotle and Ockham: "*Tota fere Aristotelis Ethica pessima est gratiae inimica. ... Occam, mein lieber Meister.*" [Almost all of Aristotle's [*Nicomachean*] *Ethics* is most hostile to grace. ... Ockham, my dear master.] Martin Luther, *Disputatio contra eebolaaticam theologiam, 1517* (WA 1: 226); idem, *An die gantze geistlickeit zu Augsburg versamlet auff den Heichstag Anno 1530* (WA 30.II.2: 300).

40 Immanuel Kant, *Grundlegung zur Metaphysik der Sitten*, 4:429–430, 439 (*KGS* 4:114, 421, 429–430, 439); John Stuart Mill, *Utilitarianism*, 2.18; 3.4–7 (*CW* 10:219–220, 228–231). The following revisionist sources read virtue ethics into Kant: Christine Korsgaard, "From Duty and for the Sake of the Noble: Kant and Aristotle on Morally Good Action," in *Aristotle, Kant, and the Stoics: Rethinking Happiness and Duty*, ed. Stephen Engstrom and Jennifer Whiting (Cambridge University Press, 1996), 203–236; Barbara Herman, *The Practice of Moral Judgment* (Harvard University Press, 1993); Barbara Herman, "Making Room for Character," ed. Stephen Engstrom and Jennifer Whiting (Cambridge University Press, 1996), 36–62; Robert B. Louden, "Kant's Virtue Ethics," *Philosophy* 61, no. 238 (Oct., 1986), 473–498; Onora O'Neill, "Kant's Virtues," in *How Should One Live? Essays on the Virtues*, ed. Roger Crisp (Clarendon Press, 1996), 77–98; Allen W. Wood, *Kant's Ethical Thought* (Cambridge University Press, 1999). Despite the fact that Bentham takes a low view of virtue as demonstrated by Annas, Driver and Hurka have given consequentialist accounts of the virtues. Julia Annas, "Should Virtue Make You Happy?," *Apeiron* 35, no. 4 (2002); Julia Driver, *Uneasy Virtue* (Cambridge University Press, 2001); Thomas Hurka, *Virtue, Vice, and Value* (Oxford University Press, 2001).

41 Norman L. Geisler, *Ethics: Alternatives and Issues* (Zondervan, 1971), 79–136; idem, *Christian Ethics: Contemporary Issues and Options*, 2nd ed. (Baker Academic, 1989), 66–115.

42 Anscombe, "Modern Moral Philosophy," 1–16; Roger Crisp, "Virtue Ethics," in *REP*, ed. Edward Craig (Routledge, 1998), 622; Louden, "Virtue Ethics," 9:687.

43 Alasdair MacIntyre, *After Virtue: A Study in Moral Theory*, 2nd ed. (University of Notre Dame Press, 1984); Nafsika Athanassoulis, "Virtue Ethics," in *Internet Encyclopedia of Philosophy: A Peer-Reviewed Academic Resource*, ed. James Fieser and Bradley Dowden (2010), https://www.iep.utm.edu/virtue; John J. Davenport, "Towards and Existential Virtue Ethics: Kierkegaard and Macintyre," in *Kierkegaard after Macintyre: Essays on Freedom, Narrative, and Virture*,

formulated the virtue ethics of the Greek philosophers with particular emphasis on Aristotle, and similarly Christian ethicists have placed emphasis on the ethics of Aristotle and Aquinas.[44] While "still a minority position," virtue ethics is now considered "an alternative model" or "'third option', competing with" the ethical theories in the traditions of Kant and Mill.[45] The impact of the eclipse and resurgence of virtue ethics on sanctification is that the pre-modern connection between virtue ethics and sanctification was lost by the modern eclipse of virtue by duty and rules, while the post-modern resurgence of virtue ethics has caused Christians to reconsider the links between virtue ethics and sanctification.

Critical Appropriation of Virtue Ethical Sanctification

This section turns from establishing the impact of the resurgence of virtue ethics on sanctification to how this insight is critically appropriated. A number of scholars have reconsidered the links between virtue ethics and sanctification including: S. Hauerwas, G. Meilaender, J. Kotva, J. Woodill, and B. Borgman.[46] Of these scholars, Hauerwas and Kotva are important for this book because: Hauerwas is currently the most influential proponent of virtue ethics from a theological view point; Kotva explicitly claims to be building on the work of Hauerwas; and they have two of the most important discussions connecting virtue ethics to sanctification.

---

ed. John J. Davenport and Anthony Rudd (Open Court, 2001), 266–268; R. Scott Smith, *Virtue Ethics and Moral Knowledge: Philosophy of Language after Macintyre and Hauerwas*, Ashgate New Critical Thinking in Philosophy (Ashgate, 2003), 3.

44 Daniel Statman, "Introduction to Virtue Ethics," in *Virtue Ethics*, ed. Daniel Statman (Georgetown University Press, 1997), 26.

45 Stephen Darwall, ed. *Virtue Ethics*, ed. Steven M. Cahn, Blackwell Readings in Philosophy (Blackwell, 2003), 5; Statman, "Introduction," 5; Karen Stohr and Christopher Heath Wellman, "Recent Work on Virtue Ethics," *American Philosophical Quarterly* 39, no. 1 (2002): 70; Trianosky, "Virtue Ethics," 337.

46 Stanley Hauerwas, *Character and the Christian Life: A Study in Theological Ethics* (Trinity University Press, 1975); Gilbert C. Meilaender, *The Theory and Practice of Virtue* (University of Notre Dame Press, 1984); Kotva, *Case for Virtue*; Joseph Woodill, *The Fellowship of Life: Virtue Ethics and Orthodox Christianity* (Georgetown University Press, 1998); Brian S. Borgman, *Feelings and Faith: Cultivating Godly Emotions in the Christian Life* (Crossway, 2009). Three post-modern liberal works that establish a link between virtue ethics and the Trinity include: Cunningham's post-liberal *These Three are One*, Jones's post-liberal *Transformed Judgment*, and Lee's pro-homosexual, feminist, "Made in the Images of God." These works are important enough to mention in passing but do not significantly contribute to this book other than establishing a general precedent for connecting the Trinity and virtue ethics. David S. Cunningham, *These Three Are One: The Practice of Trinitarian Theology*, Challenges in Contemporary Theology (Blackwell, 1998); L. Gregory Jones, *Transformed Judgment: Toward a Trinitarian Account of the Moral Life* (University of Notre Dame Press, 1990); A. Elizabeth Lee, "Made in the Images of God: Towards a Trinitarian Virtue Ethics" (Ph. D. diss., Graduate Theological Union, 2010).

In his published doctrinal dissertation, *Character and the Christian Life* (1975), Hauerwas discusses the idea of "character" within the context of a sub-discipline of philosophy called "action theory," which studies the nature and causes of actions, and within the context of his post-liberal Yale school of narrative theology.[47] As chapter 2 will explain, Hauerwas' work has a faulty philosophical basis so that his insights may only be critically appropriated. Hauerwas' philosophical basis is due at least in part to his position within the post-liberal Yale school of narrative theology. According to Kotva, Hauerwas in this work was the first resurgence scholar who "began the task of linking virtue ethics to the systematic category of sanctification."[48] Hauerwas makes the link through the thesis of his fifth chapter by claiming that when sanctification is interpreted in terms of his understanding of character, the transformation of the believer can be described in a way that does not result in a works-based salvation.[49]

Hauerwas claims that traditional Protestant views have been hesitant to describe concretely the transformation that takes place in sanctification in order to safeguard against falling into a works-based salvation.[50] For Hauerwas, the primary link between sanctification and character comes from the fact that despite their differences, Calvin, Wesley, and Edwards all agree that "the essential element in man's sanctification" is "the change of the 'person'"

---

47 Hauerwas, *Character*, xix, 111; Jennifer Hornsby, "Action," in *CREP*, ed. Edward Craig (Routledge, 2000), 5; Johannes S. Reinders, "The Meaning of Sanctification: Stanley Hauerwas on Christian Identity and Moral Judgment," in *Does Religion Matter Morally?: The Critical Reappraisal of the Thesis of Morality's Independence from Religion*, ed. Bert Musschenga, MML 2 (Kok Pharos, 1995), 147. Narrative theology and its various branches must be defined in order to understand the phrase "post-liberal Yale school of narrative theology" and how Hauerwas' position within this school contributes to a faulty basis for his thought. Narrative theology refers to a number of post-modern approaches to theology and hermeneutics in which truth or meaning is viewed as communicated through stories (narrative) rather than statements (propositions). Narrative theology consists of three schools: California, Chicago, and Yale. The Yale school is based on Barth's Neo-Orthodox existentialism as well as the ordinary language philosophy of Ludwig Wittgenstein, and some of its proponents include Hans Frei (founder), George Lindbeck, and David Kelsey. The Yale school of narrative theology produced two distinct theological movements: post-conservatism and post-liberalism. Post-liberalism is a post-modern revision of Protestant modern liberalism, which adheres to narrative theology and like earlier liberalism denies the inerrancy, authority, and sufficiency of Scripture. Some of its proponents include George Lindbeck, Hans Frei, and Stanley Hauerwas. Kevin J. Vanhoozer et al., eds., *DTIB* (Baker Academic, 2005), 531, 606, 859–860; Kevin T. Bauder et al., eds. *Four Views on the Spectrum of Evangelicalism*, Zondervan Counterpoints Collection (Zondervan, 2011), 86–89, 176; Dan R. Stiver, *Theology after Ricoeur: New Directions in Hermeneutical Theology*, 1st ed. (Westminster John Knox Press, 2001), ix, 115, 246; John J. Stackhouse, ed. *Evangelical Futures: A Conversation on Theological Method* (Baker, 2000), 76, 201.

48 Kotva, *Case for Virtue*, 71.

49 Hauerwas, *Character*, 182, 193–194.

50 Ibid., 182, 193–195.

which "has close parallels to the importance of character for ethical behavior."[51] Hauerwas views the "person" of these three theologians as his philosophical "self," which is a moral agent with character. This character is not only the result of the self's history of past chosen actions (the self's narrative history) but also an orientation that guides the self's future choice of actions.[52] Since character is not absolutely stable, but rather "open to change and growth," then Hauerwas interprets Calvin, Wesley, and Edwards' "change" as a change in character. This change in character involves growth in the believer's understanding of how to choose actions in accord with the guiding or "fundamental orientation" of being "loyal to God's act in Jesus Christ" rather than as a works-based moralism of "becoming better and better."[53]

In the *Christian Case for Virtue Ethics*, Kotva claims his presentation of the connection between sanctification and virtue ethics builds on that of Hauerwas in *Character and the Christian Life* by treating aspects of sanctification's "correlation with and correction to virtue theory ... that Hauerwas left largely unexplored."[54] In order to establish this correlation and correction, Kotva compares neo-Aristotelian virtue ethics both to systematic theology and to the biblical text. In his systematic comparison, Kotva uses the similarities among the descriptions of sanctification by three theologians (Hendrikus Berkhof, Millard J. Erickson, and John Macquarrie) in order to establish what sanctification is, and then he compares it to neo-Aristotelian virtue ethics.[55] Kotva concludes that sanctification and neo-Aristotelian virtue ethics have three similarities and two differences. The similarities include that: (1) both are teleological, which Kotva defines as being "focused on the movement from who we are to who we can be," (2) these are focused on the development of virtue, and (3) they are concerned with a process of moral transformation over a lifetime.[56]

Kotva also claims that sanctification and neo-Aristotelian virtue ethics have two differences. The first difference is that while sanctification allows for human responsibility but emphasizes the priority of God's grace, neo-Aristotelian virtue ethics omits grace and emphasizes human effort.[57] The second difference is that neo-Aristotelian virtue ethics emphasizes the idea of a *telos* (the Greek word for "end" or "goal") as "an ideal of human excellence

---

51　Ibid., 196.
52　Ibid., 117, 119, 221.
53　Ibid., 120, 220, 223, 228.
54　Kotva, *Case for Virtue*, 71, 78.
55　Ibid., 69–78.
56　Ibid., 72–78.
57　Ibid., 76.

and perfection that can never be fully actualized," but sanctification holds to a *telos* that is actualized in the next life through glorification.[58] Kotva implies that in order for neo-Aristotelian virtue ethics to be compatible with Christian sanctification, it must be modified to emphasize grace and include a *telos* in the afterlife.[59]

In addition to his systematic comparison, Kotva also compares virtue ethics to the biblical text. Kotva limits his comparison to Matthew and Paul. Some of his most relevant conclusions for this book are that virtue ethics and Matthew and Paul agree in focusing on "internal qualities" (virtues), reciprocity, a *telos*, and discipleship/training (habituation).[60]

This book critically appropriates several concepts from the work of Hauerwas and Kotva. From the work of Hauerwas, his idea of character as a link between virtue ethics and sanctification is appropriated in order to explain how Aristotelian reciprocity can explain the change in sanctification involved with acquiring and increasing in virtue in a way consistent with *sola fide*. However, the next chapter will argue that the philosophical basis upon which Hauerwas derives his idea of character and its linking function is biblically inconsistent. Therefore, this book cautiously and critically appropriates only Hauerwas' general concept of using character as a link and derives the definition of character and the nature of the link independently from his work.

Three broad concepts are appropriated from Kotva's work. First, Kotva's links between virtue ethics and sanctification are generally accepted. Second, his qualification is accepted that some aspects of virtue ethics need to be corrected or modified in order to be more biblically consistent. Third, this book builds on the exegesis Kotva used to establish links between virtue ethics and the Bible and the modifications he made to virtue ethics to harmonize it with Scripture.

The Historical Development of the Doctrine of Sanctification

The history of sanctification has not been treated as extensively or with as much attention as the histories of the Trinity, virtue ethics, or perhaps even most of the other doctrines.[61] As a result, the history of sanctification is not as

---

58 Ibid., 76.
59 Ibid., 76–78.
60 Ibid., 28, 104–108, 120–121, 126–129, 131.
61 Several different and relatively brief histories of sanctification and their various emphases include the following: Berkhof's history is structured around the separation of sanctification from justification, Bockmuehl's history is concerned to show "the whole range of aspects of the biblical teaching," Garrett's history seems designed to introduce and critique the various traditional views, Jenney's history focuses on the development of Pentecostalism,

standardized. The following selective history is constructed so as to demonstrate both the impact of virtue ethics on Trinitarian sanctification and how the position-only view of sanctification emerged. The following historiography depicts the relationship of four issues (regeneration, justification, the Trinity, and virtue ethics) to sanctification in history. While the position-only view is not a major focus of this work, it is important to consider because rejection or acceptance of it determines the nature of sanctification as having either three aspects (past positional, present progressive, and future perfective) or only one present positional aspect.

A Selective History of Sanctification

In the Patristic period, L. Berkhof aptly notes that the doctrine of sanctification was not developed much until Augustine.[62] However, the church fathers used the holiness language of the Greek and Latin NTs ("ἁγι-," "*sancta/sanctificare*") to tie explicitly sanctification to virtue.[63] For example, Clement of Alexandria (AD 155–220) defined sanctification in terms of virtue, "Ἀναγεννηθέντες

Muller's history traces the idea of perfection, and Toon's history focuses on the relationship between justification and sanctification. Louis Berkhof, *Systematic Theology* (Eerdmans, 1938), 529–531; K. Bockmuehl, "Sanctification," in *NDT*, ed. Sinclair B. Ferguson and J.I. Packer (InterVarsity, 2000), 613–616; Garrett, *Systematic Theology*, s.v. "2.8.66.3.A–C."; Timothy P. Jenney, "The Holy Spirit and Sanctification," in *Systematic Theology: A Pentecostal Perspective*, ed. Stanley M. Horton (Gospel Publishing House, 2012), ch. 12; R. A. Muller, "Sanctification," *ISBE* 4:321–331; Peter Toon, *Justification and Sanctification*, Foundations for Faith (Crossway, 1983), 45–110. In order to illustrate the relatively sparse treatment of the history of sanctification in comparison to other doctrines, one can note the short page lengths of the previous sources on sanctification in comparison to McGrath's massive, formerly three volume, and 448 page magnum opus on justification, *Iustitia Dei*. Alister E. McGrath, *Iustitia Dei: A History of the Christian Doctrine of Justification*, 3rd ed. (Cambridge University Press, 2005). For an overview of the history of sanctification as presented in this book see Table A1 in Appendix 1.

62 Berkhof, *Systematic Theology*, 529.

63 Ambrose, *Spir.* 1.16.159 (CSEL 79:82); Clement of Alexandria, *Paed.* 3.12 (SC 29, 3:164); Clement of Rome, 1 *Clem.* 30 (*PAO* 1 pt. 1:17); Tertullian, *Res.* 44.3–6 (CSEL 47:91). These examples are representative and were selected due to their clarity and to meet the rigorous and unnecessary demand of the Position-Only view that sanctification only involves the "ἁγι-" and "*sancta/sanctificare*" language, which occurs in these sources. If one does not restrict the idea of sanctification to this language and allows for other biblical language and concepts to represent sanctification, then early Patristic examples of sanctification being tied to virtue are more numerous. Some less restricted, but representative and selective examples include: Hermas, *Sim.* 6.1; 10.1 (GCS 48:59, 105–106); Justin Martyr, 1 *Apol.* 1.21 (SC 507:190); Origen, *Cels.* 3.71; 8.17 *Origenes Contra Celesum Libri VIII*, ed. J. Den Boeft et al., Supplements to Vigiliae Christianae 54 (Köln: Brill, 2001), 208, 534–535; Gregory of Nyssa, *De anima et resurrectione* in *De anima et resurrectione; Vita Macrinae*, Franz Oehler, ed., Bibliothek Der Kirchenväter 1 (Wilhem Engelmann, 1858), 86, 88, 102; idem, *De infantibus praemature abreptis* (*GNO* 3 pt. 2:83–85, 95–96); idem, *Oratio catechetica magna* 8 (*GNO* 3 pt. 4:32).

... ἁγιασθῶμεν ... κατ᾽ ἀρετὴν ἀνυπέρβλητος."[64] Although attributing sanctification to the Spirit was common, there were some Trinitarian statements.[65] For example, Origen (AD 185–254) claimed the "Trinity is the fountain of all holiness."[66] It was not uncommon for justification and sanctification to be conflated as in Barnabas and Tertullian.[67]

The conflation of justification and sanctification continued in the thought of Augustine (AD 354–430).[68] Like the tradition before him, Augustine viewed sanctification as a process of being made holy which involved growing in virtue, as demonstrated by Augustine's claim that "For having been sanctified [*sanctificati*], we burn with full and complete love ... I assert that virtue is entirely nothing except the highest love of God."[69] In his extensive discussions on virtue, Augustine develops the tradition by arguing that the virtues are infused as a supernatural gift of the Spirit to empower the believer to live righteously.[70] Augustine's thought on sanctification and virtue may have a Trinitarian element. On the basis of *De Civitate Dei* 11.28, Frederick Carney argues that Augustine's virtue ethic has a Trinitarian element in which believers are being restored into the Creator's image of eternity (Father), truth (Son), and love (Spirit) from which they have fallen due to sin.[71] In order to recognize the Trinitarian character in *Civ.* 11.28, Carney claims one must realize that often

---

64 "being regenerated ... let us sanctify ourselves ... according to perfect virtue." Clement of Alexandria, *Paed.* 3.12, (SC 29, 3:164).

65 Some authors who appropriated sanctification to the Spirit include: Clement of Alexandria, *Paed.* 1.6 (GCS 39:105); Gregory of Nyssa, *Refutatio Confessionis Eunomii* 2 (*GNO* 2:317); Tertullian, *Prax.* 2.11–14 (CSEL 47:229). Some authors who described sanctification in Trinitarian terms include: Gregory of Nyssa claimed, "Ἁγιάζει ... ὁμοίως ὁ Πατὴρ καὶ ὁ Υἱὸς καὶ τὸ Πνεῦμα τὸ Ἅγιον," "The Father and Son and Holy Spirit likewise sanctify." Gregory of Nyssa, *Ad Eustathium de sancta trinitate* 7 (*GNO* 3 pt. 1:11) and Origen, *Princ.* 1.4.2 (GCS 22:65).

66 "*quae Trinitas totius est sanctitatis fons.*" Origen, *Princ.* 1.4.2 (GCS 22:65).

67 Barnabas, *Barn.* 5 (*PAO* 1 pt. 2:50); Tertullian, *Bapt.* 7.10.27–31 (CSEL 20:209).

68 Augustine, *Bapt.* 4.24.32 (CSEL 51:259); It is well known that Augustine's view is based in part on his misinterpretation of justification as a process of being made just, when he mistakes "*justificati*" for "*justi facit*" by claiming, "*Quid est enim aliud, justificati, quam justi facit ... Unde aliter dicimus, Deus sanctificat sanctos suos.*" "What is for instance (in) some (places), to be justified, than to be made just, ... In another place it says, God sanctifies his saints" Augustine, *Spir. et litt.* 26.45 (CSEL 60:228); McGrath, *Iustitia Dei*, 46–47.

69 "*Sanctificati enim plena et integra caritate flagramus ... nihil omnino esse uirtutem affirmauerim nisi summum amorem dei.*" Augustine, *Mor. eccl.* 13.22; 15.25; see also: 13.23; 19.36; 25.46 (CSEL 90:27, 29, see also: 26–29, 40–41, 51).

70 On the attainment of *talis*, "excellence (of character)," by infusion of the Spirit see: Augustine, *Spir. et litt.* 36.66 (CSEL 60:199–200). On infusion of the virtues see: Augustine, *Conf.* 8.12.29 (CSEL 33:195); idem, *Civ.* 4.20; 5.19 (CSEL 40/1:186–187, 252); idem, *C. du. ep. Pelag.* 1.8.13 (CSEL 60:435). On love of God enabling "righteousness living," see: Augustine, *Civ.* 10.6 (CSEL 40/1:454–455).

71 Frederick S. Carney, "The Structure of Augustine's Ethic," in *The Ethics of St. Augustine*, ed. William S. Babcock, JRESR 3 (Scholars Press, 1991), 11, 15, 33; Augusitne, *Civ.* 11.28 (CSEL 40/1:554–556).

in Augustine's writings the Father is associated with eternity (*Trin.* 6.10.11), the Son with truth (*Trin.* 4.18.24), and the Spirit with love (*Trin.* 15.17.27).[72] Augustine's view generally prevails until the Reformation as seen in the work of Aquinas.[73]

In the Middle Ages, explicitly following Augustine at points, Aquinas' (1225–1274) extensive discussions of virtue argued for sanctification as involving a progress of infused virtue: "according to Augustine ... the invisible mission happens for the sanctification of the creature ... according to the progress of virtue, or an increase of grace, the invisible mission happens."[74] Aquinas also follows Augustine in conflating justification (as a process of making righteous) and sanctification.[75] Aquinas strongly appropriates sanctification to the Spirit.[76] After Aquinas, Ockham (1280–1349) and the later medieval voluntaristic nominalists helped to prepare the way for the Reformation's separation of justification and sanctification by arguing, as R. A. Muller put it, "that the remission of sins [justification] and the infusion of sanctifying grace are connected not out of necessity but because of the divine decree."[77]

---

72 Carney, "Structure," 11, 15, 33; Augustine, *Civ.* 11.28 (CSEL 40/1:554–556); idem, *Trin.* 4.18.24; 6.10.11 (CCSL 50:191–193, 241–242); idem, *Trin.* 15.17.27 (CCSL 50A:501–502).

73 Further evidence that virtue ethical sanctification prevails during this period can be found, among others, in Bernard of Clairvaux (1090–1153) and Peter Lombard (1095–1164), who both explicitly connect sanctification to virtue in their long discussions of virtue. For example, Bernard claims, "*exhibeatur etiam virtus in specie pietatis*" [let virtue produce in kind piety]. Bernard of Clairvaux, *Ad Clericos de Conversione* 37 (SC 457: 412); Bernard of Clairvaux, *Dilig. D.* 2.2–6 (SC 393: 64–74); idem, *Super Cantica Sermo* 3.3 (SC 414:106); Peter Lombard, *Discrimen* 2.27.5; 3.23–36 *The Sentences*, ed. Joseph Goering and Giulio Silano, trans., Giulio Silano, MST 43, 45 (Pontifical Institute of Mediaeval Studies, 2008, 2010), 43:135, 45:97–150, esp. 137.

74 "*secundum August. ... missio invisibilis fit ad sanctificandam creaturam ... secundum profectum virtutis, aut augmentum gratiae fit missio invisibilis.*" Aquinas, *STh.*, I q.43 a.6 s.c.; I q.43 a.6 ad.2 (*OOII* 4:451). For the infusion of virtues see: Idem., *STh.*, I–II q.110 a.3 resp. (*OOII* 7:313). Aquinas also connects sanctification and virtue in his discussion of the sacraments: "*et forma nostrae sanctificationis, quae consistit in gratia, et virtutibus*" [and the form of our sanctification, which consists in grace and the virtues]. Idem., *STh.*, III q.60 a.3 resp.; III q.79 a.4 ad.1; III q.79 a.6 (*OOII* 12:12:6, 223, 225).

75 Aquinas, *Super Epistolam B. Pauli ad Romanos lectura* C.1 L.4.69; C.9 L.3.772 ed. J. Mortensen and E. Alarcón, trans. F. R. Larcher, Under the title *Commentary on the Letter of Saint Paul to the Romans*, Latin/English ed., Biblical Commentaries 37 (The Aquinas Institute, 2012), 25, 258; Aquinas, *STh.*, I–II q.112 a.2 ad.1; I–II q.113 a.6 resp. (*OOII* 7:324, 336). The conflation may be more easily recognized when one realizes that "*gratiae infusion*" (*STh.*, I–II q.113 a.6 resp.) is conflated with "*gratiae gratum facientis*" (*STh.*, I–II q.112 a.2 ad.1). Davies elucidates, "though he [Aquinas] speaks of the division of grace, he does not mean to imply that there are different graces ... Grace, for him, is always the same thing, however we think of it." Brian Davies, *The Thought of Thomas Aquinas* (Oxford University Press, 1992), 269.

76 Aquinas, *STh.*, I q.43 a.3 (*OOII* 4:447–449).

77 Muller, "Sanctification," 327. For a similar judgment see: Alister E. McGrath, *Intellectual Origins*, 77–81.

In the time prior to the Reformation, three important features characterized sanctification: (1) sanctification is conflated with justification and regeneration, (2) sanctification is viewed as a process of being made holy which is viewed as growing in infused virtues, and (3) for some, sanctification is highlighted as a Trinitarian work.

In the Reformation, two significant developments occurred with respect to sanctification. First, the Council of Trent (1545–1563) accepted Aquinas' position on sanctification as the view of the Roman Catholic Church.[78] Second, the Reformers modified the received doctrine of sanctification.

The modifications of the received doctrine by the Reformers began with Luther and continued through Calvin. Luther (1483–1546) reinterpreted justification as the righteous status imputed by God rather than as an infused grace which makes the believer just.[79] For Luther, justification and sanctification are still conflated, but in conjunction with his idea of "at the same time righteous and sinner" (*simul iustus et peccator*), the language of "progress" refers to the reaffirmation of one's status through repentance such that "to progress is nothing other (than), if not always to begin."[80] Luther replaced the infused virtue of love with the non-infused disposition of faith as a trust that is the Spirit's instrument in union with Christ, "a supernatural habit, infused from heaven, which is charity ... These are the schoolmen's dreams. But we put in the place of that charity, faith."[81] This rejection of infused virtues that merit justification seems responsible for beginning a shift in later writers on sanctification away from virtue and toward "good works" and "the law."[82] Luther tended to appropriate sanctification to the Spirit.[83]

---

78 Henry Denzinger, Roy J. Deferrari, and Karl Rahner, ed. *The Sources of Catholic Dogma* (B. Herder Book, 1954), 251–253.

79 "*iustitiam Dei ... qua nos Deus induit, dum nos iustificat ... de imputatione,*" [the righteousness of God ... with which God clothes us, when he justifies us ... according to imputation]. Luther, *Vorrede Zum Ersten Bande Der Gesamtausgaben Seiner Lateinischen Schriften, Wittenberg 1545* (WA 54:186). "*iusti habebuntur et deputabuntur,*" [considered and regarded righteous]. Luther, *Der Brief an Die Römer* (WA 56:201).

80 "*proficere est nihil aliud, nisi semper incipere.*" Luther, *Römer* (WA 56:9, 227, 333, 441–443). Luther, *Dictata Super Paslterium: Psalmus 119:88* (WA 4:350). For a similar judgment see: Regin Prenter, *Spiritus Creator*, trans. John M. Jenson (Wipf and Stock, 1946), 39, 69–81.

81 "*habitum supernaturalem, e coelo infusum, qui est charitas, ... Haec sunt Scholasticorum somnia. Nos autem loco charitatis istius ponimus fidem*" Luther, *In Epistolam S. Pauli Ad Galatas Commentarius Ex Praeclectione* (WA 40.1:228). For a similar judgment see: Bernd Wannenwetsch, "Luther's Moral Theology," in *The Cambridge Companion to Martin Luther*, ed. Donald K. McKim, Cambridge Companions to Religion (Cambridge University Press, 2003), 129.

82 For a similar judgment see: D. Michael Cox and Brad J. Kallenberg, "Character," in *DSE*, ed. Green.

83 Luther, *Römer* (WA 56:168).

Melanchthon (1497–1560), according to P. Toon, was the first to distinguish conceptually "between justification and regeneration/sanctification," a distinction which "came to assume great importance, especially after it was adopted by John Calvin."[84] Building on Luther's foundation, Melanchthon gave a forensic interpretation of justification as an imputed status attained through the instrument of faith by means of the Spirit, but with the loss of Luther's idea of union.[85] As in the previous tradition, he conflated regeneration and sanctification as both an event/status and a process.[86] Melanchthon primarily attacked the virtues as not being a means of justification and subordinated their importance in the process of sanctification to the third use of the law.[87]

Since Calvin (1509–1564) adopted Melanchthon's view, then their positions are similar except that Calvin retained and emphasized Luther's concept of union with Christ and, based on the concept of union, clarified that justification and sanctification are distinct but inseparable.[88] This distinction made by Melanchthon and popularized by Calvin is foundational for all subsequent teaching on sanctification following in the Reformation tradition.[89] Calvin also repudiated the virtues as a means of justification and shifted the

---

84 Toon, *Justification and Sanctification*, 63. According to Franks, McGrath, and Toon, the claim of Keathley and Peterson is mistaken that Calvin was the first to make this distinction. Robert S. Franks, *The Work of Christ: A Historical Study of Christian Doctrine*, Nelson's Library of Theology (Thomas Nelson and Sons, 1962), 324–325; Kenneth Keathley, "The Work of God: Salvation," in *A Theology for the Church*, ed. Daniel L. Akin (B&H, 2007), 701; McGrath, *Iustitia Dei*, 213, 254–255; David G. Peterson, *Possessed by God: A New Testament Theology of Sanctification and Holiness*, NSBT 1 (InterVarsity Press, 1995), 93; Toon, *Justification and Sanctification*, 63. Melanchthon claimed, "*vt ad Hebraeos scriptum est. Sanctificati sumus per oblationem Iesu Christi semel. ... Item, scriptura docet, Nos coram Deo iustificari per fidem in Christum,*" [as is written according to Hebrews. We have been sanctified by the single offering of Jesus Christ ... Also Scripture teaches, we are justified before God through faith in Christ]. Philipp Melanchthon, *Confessio Augustana* (CR 26:299–300). Calvin's clearest (*Institutes* [1559] 3.16.1) and other statements that make the distinction do not appear in *Institutes* (1536) so that Melanchthon's statements in his *Confessio* (1530) and *Apologia* (1531) are earlier.

85 "*iustificare est forense verbum*" [justification is a forensic term] and "*iustificatio seu imputatio iustitiae*" [justification or the imputation of righteousness]. Philipp Melanchthon, *Loci communes theologici* (MW 2.2:359, 800).

86 For the conflation see: Melanchthon, *Apologia Confessionis Ex Editiene Principe A. 1531 4th Edita* (CR 27:429, 447, 543, 619). For a progressive concept of sanctification see: Melanchthon, *Loc. com.* (MW 2.1:239–240, 281); Melanchthon, *Loc. com.* (MW 2.2:783).

87 Melanchthon, *Loc. com.* (MW 2.2:431–433); Melanchthon, *Apol. Conf.* (CR 27:447–448, 587).

88 Calvin claims, "*Sed quia de iustitia et sanctificatione tantum quaestio est, in iis insistamus. Inter se distinguamus licet, inseparabiliter tamen utramque Christus in se continet.*" [But because so much questioning is concerning justification and sanctification, we press on with regard to them. Among ourselves we distinguish (them), it is permitted, yet no matter which, Christ in himself inseparably secures (both).] John Calvin, *Inst.* 3.16.1 (CR 30:586).

89 Peterson, *Possessed by God*, 94.

focus even more than Melanchthon to the third use of the law by increasing the emphasis on knowing God's will instead of producing virtue and by explicating the Ten Commandments, which later became the foundation of Reformed ethics.[90] Both Melanchthon and Calvin recognize that sanctification is also from Christ, but tend to appropriate it to the Spirit.[91] In general the Reformers did not emphasize sanctification as a Trinitarian work in the way Gregory of Nyssa, Origen, and others did.

As a result of the Reformer's modifications, four important features characterized sanctification by the end of the Reformation: (1) a conflation of regeneration and sanctification is distinguished from justification, (2) sanctification focuses more on obedience to the law instead of cultivating virtue, which is primarily repudiated as a means of justification, (3) sanctification is viewed as a process of increasingly holy living but not inherent holiness, and (4) sanctification's Trinitarian nature was not emphasized as it was previously. It is important to note that while a distinct shift occurs toward minimizing the role of virtue in sanctification with the Reformation, virtue was not completely eclipsed immediately and only began slowly to give way to the ideas of rules, duty, and law over the following centuries.

In the eighteenth century, debates over infant baptism and predestination, as well as the thought of Pietism and the Evangelical Awakenings, as expressed by Abraham Kuyper, drove the term regeneration away from "its *wider* sense" of "the *entire* change by grace effected in our persons" toward its "*limited* sense" as the "*starting-point* of the Christian life" in distinction from progressive sanctification as the continued change.[92] As a result of these and other factors, by the time of Charles Hodge (1797–1878), regeneration was explicitly distinguished from sanctification.[93]

---

90 Calvin rejects the virtues as a means to salvation in his discussion of free will: Calvin, *Inst.* 2.2.1–2.2.4; 2.2.9 (CR 30:175–178, 183–184). Calvin claimed, "*Tertius usus, qui et praecipuus est, ... discant quails sit Domini voluntas*" (The third use, which is also principal, ... to know what is the will of the Lord) Calvin, *Inst.* 2.7.12 (CR 30:261). For Calvin's exposition of the Ten Commandments in conjunction with the third use of the law see: Calvin, *Inst.* 2.2.8 (CR 30:266–309). For Calvin's minimization of virtue in describing the Christian life see: Calvin, *Inst.* 3.6.1 (CR 30:501–502). For a similar judgment on the Reformation's new empahsis on the Ten Commandments see: Wannenwetsch, "Luther's Moral Theology," 121.

91 Calvin, *Inst.* 3.2.8; 3.16.1 (CR 30:404, 586); Melanchthon, *Apol. Conf.* (CR 27:429, 526).

92 Emphasis original. Abraham Kuyper, *The Work of the Holy Spirit* (Funk & Wagnalls, 1900), 293. See also: Herman Bavinck, *Sin and Salvation in Christ*, vol. 3 of *Reformed Dogmatics*, ed. John Bolt, trans. John Vriend (Baker Academic, 2006), 579–584; Herman Bavinck, *Holy Spirit, Church, and New Creation*, vol. 4 of *Reformed Dogmatics*, ed. John Bolt, trans. John Vriend (Baker Academic, 2008), 55–59; Berkhof, *Systematic Theology*, 466–467; Helmut Burkhardt, "Regeneration," in *NDT*, ed. Sinclair B. Ferguson and J.I. Packer (InterVarsity Press, 2000), 574.

93 Charles Hodge, *Systematic Theology* (Logos Research Systems, 1997), 3:3, 5. Although seemingly following Calvin, sanctification appeared as a separate element in the *ordo salutis*

From the eighteenth to the twentieth centuries, seven historic evangelical views of sanctification developed, including the: Lutheran, Reformed, Wesleyan, Keswick, Pentecostal, Augustinian-Dispensational, and Contemplative views.[94] Since these historic views are only touched upon briefly by this book and since they have been extensively described and analyzed in numerous other sources, then they are broadly categorized according to the main controversy most touched upon by this book (the progressive versus two stage debate) and their relationship to virtue ethics and the Trinity is explained.[95]

As briefly mentioned in the introduction, of the issues that the seven historic views debate, the controversy over a progressive versus a two stage view of sanctification is the issue most touched on by this book and which may

in the seventeenth century. Packer aptly observes that it was still conflated with regeneration during this period. Examples of this conflation can be found in William Ames (1576–1633), Johannes Maccovius (1588–1644), Francis Turretin (1623–1687), and Robert Traill (1642–1716). J. I. Packer, "Regeneration," in *Evangelical Dictionary of Theology*, ed. Walter A. Elwell, Baker Reference Library (Baker, 2001), 1001; William Ames, *The Marrow of Theology* (Baker, 1997), ch. 26.19; Johannes Maccovius, *Loc. Com.* 70 (626–627); Robert Traill, "Sermon VI: 1 Peter 1:2," in *Works of the Late Reverend Robert Traill* (J. Ogle, 1810), 4:71; Francis Turretin, *Inst.*15.4.13 (2:459–460). However, two possible exceptions are John Owen (1616–1683) and Walter Marshall (1628–1680), who *may* distinguish between regeneration and sanctification. If as Ferguson contends, Owen distinguished between regeneration and sanctification in his *ordo salutis*, then Owen *might* be the first to make this distinction, but general or at least wider acceptance of such a distinction does not seem to have occurred until Hodge. Sinclair B. Ferguson, *John Owen on the Christian Life* (Banner of Truth, 1987), 35; Walter Marshall, *The Gospel-Mystery of Sanctification* (Southwick and Peluse, 1811), 43–44, 127, 137; John Owen, Πνευματολογια· or, a Discourse Concerning the Holy Spirit, Works 3:366–367, 387, 393, 397, 408. In *Holiness* (1877), published just after Hodge's *Systematic Theology* (1871–1873), J. C. Ryle (1816–1900) explicitly distinguishes between sanctification and regeneration, thus further demonstrating that the two terms had become differentiated by the time of Hodge. J. C. Ryle, *Holiness: Its Nature, Hindrances, Difficulties and Roots* (William Hunt and Company, 1889), 26.

94 Alexander and Gundry agree on the importance of the Reformed, Wesleyan, and Pentecostal views, but Alexander has the Lutheran and Contemplative views and Gundry the Keswick and Augustinian-Dispensational views. While the authors in these two studies differentiate between the Pentecostal and Charismatic movements, they group them under a single view. The contemplative view predates this period, but it is included with the other views so that they can all be discussed together. Donald Alexander, ed. *Christian Spirituality: Five Views of Sanctification* (InterVarsity, 1988); Gundry, ed. *Five Views on Sanctification*.

95 Readers who are either unfamiliar with the seven historic views or wish to refresh their memories may consult the following excellent sources which describe and analyze these views: Alexander, *Christian Spirituality*; Garrett, *Systematic Theology*, s.v. "2.8.66.3.A–C"; Gregory A. Boyd and Paul R. Eddy, *Across the Spectrum: Understanding Issues in Evangelical Theology*, 2nd ed. (Baker Academic, 2009), 161–182; Pamela D. Green, "The Function of Romans 6–8 in Four Models of Sanctification: A Critical and Exegetical Analysis" (M.A. Th. thesis, Southwestern Baptist Theological Seminary, 2005); Gundry, *Five Views on Sanctification*; H. Wayne House, *Charts of Christian Theology and Doctrine* (Zondervan, 1992), 92–94; James M. Howard, *Paul, the Community, and Progressive Sanctification: An Exploration into Community-Based Transformation within Pauline Theology*, ed. Hemchand Gossai, StBibLit 90 (Peter Lang, 2007), 11–25; Robert N. Wilkin, "We Believe In: Sanctification: Part 3: Present Sanctification: God's Role in Present Sanctification," *JGES* 7, no. 12 (1994), http://www.faithalone.org/journal/; Internet.

be used to categorize the seven views. This controversy entails the competing ideas of whether progressive sanctification following conversion is to be understood as a single continuous process of growing in holiness or whether this process consists of two distinct stages separated by an instantaneous crisis-event. Of the seven historic views, the Lutheran, Reformed, Augustinian-Dispensational, and Contemplative views may be construed as viewing sanctification as a single stage process.[96] The Wesleyan, Keswick, and Pentecostal views have different descriptions of the instantaneous crisis-event (entire sanctification, crisis experience, baptism of the Holy Spirit), but for each of these three views, this crisis-event divides sanctification into an initial stage characterized by struggle with sin and relatively little spiritual growth and a second stage characterized by victory over sin and relatively vigorous spiritual growth.[97] In chapter 4 of this book, the virtue ethical concept of habituation is related to this debate.

Since the historical development of two (justification and regeneration) of the four issues this history sought to relate to sanctification have been fully described, then the relationship of virtue ethics and the Trinity to the seven

---

96 Forde's Lutheran view, that "Sanctification ... is a matter of getting used to justification," and Luther's view, *proficere est nihil aliud, nisi semper incipere,* "to progress is nothing other (than), if not always to begin," might be construed as a Position-Only view, but Forde interprets Luther as arguing for "a kind of growth and progress." Furthermore, other Lutherans such as Pieper and Mueller (396–400) have a process similar to the Reformed view so that the Lutheran view can be characterized as having a process. Gerhard O. Forde, "The Lutheran View," in *Christian Spirituality: Five Views of Sanctification,* ed. Alexander, 22–23, 27–30; Luther, *Dictata Paslterium* (WA 4:350); John Theodore Mueller, *Christian Dogmatics* (Concordia Publishing House, 1999), 396–400; Franz Pieper, *Christliche Dogmatik* (Evangelisch-Lutherischen Synode von Missouri und Anderen Staaten, 1946), 518. House's chart "69. Views of Sanctification" might give the false impression that the dispensational view holds to a two-stage sanctification. However, in light of Chafer and Walvoord's one-stage view, House's chart is best understood as merely reflecting the fact that in the later Lordship salvation debate that the Free Grace view of the dispensational tradition holds that repentance logically not chronologically comes later in the *ordo salutis*. Lewis Sperry Chafer, *Systematic Theology* (Kregel, 1948), 6:45–46, 284–285; 7:274–284; House, *Charts,* 111; Howard, *Progressive Sanctification,* 11–25; John F. Walvoord, "The Augustinian-Dispensational Perspective," in *Five Views on Sanctification,* ed. Gundry, 215–222; Wilkin, "Part 3: Present Sanctification." For a good overview and analysis of the Lordship salvation debate see: Millard J. Erickson, "Lordship Theology: The Current Controversy," *SWJT* 33, no. 2 (1991). Since Bernard of Clairvaux has four degrees of love and John of the Cross has ten steps or degrees of love, then the Contemplative view might be interpreted as being a multi-stage sanctification, but it also might be construed as a single stage view in which distinct degrees of spiritual growth are recognized. Bernard of Clairvaux *De Diligendo Deo* 2.2–6 (SC 393:64–74); John of the Cross, *Dark Night of the Soul,* trans. E. Allison Peers (Neeland Media, 2010), 84–110; E. Glenn Hinson, "The Contemplative View," in *Christian Spirituality: Five Views of Sanctification,* ed. Alexander, 180–185.

97 Alexander, *Christian Spirituality,* 86, 101–102, 107, 116, 121–122, 125, 136–137; Boyd and Eddy, *Across the Spectrum,* 172–174, 179–180; Gundry, ed., *Five Views on Sanctification,* 14, 42, 48, 123–126, 128–134, 171, 178; House, *Charts,* 111.

historic views of sanctification remains to be explained. The relationship of virtue ethics to sanctification in the later Lutheran and Reformed views generally is similar to that in Melanchthon and Calvin. In the later Lutheran and Reformed views, the virtues typically receive little if any attention, but when they are discussed, the treatment includes attacks on the virtues as a means of justification and subordinating the virtues to the law, the will of God, and good works.[98] The relationship of virtue ethics to sanctification is the same for each of the remaining five historic views and is generally characterized by earlier authors making some mention of virtue in their discussion of sanctification (but the amount of mention is less than authors prior to the Reformation) and later authors making little or no mention of virtue.[99] For example, John Wesley (1703–1791), the founder of Wesleyanism, spoke of "that habitual disposition of the soul, which in the sacred Writings is termed holiness, ... the being endued with those virtues, which were in Christ Jesus," but later Wes-

---

[98] Berkhof, *Systematic Theology*, 428–429, 433, 523, 533, 540–541; G. C Berkouwer, *Faith and Sanctification*, Studies in Dogmatics (Eerdmans, 1952), 38; Forde, "The Lutheran View," 27, 29–30; Hodge, *Systematic Theology*, 3:148, 153, 217, 226–227, 232, 236–237; Mueller, *Christian Dogmatics*, 380, 400–406; Pieper, *Christliche Dogmatik*, 480, 510–111, 521–524, 545–546; William Greenough Thayer Shedd, *Dogmatic Theology*, ed. Alan W. Gomes, 3rd ed. (P&R, 2003), 803–804, 808. Two exceptions are Edwards, who devoted an entire work to virtue in which he equated sanctification to virtue, and Jenson, who seems to revive virtue to a limited extent. Jonathan Edwards, "A Dissertation Concerning the Nature of True Virtue" (Works 1:139); Robert W. Jenson, *The Works of God*, vol. 2 of *Systematic Theology* (Oxford University Press, 1999), ch. 18, 22, 25, 30.

[99] For the Wesleyans, see the next footnote. For the Keswick movement, compare Asa Mahan to J. Robertson McQuilkin: Asa Mahan, *Out of Darkness into Light* (Amazon Digital Services, 2010), pt. 1, ch. 3, 4; pt. 2, ch. 1; idem, *Christian Perfection* (Amazon Digital Services, 2012), s.v. Discourse 1.2; 3.I.7; 5; 8; J. Robertson McQuilkin, "The Keswick Perspective," in *Five Views on Sanctification*, ed. Gundry, 149–183. For Pentecostals, compare Charles Finney to Stanley M. Horton, Timothy P. Jenney, Russell P. Spittler: Charles Finney, *Principles of Sanctification* (Bethany House, 1986), ch. 2.19; 3; 12; idem, *Systematic Theology*, Original, Unabridged 1851 ed. (Holiness Publishing, 2011), s.v. Lecture 3.3; 4.III.4; 5.III.29, 39; 5.IV.2; idem, *The Works of Charles Finney* (Packard Technologies, 2004), s.v. Lecture XVII.II.4; XXIII.I.2, II.2, V.2; ch. 13.IV.3; Stanley M. Horton, "The Pentecostal Perspective," in *Five Views on Sanctification*, ed. Gundry, 103–135; Jenney, *Sanctification*, ch. 12; Russell P. Spittler, "The Pentecostal View," in *Christian Spirituality*, ed. Alexander, 133–170. For the Augustinian-Dispensationalists compare Lewis Sperry Chafer to John F. Walvoord: Chafer, *Systematic Theology*, 1:48, 234–237, 303, 317; 2:5, 74, 163, 202; Lewis Sperry Chafer, *He That Is Spiritual: A Classic Study of the Biblical Doctrine of Spirituality* (Kessinger Publishing, 2010), ch. 3, 4; Walvoord, "Augustinian-Dispensational Perspective," 197–226; John F. Walvoord, *The Holy Spirit: A Comprehensive Study of the Person and Work of the Holy Spirit* (Zondervan, 2010), ch. 21, 23. For the Contemplatives compare Bernard of Clairvaux, John of the Cross, and Ignatius Loyola to Thomas Merton and E. Glenn Hinson: Bernard of Clairvaux, *Dilig. D.* 2.2–6 (SC 393: 64–74); John of the Cross, *Dark Night of the Soul*, 15–32, 40–42, 47–48, 67–68, 96, 110–113; Lawrence S. Cunningham, ed. *Thomas Merton: Spiritual Master, the Essential Writings* (Paulist Press, 1992), 15, 31, 80, 92–93, 153; Hinson, "The Contemplative View," 174; Ignatius Loyola, *The Spiritual Exercises of St. Ignatius Loyola; Spanish and English with a Continuous Commentary*, ed. and trans. Joseph Rickaby (Burns & Oates, 1915), 73, 94, 112, 170, 215, 217.

leyan authors such as Melvin Dieter and Laurence Wood make no mention of virtue in their discussions of sanctification.[100]

The relationship of the Trinity to the seven historic views of sanctification is that the Trinitarian nature of sanctification is generally not emphasized by the historic views until the time of the contemporary Trinitarian proponents. In fact, prior to and even in some instances after the rise of the contemporary Trinitarian proponents, a number of adherents from the historic views of sanctification so emphasized the role of the Spirit in sanctification that they neglected the Father and the Son.[101] For instance, in *Five Views on Sanctification*, only Hoekema has a truly Trinitarian sanctification, Stanley M. Horton and J. Robertson McQuilkin explicitly downplay the Trinity to highlight the Spirit to varying extents, Walvoord only mentions union with Christ (Christ and Spirit), and M. Dieter merely appropriates sanctification to the Spirit.[102]

One potential cause of this overemphasis on appropriating sanctification to the Spirit or neglect of the Trinity is the frequent description of Christ's role in progressive sanctification as being primarily and in many instances exclusively passive.[103] In these instances, one way Christ's work in progressive

---

100 John Wesley, "A Plain Account of Christian Perfection," in *The Works of John Wesley*, ed. Thomas Jackson (Wesleyan Methodist Book Room, 1872), 367. Muller and Collins see a significant role for virtue in Wesley's thought. Kenneth Collins, "A Hermeneutical Model for the Wesleyan Ordo Salutis," *Wesleyan Theological Journal* 19, no. 2 (1984): 24; Muller, "Sanctification," 329; Melvin E. Dieter, "The Wesleyan Perspective," in *Five Views on Sanctification*, ed. Gundry, 9–46; Laurence W. Wood, "The Wesleyan View," in *Christian Spirituality*, ed. Alexander, 95–118.

101 Berkhof, *Systematic Theology*, 527, 532, 535; Berkouwer, *Sanctification*, 78–79; Millard J. Erickson, *Christian Theology*, 3rd ed. (Baker Academic, 2013), 897; Mueller, *Christian Dogmatics*, 384–386; John Murray, *Redemption: Accomplished and Applied* (Eerdmans, 1954), ch. 7; Pieper, *Christliche Dogmatik*, 501–502, 506, 508, 513; Augustus Hopkins Strong, *Systematic Theology* (American Baptist Publication Society, 1907), 3:869; Shedd, *Dogmatic Theology*, 803–804. Three notable exceptions to the primary appropriation of sanctification to the Spirit in this period are Bavinck, Hodge, and Kuyper. Bavinck, *Spirit, Church, and Creation*, 4:235, 248–250, 252; Hodge, *Systematic Theology*, 3:213, 215, 218, 228–231; Kuyper, *Holy Spirit*, 457–463.

102 Gundry, ed., *Five Views on Sanctification*, 16, 68–70, 95–96, 125–127, 139, 155, 175, 221. The situation is similar in Alexander's *Christian Spirituality*. To qualify, Horton does have a Trinitarian sanctification in his presentation, but he spends far more time on the Spirit and in his response to Hoekema he downplays Trinitarian sanctification in order to emphasize the Spirit. The following claims serve as further illustration of the neglect of the Trinity among the historic views of sanctification: "Of the members of the Trinity, it is He [the Spirit] who sanctifies the believer" (McQuilkin), "Specifically it is the Holy Spirit who is the agent of sanctification" (Murray), and "Sanctification results from the continuation of the agency of the Holy Spirit after the act of regeneration" (Shedd). McQuilkin, "The Keswick Perspective," 155; Murray, *Redemption*, pt. 2, ch. 7; Shedd, *Dogmatic Theology*, 803.

103 The standard story of Trinitarianism would suggest that scholars were reticent to involve the Trinity in their theology such as sanctificaiton due to the anti-Trinitarianism that emerged in the Reformation and climaxed in the Englightenment, but the revisionists would deny this claim. If there was no eclipse of the Trinity due to anti-Trinitarianism, it is still possible that sanctification became less Trinitarian due to anti-Trinitarianism or due to a combina-

sanctification is described as passive is that Christ's death on the cross (his "finished work") accomplishes positional sanctification which serves as the passive basis for the Spirit to apply actively progressive sanctification.[104] For example, Kuyper claims "that Christ has *obtained* sanctification, ... the Holy Spirit *imparts* it."[105]

The seven historical views of sanctification generally adhere to the Reformation characterization of sanctification as well as the eighteenth century modifications including: (1) justification is distinguished from sanctification, (2) sanctification is differentiated from regeneration, (3) the Trinitarian nature of sanctification typically is not emphasized as it was in the Patristic era until the time of the contemporary Trinitarian proponents, and (4) if virtue is mentioned, it is usually repudiated as a means of salvation or subordinated to the law.[106] Additionally, the historic views normally interpret sanctification as

---

tion of factors that might include: eclipse of union with Christ, use of Oden's "Triune premise," the concept of the "final work of Christ" in coordination with the idea of "redemption accomplished in Christ and applied by the Spirit," and/or other issues. This book is not primarily concerned with *why* many scholars began almost exclusively to appropriate sanctification to the Spirit, but rather with responding to this historic occurrence by emphasizing the importance of virtue ethics for sanctification and highlighting the role of Christ in order to describe sanctification as a more Trinitarian process.

104 For a simlar judgment see: Webster, *Holiness*, 80–81. Berkouwer, *Sanctification*, 92–93; Calvin, *Inst.* 3.1.1; 3.14.9; 4.18.3 (CR 30:393, 570, 1053–1054); Hodge, *Systematic Theology*, 3:213, 215; Kuyper, *Holy Spirit*, 462; Mueller, *Christian Dogmatics*, 319, 446; Murray, *Redemption*, pt. 1, ch. 4; pt. 2., ch. 1; pt. 2, ch. 7; Pink, *Sanctification*, 124; Strong, *Systematic Theology*, 1:317; 3:869, 872. Someone might object that in *Institutes* 2.15.6; 3.20.18, Calvin has an active role for Christ in his heavenly intercession, but as chapter 5 will futher explain, Calvin is following the tradition of Gregory of Nazianzus' interpretation of Christ's intercession in which the intercession is Christ's past sacrifice represented by his passive presence in heaven rather than an active prayer as in the Lutheran tradition represented by Chemnitz and Mueller. Careful observation of Calvin's empahsis on Christ's past "sacrifice" making believer's present prayers acceptable and providing the believer "access" confirm Christ's passive role for Calvin. Another way that Christ's work in progressive sanctification is described as passive is the historical tendency of making union with Christ the passive basis upon which the Spirit actively applies progressive sanctification. Union does not have to result in a passive description of progressive sanctification, but historically this has been the tendency. Since union is such a broad issue, it is passed over in this argument in favor of pursuing its impact on sanctification as an area for future research.

105 Emphasis original. Kuyper, *Holy Spirit*, 462.

106 This characterization describes the majority of authors, but there are some exceptions in each case. For example, Edwards and Jenson were mentioned as exceptions to the characterization regarding virtue ethics and Bavinck, Hodge, and Kuyper were mentioned as exceptions to the characterization regarding the Trinity. To these might also be added the Trinitarian sanctification emphasis found in Marshall and Ryle: Marshall, *Gospel-Mystery*, 70, 277–278; Ryle, *Holiness*, 89, 444–448.

having three aspects: past positional, future perfective, and present progressive, which includes a present process of moral transformation.[107]

Since the emergence of the seven historical views, developments in the field of biblical studies have caused scholars to question how sanctification should be defined.[108] In biblical studies, several factors have likely contributed to an increasing number of scholars questioning the definition of sanctification: (1) the increased knowledge of and more exacting scientific definition of terms has contributed to this questioning, (2) changes in how Greek tenses are to be understood has added to such inquires, and (3) greater emphasis on reading the NT in light of the OT as well as second temple Judaism has been conducive to such queries.[109] In light of these and likely other factors, a position-only view of sanctification has emerged which claims that the theological use of the term "sanctification" as "a process of moral and spiritual transformation" does not match the NT usage of the term, which is said to refer only to the initial position or status of believers.[110]

The Definition of Sanctification: Positional and Progressive

Due to the controversial nature of the position-only view, it is important to understand what positional sanctification is and the definition of progressive sanctification that is developed in the following chapters. Positional sanctification may be defined as the position or status (1 Cor 6:11; Rev 22:17) of

---

107 Arthur L. Farstad, "We Believe in Sanctification–Part 1: Introduction," *JGES* 5, no. 2 (1992); Richard L. Mayhue, "Sanctification: The Biblical Basics," *MSJ* 21, no. 2 (2010): 146–148, 150, 153–156; Zondervan, "Foreword," in *Five Views on Sanctification*, ed. Gundry, 7.

108 After the rise of the seven historic views, Packer claims that another important development is the "relative eclipse" of sanctification in contemporary theology. Porter claims that there has been a resurgence of interest in sanctification, but under new terms in the field of spiritual formation rather than theology proper. J. I. Packer, *Keep in Step with the Spirit* (F. H. Revell, 1984), 97, 99, 101; Steven L. Porter, "On the Renewal of Interest in the Doctrine of Sanctification: A Methodological Reminder," *JETS* 45, no. 3 (2002): 415–416, 426. More recently, while there has not been a resurgence of interest in sanctification in theology proper, there have been a number of recent dissertations on sanctification (Pratt, 1999; Kwon, 2002; Kettenring, 2005; Owens, 2008; Reeder, 2009; Walter, 2009; Wilson, 2009; Bosson, 2010) and articles published in series (a five part series in the *Journal of the Grace Evangelical Society* 5–8 (1992–1995); a six part series in *Banner of Truth* 509–512 (2006); a six part series in *TableTalk Magazine* 34, no. 5 (May 2010): 2–25, a six part series in the *MSJ* 21, no. 2 (2010): 143–236) which may indicate a growing interest and may be found in the bibliography.

109 Daniel B. Wallace, *Greek Grammar Beyond the Basics: Exegetical Syntax of the New Testament* (Zondervan, 1999), 4, 363, 714; Stanley N. Gundry, ed. *Three Views on the New Testament Use of the Old Testament*, Counterpoints (Zondervan, 2008); R. T. France, "The Church and the Kingdom of God: Some Hermeneutical Issues," in *Biblical Interpretation and the Church: Text and Context*, ed. D. A. Carson (Paternoster, 2000), 37.

110 Peterson, *Possessed by God*, 13, 27, 81.

holiness conferred by God on the believer by which the believer is elected to be God's possession (Deut 7:6).[111] Broadly following the Aristotelian-Augustinian-Thomistic tradition, virtue ethics and Trinitarian progressive sanctification are taken as partial synonyms that refer to the teleological process based on natural law ("the view that there are innate or natural moral laws known by all men") and requiring metaphysical realism in which the believer actualizes their positional holiness (Rom 6:22) by imitating (Matt 4:19; 1 Cor 11:1) the nature/character of the Father as expressed in the creation (Ps 19:1; Acts 14:17; Rom 1:20) and the Son (John 8:38; 14:9–10) by habitually (Luke 6:40; 1 Tim 4:7; Heb 5:14) acting in accordance with created purposes through the power of the Holy Spirit (Rom 5:6; 8:3), prayer-help of Christ (Luke 22:31; Rom 8:34; Heb 2:14–18), and motivation of Spirit-empowered virtues (Luke 8:1–15; Rom 12:1–2, 9), to be transformed (Rom 12:1–1; Col 3:10) into the *telos* or end of the good, the image of Christ (Mark 10:18; Rom 8:29).[112] The position-only view is assessed with this understanding of the difference between positional (sometimes called definitive) and progressive sanctification in mind.

Assessment of the Position-only View

By claiming that in biblical use, sanctification only refers to the past positional aspect, the position-only view of sanctification represents a challenge to the seven historic views, which normally interpret sanctification as having three aspects: past positional, future perfective, and present progressive (a present process of moral transformation).[113] While the position-only view is not a major focus of this book, it is important to consider since acceptance or rejection of the position-only view is determinative of the nature of sanctification, and because there are currently no known responses to it. There are a number of scholars who have argued for the position-only view of sanctification and whose work may mark an emerging trend.[114] This discussion

---

111 John Murray, "Definitive Sanctification," *CTJ* 2, no. 1 (1967): 5, 12; Peterson, *Possessed by God*, 20, 23–24, 34.

112 On natural law see: Norman L. Geisler and Paul D. Feinberg, *Introduction to Philosophy: A Christian Perspective* (Baker, 1980), 432. This definition of virtue ethics is not comprehensive and does not entail all that is involved with this term. These terms are explained further in chapter three.

113 William G. Coberly, "An Exegetical Argument for the Position-Only View of Sanctification" (M.T. thesis, The Master's Seminary, 2004), 1–2.

114 Coberly, "An Exegetical Argument for the Position-Only View of Sanctification," 1–4; Clarence Tucker Craig, "Paradox of Holiness," *Interpretation* 6 (1952): 151, 153, 160–161; Victor Paul Furnish, *Theology and Ethics in Paul*, The New Testament Library (1968; repr., Westminster John Knox, 2009), 123, 155, 239–241; David G. Peterson, *Possessed by God: A New Testament Theology of Sanctification and Holiness*, NSBT 1 (InterVarsity, 1995), 13, 24–25, 103, 115–116, 123, 125,

will focus on D. G. Peterson, an Anglican NT scholar at Moore Theological College, Sydney, Australia and who may be better known for his work on the book of Hebrews. Peterson's work is important because it is likely responsible for popularizing the position-only view (as evidenced by Coberly's appropriation of it), and because his work represents one of the most comprehensive and conscious arguments for the position-only view as a systematic view in competition with the traditional view.

In *Possessed by God*, Peterson argues against the misunderstanding of sanctification as "moralistic perfectionism" achieved by "human effort," which he believes is the perspective of the seven historic views of sanctification.[115] According to Peterson, these views have misunderstood sanctification as "a process of moral and spiritual transformation following conversion."[116] They have failed to recognize that the sanctification language of "the New Testament ... refers to God's way of taking possession of us in Christ" through "a status ... which God imparts" that is to be "expressed and maintained" and that such language does not refer to renewal and transformation."[117] Although Peterson uses qualifications such as "primarily" and "possible," his argument to a large extent is a *terminological* rejection of progressive sanctification, "biblical terminology must not be obscured by confusing it with other terms."[118] Peterson holds to positional sanctification and takes the idea of "transformation and growth" as a separate concept, language group, or rubric apart from sanctification.[119] Peterson claims that he has "doubts about ... the progressive aspect of sanctification ... and the implication that there is a graded form of progress that can lead to ever-increasing measures of holiness" because "instead of speaking in terms of progressive sanctification, the New Testament more

---

133–137. Coberly lists a number of additional scholars whom he claims adhere to the position only view including Wilkin. However, Wilkin claims that Coberly has misclassified him as adhering to the position-only view when in fact Wilkin explicitly supported the traditional three aspect view in his two relevant articles in the *Journal of the Grace Evangelical Society*. As a result of this misclassification, Coberly's other classifications are suspect and only those whose adherence seems certain are cited. Coberly, "Position-Only," 25–36; Robert N. Wilkin to Ronald M. Rothenberg, "Question about Sanctification Articles," 26 June 2012, e-mail; Wilkin, "Part 3: Present Sanctification"; Robert N. Wilkin, "We Believe In: Sanctification: Part 4: Man's Role in Present Sanctification," *JGES* 7, no. 13 (1994), http://www.faithalone.org/journal/.

115 Peterson, *Possessed by God*, 12, 91, 137, 144.

116 Ibid., 27, 136.

117 Ibid., 22–23, 27, 67, 78–79, 125–126, 132–133, 136–137, 140, 143–144.

118 Ibid., 135, cp. 68, 70, 136. The only real possible exception Peterson seems to give for a process passage is the highly controversial v. 1 Tim 2:15. Ibid., 24, 27, 67, 133, 136, 141. Coberly even more explicitly draws out the fact that Peterson's dispute has a great deal to do with terminology when he claims, "The question remains as to what is the appropriate biblical *terminology* for what theology calls sanctification." Coberly opts for the term "walking worthily." Emphasis added. Coberly, "Position-Only," 6, 130.

119 Peterson, *Possessed by God*, 115–137.

regularly employs the language of renewal, transformation, and growth, to describe what God is doing with us here and now."[120] Peterson supports his rejection of progressive sanctification methodologically, exegetically, and historically.

Before responding to Peterson and recognizing that interaction in this context with his works will be limited, it is important to briefly address his essay on holiness in the *New Dictionary of Biblical Theology*, because many readers may be more familiar with this standard reference than with his primary work advancing the position-only view, *Possessed by God*.[121] Despite appearances to the contrary in that essay, Peterson does not argue for the traditional view of three aspects of sanctification, but rather, as consistent with and seemingly as a summary of *Possessed by God*, in his dictionary article he also promotes the position-only view of sanctification for at least two main reasons.

First, the title or subject of the essay is holiness and not sanctification. While sanctification and holiness are very closely related, they are not the same thing. Traditionally, holiness is a communicable attribute of God's character (Lev 19:2) and sanctification deals with the participation of people in the quality of that divine attribute (2 Pet 1:4).[122] In his essay, the distinction between these terms allows Peterson to *subtly* limit the term sanctification to the past "redemptive work of Jesus Christ ... regularly portrayed as *a once-for-all, definitive act* [that] is *primarily* to do with the holy status or position of those who are 'in Christ.'"[123] Despite Peterson's affirmation that sanctification "clearly has a present and a future aspect," this statement does not mean what it appears because in his book, he explicitly draws an alleged distinction between the theological meaning of the term sanctification and the NT usage.[124] As in his book, so also in his essay, Peterson redefines (transfers and transforms) the traditional present and future aspects of sanctification from a participation in holiness respectively into the related concepts of a present pursuit and expression of the position of holiness and a future transformation into holiness, representing the eschatological actualization of the

---

120 Ibid., 70, 136.
121 D. G. Peterson, "Holiness," in *New Dictionary of Biblical Theology*, ed. T. Desmond Alexander and Brian S. Rosner (InterVarsity, 2000), 544–550.
122 Walter A. Elwell, ed. *Baker Encyclopedia of the Bible* (Baker, 1988), s.v. "God, Being and Attributes of"; Michael Horton, "God," in *Evangelical Dictionary of Theology*, ed. Daniel J. Treier and Walter A. Elwell (Baker Academic, 2017), 343, 347. Turretin, *Inst.* 3.6.5 *Instutio Theologiae Elencticae*, Francisci Turrettini Opera (John D. Lowe, 1847); 1:172.
123 Peterson, "Holiness," emphasis added, 547, cp. Idem, *Possessed by God*, 24–25.
124 Ibid., 550; cp. idem, *Possessed by God*, esp. 13, 67, 133, 136–137.

believer's position.¹²⁵ Since Peterson speaks about present and future aspects of holiness, then he appears to hold to the traditional threefold view of sanctification, but he does not because he holds to the position-only view. For Peterson, there is no present progressive sanctification or progress/participation in holiness through improved character and there is no future completion of this progress. Rather there is a present *expression* of one's position or relationship with God and a future *transformation* or actualization of the position or status conferred on believers in the past. However, in his book, Peterson clarifies that the present and future aspects of sanctification are better expressed under the terms growth, renewal, and transformation as separate categories rather than under sanctification.¹²⁶ Consequently, when Peterson speaks about present and future sanctification in his essay, he means something different from what is traditionally understood, and he has transferred and modified the traditional sanctification concepts into the separate categories of growth/renewal and transformation.

Second, in order to recognize this shift/transfer and modification of theological concepts, and as consistent with his terminological argument in *Possessed by God*, Peterson does not mention the term progressive sanctification in his essay and only mentions glorification once when he subtly separates it from sanctification. He transfers and transforms these concepts into holiness as a separate category. For Peterson, the traditional concept of progressive sanctification as a present process of moral transformation is transferred to and modified into the concept of a present pursuit of holiness as an expression of one's past position of sanctification. Just like in his book, Peterson uses the qualifying language of "primarily" to cosmetically mediate any impression of position-*only,* but then proceeds to reinterpret *every* NT passage he covers (the same ones from his book) from the traditional understanding of a present progressive process of moral transformation to a present pursuit of holiness "as a practical *expression* of their sanctification [status or position, *sic.*] in Christ."¹²⁷ In his essay, the closest Peterson gets to openly denying the progressive nature of sanctification, as he explicitly does in his book, is with regard to his interpretation of 1 Cor 1:30, "this text is not describing a *sequence*," and his rejection of Wesleyan entire sanctification from 1 Thess 5:23, "'entire sanctification' is not a crisis moment in the *process of Christian maturation*, as some have proposed."¹²⁸ Similarly with regard to glorification and as in his book, Peterson does inconsistently use the word sanctification

---

125 Cp. Peterson, *Possessed by God*, 67.
126 Peterson, *Possessed by God*, 115–116, 125, 133–137.
127 Peterson, "Holiness," emphasis added, 547, 549, cp. 548.
128 Ibid., emphasis added, 548, 550; cp. idem, *Possessed by God*, 70, 81, 115, 136.

occasionally to refer to the final state of believers "in the new creation" and "consummation," but his preferred and standard description is not glorification as a final step in a process of sanctification, but rather a future *transformation* into holiness or "to be *transformed* into his likeness (*cf.* 1 John 3:2)."[129] Peterson subtly separates glorification from sanctification by describing it as a "*later* teaching."[130]

Therefore, in his essay as in his book, Peterson's terminology and some of his concepts may be similar to and may give the *appearance* that he is presenting the traditional threefold view of sanctification as past positional, present progressive, and future glorification, but a careful reading of his essay and particularly in comparison with his much longer and more explicit book demonstrates that he is denying such a view. Peterson is sometimes inconsistent in his descriptions and occasionally lapses back to or does not sufficiently break from traditional/theological language or patterns in both of his works. However, the major thrust of his argument indicates that for him, sanctification in the NT is not a process of moral transformation beginning in the past, continuing in the present, and completed in the future, but rather is *only* a past act that merely confers a status, which is expressed in pursuing holiness and realized or actualized in a future transformation into holiness. For Peterson, sanctification is a past position/status and the present and future divine work in the believer's life is described under the separate terms/categories of growth, renewal, and transformation rather than sanctification, which are "linked" and have a "relationship" to sanctification, but are not identical with it.[131] Even if one wants to object that the label "position-*only*" is a misnomer with regard to both his book and essay, and it does not seem to be, at the very least, the moniker serves the important function of indicating that Peterson's view of sanctification is and particularly its present and future aspects are significantly different from the traditional view so that his interpretation deserves both separate classification and rejection.

While it is not possible to give a full response to Peterson in this context, a preliminary response may be made to the most significant aspect of his argument, the exegetical portion. Peterson has made a positive contribution to scholarship by highlighting the neglected aspect of positional sanctification and its prominence in the biblical text through his thoughtful and replete exegesis. While it is not possible to review every passage Peterson covers in detail, it can be noted that not everyone has been persuaded by his interpre-

---

129 Peterson, "Holiness," emphasis added, 547, 549.
130 Ibid., 550; cp. idem, *Possessed by God*, 67.
131 Ibid., 54, 136.

tations.¹³² Furthermore, two key passages that stand against the position-only view in favor of a virtue ethical view of Trinitarian progressive sanctification are 1 Pet 1:13–16 and Eph 5:25–33.

In 1 Pet 1:13–16, the passage is marked as a textual unit by the "therefore" in v. 13 and the OT quotation in v. 16. The interpretation of the passage turns on whether one takes the three relevant participles (ἀναζωσάμενοι, "girding up," νήφοντες, "being sober," and συσχηματιζόμενοι, "conforming" [v. 13–14]) as imperatives or as adverbs.¹³³ However, both interpretations support a virtue ethical view of Trinitarian progressive sanctification. If the participles are taken as imperatives, as they are in most of the current major translations (NIV, NAS, NLT), then, including the relevant main verbs (ἐλπίσατε, "set your hope" and ἅγιοι ... γενήθητε, "be holy" [v. 13, 15]), a series of five commands is summarized by the final command to be holy (v. 15), which is emphasized as the main point through the OT quotation (v. 16). In this case, holiness is defined in part by the virtues of a prepared mind, soberness, and hope (v. 13).

If the participles are taken as adverbs of means which describe how the main verbs take place, i.e. "set your hope by being sober," as favored by some translations (KJV, NKJV, ESV) and some commentators, then the flow of the argument in the immediate context indicates that holiness is a result of hoping in the grace received at the return of Christ.¹³⁴ In this case, the phrase "be holy in all [your] conduct" (v. 15) is key because by it the OT cultic concept of the religious sphere, holiness, is, according to J. Ramsey Michaels, "boldly translated here into positive ethical virtues" in the sphere of mundane everyday life.¹³⁵ For in the wider context of the remainder of the letter, Peter fre-

---

132 While the following athors do not reject the postion-only view, they seem to be familiar with it but adhere to the traditional three aseptcs of the seven historic views. Keathley, "Salvation," 758–759; Mayhue, "Biblical Basics," 145, 150–151, 155. William D. Barrick, "Sanctification: The Work of the Holy Spirit and Scripture," *MSJ* 21, no. 2 (2010): 180, 182–184, 186–188; John J. Murray, "Sanctification: 3. Through the Power of the Spirit," *BoT* 511 (Apr 2006): 4–6. Johnson, like Peterson's reviewers, seems to approve of him because Johnson has misread Peterson as basing progressive on positional sanctification, when in fact Peterson rejects progressive sanctification. Eric L. Johnson, "Rewording the Justification/Sanctification Relation with Some Help from Speech Act Theory," *JETS* 54, no. 4 (2011): 769.

133 Roger M. Raymer, *1 Peter*, in BKC, ed. John F. and Roy B. Zuck Walvoord (Victor Books, 1985), 2:842–843. Wallace, *Greek Grammar*, 616–617.

134 Karen H. Jobes, *1 Peter*, BECNT (Baker Academic, 2005), 109–111; I. Howard Marshall, *1 Peter*, IVPNTC (InterVarsity, 1991), s.v. "1 Pe 1:13"; J. Ramsey Michaels, *1 Peter*, WBC 49 (Word, 1998), 55; Thomas R. Schreiner, *1, 2 Peter, Jude*, NAC (B&H, 2003), 77–78; Wallace, *Greek Grammar*, 616–617, 623, 626, 627–629.

135 Michaels, *1 Peter*, 59. One might also note that whereas the term "obedience" in v. 14 might connote duty to laws, in v. 16 the OT quote claims the reason for being holy is God's holiness or nature and in the first half of v. 15, the idea is that believers are to imitate God's holiness as the pattern of their character. Verses 15–16 focus on character as the locus of holiness, an idea consistent with virtue. Jobes, *1 Peter*, 112–113; Craig S Keener, *The IVP Bible Background*

quently speaks of this conduct (ἀναστροφῇ, 1:15; 1:18; 2:12; 3:1–2, 12; see also 2 Pet 2:7; 3:11) and explicitly defines being "holy in all [your] *conduct*" (2:15) as possessing and displaying the virtues of purity and reverence (3:2) and perhaps goodness (2:12; 3:16).[136] Moreover, Clement of Rome was likely interpreting 1 Pet 1:13–16 when he connected virtue to sanctification by defining "do all the things of holiness" in terms of avoiding a list of vices and "being clothed" with a list of virtues.[137] Having defined holiness in terms of possessing certain virtues in 1 Pet 1:13–16, in 2 Pet 1:5–9, Peter indicates a progressive idea of sanctification through the ideas of "adding to your faith virtue (ἀρετήν)" (2 Pet 1:5) and through his mention of virtues increasing ("for if these [virtues] are yours and increasing," 2 Pet 1:8; cp. 1 Thess 3:12, 2 Thess 1:3).

While Eph 5:25–33 is explained in more detail in chapter 4, it is important to note now that a key factor in the interpretation of the passage is whether one takes the participle καθαρίσας, "having purified," as antecedent (action prior to) or coincident (action simultaneous with) to the main verb ἁγιάσῃ, "to make holy" (v. 26). In favor of the antecedent view, Peterson generally seems to claim that "Purification is the basis of sanctification" and similarly Coberly explicitly interprets Eph 5:26 such "that cleansing is ... likely, the *cause* of the sanctification ... nor is sanctification here equivalent to purifying."[138] In the immediate context of marriage, J. Muddiman argues that if the "washing with water" (v. 26) is a reference to the Jewish custom of a *prenuptial* bridal bath (Ezek 16:8–14), then the cleansing "definitely precedes" the sanctifying, which in the metaphor would be a post-nuptial event.[139]

However, the grammar, immediate context, and canonical context, all favor the coincident interpretation. Grammatically, since the participle "cleansing" follows the main verb "sanctify," then it is best understood as a coincident "participle of means" or "an *epexegetical* participle in that it *defines* or *explains* the action of the controlling verb," such that the sanctifying takes place by the means or instrument of the cleansing.[140] In the immediate context, since the "cleansing" and "washing with water" take place "by the

---

Commentary: New Testament (InterVarsity, 1993), s.v. "1 Pet 1:15–16"; Marshall, *1 Peter*, s.v. "1 Pet 1:15–16."

136 Marshall, *1 Peter*, 1 Pet 1:16; Michaels, *1 Peter*, 59.

137 "ποιήσωμεν τὰ τοῦ ἁγιασμοῦ πάντα" (1 *Clem.* 30, *PAO* 1 pt. 1: 17); J. N. D. Kelly, *The Epistles of Peter and of Jude*, BNTC (Continuum, 1969), 69; Michaels, *1 Peter*, 59.

138 Emphasis added. Coberly, "Position-Only," 52–53; Peterson, *Possessed by God*, 34.

139 John Muddiman, *The Epistle to the Ephesians*, BNTC (Continuum, 2001), 265. Among others, Hoehner seems to support the antecedent view: Harold W. Hoehner, *Ephesians: An Exegetical Commentary* (Baker Academic, 2002), 752.

140 F. F. Bruce, *The Epistles to the Colossians, to Philemon, and to the Ephesians*, rev. ed., NICNT (Eerdmans, 1984), 387; Andrew T. Lincoln, *Ephesians*, WBC 42 (Word, 1990), 375; Stanley E. Porter, *Verbal Aspect in the Greek of the New Testament: With Reference to Tense and Mood*,

word" (v. 26) and since the "the word" is likely a reference to the gospel (John 15:3; 17:7; Eph 6:17; Rom 10:8, 17; Heb 6:5; 1 Pet 1:25), then the sanctifying and cleansing are best thought of as taking place simultaneously with justification upon the moment of believing the Gospel or in the metaphor at the marriage ceremony (Rom 10:17; 1 Cor 6:11; Eph 1:13–14).[141] In the canonical context, Craig notes that in 1 Thess 4:7, "Holiness is simply the antithesis to uncleanness."[142] If impurity (ἀκαθαρσίᾳ) is the opposite of sanctification, this contrast implies that purity is somehow synonymous with sanctification. Ephesians 5:26 defines the synonymous nature, by explaining that sanctification occurs by the means of cleansing.[143] Contrary to the position-only view, since there are passages in which purification takes place in the present within a moral context (1 Cor 5:7; 2 Cor 7:1; James 4:8; 1 John 1:9) and since purification is one aspect of sanctification (Eph 5:26), then sanctification has a present aspect consistent with the idea of a present moral process. Therefore, there seems to be biblical grounds for rejecting Peterson's proposal. Furthermore, Peterson's revision of the doctrine of sanctification not only drives a wedge between theological and biblical studies, but is also a repudiation of virtually the entire tradition.[144] For these reasons, the position-only view is rejected in favor of the traditional view of sanctification as involving three aspects, including a present process of moral transformation.

Conclusion

Five important observations arise from the histories of these three doctrines which highlight their interconnectedness and the impact of virtue ethics on Trinitarian sanctification. First and foremost, the nature of sanctification is radically changed by the eclipse and resurgence of virtue ethics. While pre-Reformation sanctification involved and was at points identical to virtue ethics, post-Reformation sanctification generally has not involved virtue ethics. The resurgence in virtue ethics is currently moving back toward the

---

ed. D. A. Carson, SBG 1 (P. Lang, 1989), 383–384; Frank Thielman, *Ephesians*, BECNT (Baker Academic, 2010), 383; Wallace, *Greek Grammar*, 624–625, 628–629.

141 Lincoln, *Ephesians*, 375–376.

142 Craig, "Paradox," 152.

143 The interpretation of at least partial synonymity between cleansing and sanctification is consistent with Owen, Pink, and Smeaton, who all define purification as an aspect of sanctification. Owen, *Holy Spirit* (Works, 3:422–424); Pink, *Sanctification*, 84; George Smeaton, *The Doctrine of the Atonement as Taught by Christ Himself*, 2nd ed. (T&T Clark, 1871), 251–252.

144 Carl Trueman, "A Man More Sinned Against Than Sinning? The Portrait of Martin Luther in Contemporary New Testament Scholarship: Some Casual Observations of a Mere Historian," http://www.crcchico.com.

pre-Reformation involvement of virtue in sanctification. Second, virtue ethical Trinitarian sanctification is a development of the current discussion in the fields of theology, ethics, and philosophy. Third, particularly during the modern period, some overemphasized the role of the Spirit in progressive sanctification by neglecting Christ and the Father, resulting in a non-Trinitarian description of sanctification. Fourth, others have depicted Christ as having a primarily passive role in progressive sanctification, perhaps due to the idea of Christ's finished work. Fifth, there are sufficient reasons to question, if not reject the position-only view in favor of accepting the traditional three aspect view of sanctification.

With respect to the first observation, in their reaction to the Roman Catholic doctrine of work-based salvation, the Reformers properly recognized that virtue was involved in the Roman Catholic presentation of the doctrine, but they incorrectly threw out the baby of virtue with the bath water of works-based salvation. Since it has been demonstrated that the Bible itself contains virtue ethical ideas (Kotva's work) and even presents sanctification in terms of virtue (1 Pet 1:13–16; 2 Pet 1:5–9; 1 Thess 3:12; 2 Thess 1:3), then virtue ethics is key to Trinitarian sanctification in a way which does not violate *sola fide*. Chapters four and five of this book build upon this conclusion and provide a description of virtue ethical Trinitarian sanctification that is consistent with *sola fide*.

While many factors are likely involved in the third and fourth observations, perhaps the neglect of Christ and subsequent non-Trinitarian description of sanctification as well as Christ's relegation to a passive role in progressive sanctification were due in part to the eclipse of virtue ethics. For instance, in virtue ethical sanctification, the importance of Christ's example is that virtue is understood by observing and gained by following his virtuous example. However, in sanctification involving rules, the power of Christ's example of obedience to the law is reduced from its original epistemological and existential function of producing character to that of merely inspiring obedience. Since in rule or duty based sanctification, the example loses its original meaning, then it becomes more important to emphasize the Spirit's empowerment to obey the rules rather than Christ's inspiring believers to obedience. Therefore, in virtue ethical sanctification, Christ's example has an epistemological and existential function in relation to exemplifying virtue or being sanctified, while in rule based sanctification, Christ's example merely inspires people to obey the rules in order to be sanctified. Some might object that examples are important in rule based systems to understand the application of rules to concrete situations so that they can be obeyed. In response, it should be noted that while examples do play some secondary role in rule based sanctification, the rules are primary. Examples play a primary role in virtue ethical sanctification and rules are secondary. Additionally, in practice, when rule based sanctification is explained, scholars tend to fail either in drawing any connection between Christ's example and the believer's obedience to the law/rules (they typically do not mention the inspiration or any other purpose of the example) or they omit Christ's example and focus on the Spirit's empowerment.

Moreover, the third and fourth observations regarding the neglect of the Trinity and passive role for Christ due in part to the idea of the finished work of Christ warrant two conclusions. While it is true that Christ's work is "finished" (nothing can be added to his redemptive work on the cross to obtain salvation), he has not finished working in that he still has an active role in applying his finished work as part of a Trinitarian action through his roles as a teacher and example of virtue and by his heavenly intercession.[145] Some might object that Christ's teaching and example are part of his "finished" work in the sense that they are merely recorded in the Scriptures such that these aspects of Christ's work are also passive. In response, it is important to consider the nature of Scripture and the purpose of Christ's teaching and example in this book. Although it is true that Christ's teaching and example are currently passive in a sense because they are part of the finished canon of Scripture, it is also true that as part of Scripture, they are "living and active" (Heb 4:12) in a sense different from how the record of Christ's death and resurrection are "active" as a part of the Scriptures. Exactly how Christ's teaching and example have a "living and active" (Heb 4:12) sense is explored in Chapter 4. Additionally, in the argument of this book, Christ's teaching and example of virtue serve the primary purpose of demonstrating how sanctification is a Trinitarian work and only secondarily serve the purpose of emphasizing an active role for Christ in sanctification. While Christ's teaching and example are less active than his heavenly ministry of intercession, they have some active sense and Christ's active role is not typically emphasized in discussions of sanctification. By emphasizing the active sense of these roles of Christ, his active participation in sanctification is highlighted in a manner not commonly done elsewhere.

Therefore, virtue ethics is key to understanding Trinitarian progressive sanctification because the Trinity, virtue ethics, and sanctification are historically part of and conceptually interconnected in the tradition of interpretation and Scripture. The three histories are intricately connected in

---

145 For a similar judgment see: Gary Brady, *What Jesus Is Doing Now* (EP Books, 2012), 28.

that the eclipse and resurgence of virtue ethics has radically changed the nature of sanctification and the Trinitarian description of sanctification has been impacted by the contemporary Trinitarian proponents and perhaps by the eclipse of virtue. By critically appropriating some of the insights of the contemporary Trinitarian proponents and the retrieval of virtue by the resurgence ethicists, a virtue ethical view of Trinitarian sanctification is constructed in the following chapters of this book. The key role of virtue ethics is demonstrated through its use in providing a Trinitarian explanation of sanctification by emphasizing Christ's roles as teacher, example, and priest that give Christ an active role in progressive sanctification along with the Father and Spirit. The next chapter argues that virtue ethics is key to understanding Trinitarian progressive sanctification by demonstrating that only virtue ethics and only a particular type of virtue ethics is the most biblically consistent ethical framework for Trinitarian progressive sanctification.

CHAPTER 2

DEFINING VIRTUE ETHICS IN SANCTIFICATION: NATURE AND FUNCTION

The main claim of this chapter is that virtue ethics is key to understanding Trinitarian progressive sanctification, because virtue ethics based on metaphysical realism is the most biblically consistent ethical framework for Trinitarian progressive sanctification. As was argued in chapter two, if sanctification includes a progressive aspect that involves moral transformation, then some type of ethics is involved in sanctification. The problem for the contemporary Christian living in a pluralistic society is that numerous types of ethical theories exist, several of which claim to be biblical, from which one can choose as the type of ethical theory involved in progressive sanctification. In the following process of defining the nature and function of virtue ethics in Trinitarian progressive sanctification, the criterion of metaphysics is suggested as the basis which enables believers to determine which ethical theories are biblically consistent and which are not. This criterion of metaphysics is used to argue that virtue ethics is the most biblically consistent ethical theory.

The process of defining the nature and function of virtue ethics in Trinitarian progressive sanctification unfolds in three stages. First, virtue ethics is located as an ethical theory within the field of ethics. This location involves understanding the various areas of study within the field of ethics and how ethical theories are classified within contemporary ethics. In this stage, metaphysical realism as well as other key terms such as teleology, deontology, and nominalism are defined. Since the current classification method seems inadequate, then the replacement method of classifying by an ethical theory's metaphysical basis is suggested which provides a criterion that not only properly classifies virtue ethics but also serves as a means to determine which ethical theories are biblically consistent and which are not. Before using the criterion to determine which types of ethical theories are biblically consistent, it is noted that the virtue ethics resurgence has developed several types of virtue ethics. Arguments from history, theology, and exegesis then use the criterion to defend the claim that virtue ethics based on metaphysical realism is the most biblically consistent ethical framework for Trinitarian progressive sanctification.

The second stage moves toward a more precise definition of virtue ethics by drawing on the virtue ethics of the Aristotelian-Augustinian-Thomistic tradition by characterizing the virtue ethics of Aristotle, Augustine, and Aquinas through selective sketches. These characterizations uncover at least one function of virtue ethics in sanctification. In the third stage, a comparison of the three sketches of Aristotle, Augustine, and Aquinas' virtue ethics to the definition of virtue ethics given in chapter 2 demonstrates how these characterizations are being critically appropriated to construct a working definition of virtue ethics.

Toward a Definition of Virtue Ethics:
Contemporary Issues in Ethics

In order to move toward defining "virtue ethics," it is important to locate virtue ethics in the field of ethics. According to the classical Aristotelian divisions, ethics is one branch of philosophy, which can be construed as consisting of four interconnected branches: logic, metaphysics, epistemology, and ethics.[1] In contemporary ethics, at least since G. E. Moore's (1873–1958) *Principia Ethica* (1903), there are three divisions within ethics: metaethics, normative ethics, and applied ethics.[2] Metaethics might be defined as the "foundations of ethics" or the philosophical presuppositions upon which normative ethics are "grounded" and includes such metaphysically related questions as whether or not "moral facts ... are independent of our beliefs about what is right and wrong."[3] Normative ethics deals with ethical theories, such as virtue ethics, and "concerns judgments about what is good and how we should act."[4]

---

1 T. H. Irwin, "Aristotle (384–322 BC)," in *CREP*, ed. Edward Craig (Taylor & Francis, 2002), 50–51.

2 Roger Crisp, "Ethics," in *CREP*, ed. Edward Craig (Taylor & Francis, 2002), 256–258; G. E. Moore, *Principia Ethica*, ed. Thomas Baldwin, rev. ed. (Cambridge University Press, 1993), iii, 53–88, 89–191, 192–231; Peter Railton, "Analytic Ethics," in *CREP*, ed. Edward Craig (Taylor & Francis, 2002), 28.

3 David O. Brink, *Moral Realism and the Foundations of Ethics* (Cambridge University Press, 1989), 5–7. See also: Crisp, "Ethics," 256; Railton, "Analytic Ethics," 28.

4 Railton, "Analytic Ethics," 28. See also: Crisp, "Ethics," 257–258.

Applied ethics is the application of normative ethical theories to "particular issues of contemporary practical concern" such as "abortion, euthanasia, personal relationships, the treatment of nonhuman animals, and matters of race and gender."[5] Since virtue ethics is an ethical theory, then defining it involves normative ethics. However, as D. O. Brink has observed, "metaethics and normative ethics ... are interdependent," so the definition of virtue ethics also involves metaethics, which, itself, is grounded in metaphysics.[6]

In contemporary normative ethics, all ethical systems are classified as being either teleological or deontological.[7] Philosophers routinely classify both utilitarianism (also called "consequentialism") and virtue ethics as teleological and I. Kant's ethics as deontological.[8] While the basic language of making a distinction between teleological and deontological ethics is affirmed, this classification fails because it ignores the historic definitions of the terms "teleological" and "deontological" and their metaphysical bases. There seems to be a growing recognition that this distinction is problematic as defined because the "end" in virtue ethics is the "final cause" of Aristotle's metaphysical "chain of causation," while the "end" in utilitarianism is the "consequence" of an action.[9]

By attending to the historic definitions of the terms "teleology" and "deontology" and their metaphysical bases, the confusion between ends and consequences may be removed and a less problematic classification method may be established. According to the *Oxford English Dictionary*, "teleology" refers

---

5 Brenda Almond, "Applied Ethics," in *CREP*, ed. Edward Craig (Taylor & Francis, 2002), 42; Crisp, "Ethics," 258.

6 Brink, *Moral Realism*, 5.

7 Thomas Hurka, "Teleological Ethics," in *MEP*, ed. Donald M. Borchert (Macmillan, 2006), 9:382; Christine M. Korsgaard, "Teleological Ethics," in *REP*, ed. Edward Craig (Routledge, 1998), 9:294. According to Louden, this now standard classification was established by C. D. Broad in *Five Types of Ethical Theory* (1930). Robert B. Louden, "Virtue Ethics," in *MEP*, ed. Donald M. Borchert (Macmillan, 2006), 9:687; C. D. Broad, *Five Types of Ethical Theory*, ILPPSM 204 (Routledge, 1951), 206–208. Korsgaard traces the distinction to J. H. Muirhead, *Rule and End in Morals* (1932), but Broad (1930) is earlier. Korsgaard, "Teleological Ethics," 9:295. The argument in this section, "Toward a Definition of Virtue Ethics," generally follows Mitchell's line of thought in his unpublished work: Craig Mitchell, "Overview of Ethical Theory," (Classroom lecture notes, Ethic 7624-A—Metaethics, Fall 2009, Electronic PowerPoint Presentation).

8 Hurka, "Teleological Ethics," 9:382; Korsgaard, "Teleological Ethics," 9:294. Anscombe coined the term "consequentialism" to refer to utilitarianism. G. E. M. Anscombe, "Modern Moral Philosophy," *Philosophy* 33, no. 124 (1958): 12.

9 Hurka, "Teleological Ethics," 9:382; Korsgaard, "Teleological Ethics," 9:294; Louden, "Virtue Ethics," 9:687. In Aristotle's chain of causation, there is a first cause, a formal cause, a material cause, an efficient cause, and the final cause, which is the purpose of the thing caused and "βέλτιστον καὶ τέλος τῶν ἄλλων" [the greatest good and end of the others (causes)] (Aristotle, *Metaph.* 2.2.994b.5–10; 5.2.1013b.20–29 [*AO* 8:36, 84]). Broad seems to be the one responsible for obscuring the metaphysical difference between ends and consequences. Broad, *Five Types*, 206–207.

to the "doctrine or study of ends or final causes" and "deontology" refers to the "science of duty; that branch of knowledge which deals with moral obligations."[10] In ethics, it is well known that virtue ethics is teleological because it deals with final causes, and Kantian type ethics are deontological because they deal with duty, but what is overlooked is that in constructing the system of utilitarianism Bentham coined the term deontology as the "field, where the business consists chiefly in the proper distribution of obligations."[11] Therefore, by definition, not only Kant's ethics, but also utilitarianism is deontological and virtue ethics is teleological.

These historical classifications of teleology and deontology are not mere arbitrary designations, but rather have an objective basis in metaphysics that serves as the ground of the distinction. For the purposes of this argument, metaphysics can be conceived of as having two primary positions: realism and nominalism. In the pre-Kantian era, realism was understood as the affirmation of the existence of universals (Plato) or forms (Aristotle) such as properties, facts, or states of affairs and of concrete particulars or individual things such as people, planes, poodles, and pears.[12] During this time frame,

---

10 OED, s.v. "Deontology"; s.v. "Teleology." According to the Oxford English Dictionary, Christian Wolff (1679–1754) coined the term "teleology" in 1728 to describe Aristotle's final cause in his chain of causation that is part of his realist metaphysics: "quae fines rerum explicat … Dici posset Teleologia." [(that) which explains final causes … we may call teleology]. Christian Wolff, Philosophia rationalis, sive Logica: methodo scientifica pertractata et as usum sicentiarum atque vitae aptata, 3rd ed. (Ex Typographia Dionysii Ramanzini, 1935), 25, 31–33; For a similar judgment see: Jonathan Cohen, "XI.—Teleological Explanation," Proceedings of the Aristotelian Society: New Series 51 (1950–1951), 255;

11 Jeremy Bentham, Deontology or the Science of Morality, ed. John Bowring (Longman, Rees, Orme, Browne, Green, and Longman; William Tait, 1834), 1:21, 135. In Aristotle's virtue ethics for example, the final cause or greatest good of happiness is the end or purpose for which people live and toward which they are being conformed by acting virtuously. Aristotle, Eth. nic. 1.4.1095a.15–30; 1.6.1097b.1–1098a.20 (AO 9: 3–4, 9–11); Immanuel Kant, Grundlegung zur Metaphysik der Sitten 4:429–430, 439 (KGS 4:429–430, 439). According to the Oxford English Dictionary, Jeremy Bentham (1748–1832) coined the term "deontology" in 1826. OED, s.v. "Deontology"; For a similar judgment see: Henry S. Richardson, "Deontological Ethics," in MEP, ed. Donald M. Borchert (Macmillan, 2006), 2:713. In Bentham's book Deontology, he claims "Deontology is derived from the Greek words, δεον (that which is proper) and λογια, knowledge— meaning the knowledge of what is right or proper; … applied to the subject of morals, …the Deontological field, where the business consists chiefly in the proper distribution of obligations." Bentham, Deontology, 21, 135; see also 23–24. For an example of overlooking Bentham, see McNaughton, who does not mention Bentham in either his article or bibliography: David McNaughton, "Deontological Ethics," in REP, ed. Edward Craig (Routledge, 1998), 2:890–892.

12 William P. Alston, "What Metaphysical Realism is Not," in Realism and Antirealism, ed. William P. Alston (Cornell University Press, 2002), 97; Jonathan Barnes, ed. The Cambridge Companion to Aristotle (Cambridge University Press, 1995), 96–98, 113; Vasilis Politis, Routledge Philosophy Guidebook to Aristotle and the Metaphysics (Routledge, 2004), 199, 299–300, 309; Richard Kraut, ed. Cambridge Companion to Plato (Cambridge University Press, 1992), 122–123, 259, 482–483.

realism was contrasted with nominalism, which is a denial of realism or a denial that universals/forms exist and an affirmation that only concrete particulars exist.[13] In the present post-Kantian period, realism is often contrasted with idealism, where realism, as defined by Brink, is the two part claim that "[1] there are facts of a certain kind [2] that are in some way mind-independent or independent of human thought" and idealism is a denial of realism or, according to Sprigge, "a philosophy which makes the physical world dependent upon mind."[14] In the post-Kantian period, most idealists are generally nominalists. Consequently, although both definitions of realism are important for determining which ethical system is most biblically consistent and compatible with Trinitarian progressive sanctification, the important contrast is ultimately between realism and nominalism. In general, virtue ethics (such as Aristotle's ethics) require metaphysical realism and deontological ethics (such as utilitarianism and Kantianism) are consistent with metaphysical nominalism.[15] Since most contemporary ethical systems follow

---

13 Michael J. Loux, "Nominalism," in *REP*, ed. Edward Craig (Routledge, 1998), 8:17.

14 Brink, *Moral Realism*, 14; T.L.S. Sprigge, "Idealism," in *CREP*, ed. Edward Craig (Taylor & Francis, 2002), 379. Brink defines the term "moral realism" "as a special case of a global realist metaphysical view" in which the "facts" in view in the preceding definition of realism are simply moral facts. In the pre-Kantian period, Plato was an idealist who was a realist.

15 For example, Aristotle's virtue ethics are an example of a teleological ethical system based on metaphysical realism, because in keeping with the definition of realism (affirmation of forms *and* concrete particulars), not only does Aristotle explicitly affirm the existence of particulars (ἕκαστον) in *Int.* 7.17a38–40, but he also involves forms (εἶδος), and substances (οὐσία) in his discussions concerning causation. Aristotle, *Int.* 7.17a.38–40 (*AO* 1:42–43); idem *Metaph.* 5.2.1013b.20–29; 8.1.1042a.20–24; 8.2.1043a.1–19 (*AO* 8:84, 155, 157); idem *Phys.* 2.3.194b.16–195b30; 2.7.198a.14–198b.9 (*AO* 2:27–30, 35–36). His causation discussions are the conceptual framework underling his virtue ethics which involve a "final cause," or the "βέλτιστον καὶ τέλος" [greatest good and end] of a caused thing that is tied to the form of the nature and purpose of a thing. Arist. *Metaph.* 2.2.994b.5–10; 5.5.1013b.20–29 (*AO* 8:36, 84); idem *Eth. Nic.* 1.1.1094a.19; 3.7.1115b.20–24; 6.2.1139a.15–19; 9.9.1170a.24–25; (*AO* 9 [1837]: 1, 54, 113, 191). As an example that utilitarianism is nominalistic, Mill explicitly affirms nominalism and denies the existence of universals/forms, "General concepts, therefore, we have, properly speaking, none; we have only complex ideas of objects in the concrete." John Stuart Mill, *An Examination of Sir William Hampton's Philosophy* 17 (*CW* 9:310). Since Mill is a nominalist, he bases morality on utility or the greatest happiness principle, "the principle of utility, or ... the greatest happiness principle, ... the fundamental principle of morality, and the source of moral obligation." Mill *Utilitarianism* 2.4 (*CW* 10:207). Moreover, Kant denies realism by affirming idealism when he argues for " *transzendentalen Idealism*," which he defines as the doctrine "*daß alles, was im Raume oder der Zeit angeschaut wird, mithin alle Gegenstände einer uns möglichen Erfahrung, ... außer unseren Gedanken keine an sich gegründete Existenz haben*" [transcendental idealism ... that everything, what is viewed in space or time, consequently all materials of our possible experience ... have no established existence in themselves apart from our thoughts] Immanuel Kant, *Kritik Der Reinen Vernunft* A518/B357 (*KGS* 3:338). Consistent with nominalism in that universals and moral facts do not really exist since they are merely products of the mind, Kant's ethic is deontological in that he makes morality based on reason alone, "*die moralische Zwecklehre, die von Pflichten handelt, auf a priori in der reinen praktischen Vernunft gegebenen Principien be-*

in the broad traditions of utilitarianism or Kantianism and since the majority of recent philosophers are nominalists, then nearly all ethical systems are deontological. Therefore, virtue ethics or at least Aristotelian virtue ethics (and generally those whose ethics have some consistency with the Aristotelian virtue tradition such as Augustine and Aquinas) are teleological and based on metaphysical realism, while other ethical systems are deontological and consistent with nominalism.[16]

Someone might object that in addition to virtue ethics, some forms of naturalism or divine command theory are also teleological and so are candidates for being biblically consistent ethics. According to Sturgeon, naturalism in ethics refers to the idea "that ethical facts are simply natural facts and that ethical thought succeeds in discovering them."[17] The term "divine command theory" refers to those "[e]thical theories holding that at least one of the reasons that actions are right or wrong is that they are commanded or forbidden by God."[18] In response, most forms of contemporary naturalism and divine command theory generally are not consistent with virtue ethics that are based on realism because they do not deal with virtue, they are consistent with nominalism, or they have other incompatible features. Since Augustine, Aquinas, and J. Kotva all demonstrate that the Bible contains at least virtue ethical elements (if not some sort of system of virtue ethics) and since this book argues that only realism is consistent with the Bible, then these two theories (naturalism and divine command theory) cannot be consistent with the Bible's Trinitarian progressive sanctification and are passed over in the following discussion for these reasons.[19]

---

ruht" [the moral doctrine of ends, which treats of duties, is based on principles given *a priori* in pure practical reason]. Immanuel Kant, *Metaphysik der Sitten* 6:385, (*KGS* 6:385). Some such as Abbot and Peirce label Kant a nominalist. Francis Ellingwood Abbot, *Scientific Theism*, rep. ed. (Kessinger, 2004), 3–5, 8–9, 26; Charles Sanders Peirce, *Principles of Philosophy and Elements of Logic (Volumes 1 and 2)*, vol. 1 of *Collected Papers*, ed. Charles Hartshorne and Paul Weiss, rep. ed. (Belknap Press of Harvard University Press, 1958), 5.

16 Although Augustine's thought is based heavily on the neo-Platonic thought of Plotinus, this book demonstrates in the following section on "Augustine's Virtue Ethics" that Augustine's virtue ethics have some consistency with Aristotle's ethics. This consistency is to be expected since the ethics of Plato and Aristotle have many consistencies despite their differences.

17 Norman L. Geisler and Paul D. Feinberg, *Introduction to Philosophy: A Christian Perspective* (Baker, 1980), 432; Nicholas L. Sturgeon, "Natualism in Ethics," in *CREP*, ed. Edward Craig (Taylor & Francis, 2002), 615.

18 C. Stephen Evans, *Pocket Dictionary of Apologetics & Philosophy of Religion* (InterVarsity, 2002), s.v. "divine command theories."

19 Most contemporary versions of divine command theory are somehow related to Ockham's form of the theory. While not all agree, some scholars (such as Holmes and O'Donovan) hold that Ockham's version of divine command theory is consistent with nominalism and that Duns Scotus' divine command theory is based on realism. Since Ockham's theory is consistent with nominalism and this book argues that only realism is consistent with the Bible,

Therefore, in general, virtue ethics is a teleological theory based on metaphysical realism, while other ethical systems are deontological and consistent with nominalism.[20] In the contemporary resurgence of virtue ethics, however, there has been a proliferation of theories of virtue ethics, not all of which are teleological.

Three Types of Virtue Ethics

The contemporary resurgence of virtue ethics has produced three main types of virtue ethics: (1) neo-Aristotelian, (2) agent-based, and (3) linguis-

---

then Ockham's theory and the contemporary forms of it may be set aside. Duns Scotus' divine command theory based on realism also contains elements of virtue ethics (as does Ockham's). Duns Scotus' version may be set aside on at least one of three grounds. First, contemporary divine command theories generally do not follow Scotus' version and do not include virtue elements. Second, Duns Scotus' version is an exception and may be worth considering further in a future work. Third, while Duns Scotus' divine command theory contains virtue elements, these elements are generally consistent with the broad Aristotelian, Augustinian, and Thomistic virtue tradition. Since the scope of this book is limited to focusing on the key figures of Aristotle, Augustine, and Aquinas from the virtue tradition, then Scotus is omitted in the argument due to this limitation. Arthur F. Holmes, *Fact, Value, and God* (Eerdmans, 1997), 71; Oliver O'Donovan, *Resurrection and Moral Order: An Outline for Evangelical Ethics*, 2nd ed. (Eerdmans, 1994), 42, 134. Furthermore, it is important to note that rules, laws, or divine commands do have a place in a teleological and biblical virtue theory of sanctification. This place is exemplified by the fact that Aristotle has a place for rules and Augustine and Aquinas have a place for divine laws or commands within their thought. Aristotle, *Eth. nic.* 2.2.1103b.26–1104a.10; 2.9.1009b.14–25 (*AO* 9: 25, 39); Aquinas, STh., I–II q.91 a.1 resp.; STh., I–II q.91 a.4 resp. (*OOII* 7: 153, 156); Augustine *Civ.* 15.16.2 (CSEL 40/2: 94); idem, *Lib.* 1.7.50 (CCSL 29: 220). More importantly, rules/commands can function much like moral exemplars to point to the character of God, which is to be imitated by the believer. For example, in Leviticus 19:2, the reason for the command to "be holy" is the holiness of God, which implies that believers are to imitate God's holiness. For a similar judgment see: John E. Hartley, *Leviticus*, WBC 4 (Word, 1998), 312; Mark F. Rooker, *Leviticus*, NAC (B&H, 2000), 252. Someone might object that not all divine laws or commands so clearly point to a characteristic or virtue of God to be imitated as does Lev 19:2. In response, although it is true that not all divine laws or commands *clearly* point to a divine attribute to be imitated, it seems that for many if not most of the biblical laws, some connection can be made between a divine virtue and the divine command given, and believers are given a general command to imitate God (Eph 5:6). For example, human love is commanded based on God's love (1 John 4:7–8), the adultery prohibition (Exod 20:14) relates to God's faithfulness (1 Cor 1:9), the lying prohibition (Exod 20:16; Col 3:9–10) relates to God's truthfulness (Titus 1:2; John 14:6), and the prohibition against murder (Exod 20:13) is explicitly linked to the ontology of God's image (Gen 9:6).

20 Like all other ethical theories, there are numerous "standard" objections to virtue ethics as an ethical theory which have received responses in the literature. For some these discussions see: Joseph J. Kotva, Jr., *The Christian Case for Virtue Ethics* (Georgetown University Press, 1996), 143–166; Robert B. Louden, "On Some Vices of Virtue Ethics," *APQ* 21, no. 3 (1984): 227–236; Daniel Statman, "Introduction to Virtue Ethics," in *Virtue Ethics*, ed. Daniel Statman (Georgetown University Press, 1997), 18–26.

tic.²¹ Some representatives of the neo-Aristotelian camp include G. E. M. Anscombe, C. Pincoffs, P. Foot, M. Nussbaum, R. Hursthouse, and J. Kotva.²² Kotva has adeptly observed that "no single author develops adequately all the elements" of what constitutes a neo-Aristotelian virtue ethic so that a synthetic description is necessary for this position.²³ A synthetic description of a neo-Aristotelian virtue ethic includes at least these characteristics:²⁴ (1) the end of human beings is *eudiamonia*, which can be described as "happiness" or "human flourishing" and which results from acting "in conformity with the virtues,"²⁵ (2) rather than right action conforming to moral obligation, virtue is what "makes its possessor good" and virtue depends on the "natural goodness" of a thing or one should base "ethics ... on considerations of human

---

21 The fact that Athanassoulis, Statman, and Yearly have different categorizations indicates that currently there is no standard taxonomy of virtue ethics. Athanassoulis, *Virtue Ethics*, Internet Encyclopedia of Philosophy, https://www.iep.utm.edu/virtue; Statman, "Introduction," 8–10; Lee H. Yearly, "Recent Work on Virtue," *RelSRev* 16 (1990): 1. The taxonomy in this book divides the types of virtue ethics based on their metaphysics. Statman correctly categorizes the so called feminist "ethics of care" of "Carol Gilligan, Nel Noddings, Annette Baier and others" as a related development rather than a form of virtue ethics. Carol Gilligan, *In a Different Voice: Psychological Theory and Women's Development* (Harvard University Press, 1982); Annette Baier, *Postures of the Mind: Essays on Mind and Morals* (University of Minnesota Press, 1985); Nel Noddings, *Caring: A Feminist Approach to Ethics and Moral Education* (University of California Press, 2003); Statman, "Introduction," 17. Due to the revisionist accounts of Aristotle and Kant and the attempts of Kantianism and utilitarianism to incorporate the virtues, it has become necessary to distinguish between "virtue theory" and "virtue ethics" but the exact nature of the distinction varies. Cp. Rosalind Hursthouse, "Virtue Ethics," in *The Stanford Encyclopedia of Philosophy*, ed. Edward N. Zalta http://plato.stanford.edu; Lawrence J. Jost, "Virtue and Vice," in *MEP*, ed. Donald M. Borchert (Macmillan, 2006), 9:679.

22 In the preface of the second edition of *Fragility*, Nussbuam herself acknowledges that she is more Aristotelian in her earlier thought before her turn to the Stoics in her later writings such as *Upheavals of Thought*. Martha C. Nussbaum, *The Fragility of Goodness: Luck and Ethics in Greek Tragedy and Philosophy*, 2ⁿᵈ ed. (Cambridge University Press, 2001), xv, xix; Martha C. Nussbaum, *Upheavals of Thought: The Intelligence of Emotions* (Cambridge University Press, 2001), 4–5.

23 Kotva, *Case for Virtue*, 16.

24 Just as there are different taxonomies of virtue ethics, descriptions of virtue ethics vary as seen in the characterizations of Kotva, Statman, Spohn, and Yearley. Ibid., 16–47; William Spohn, "The Return of Virtue Ethics," *TS* 53 (1992): 61; Statman, "Introduction," 7–16; Yearly, "Recent Work," 2. The characterization of neo-Aristotelian virtue ethics in this book draws on the elements of these four descriptions, it also draws on the primary sources, and it emphasizes the characteristics most relevant for the present book.

25 Philippa Foot, *Natural Goodness* (Oxford University Press, 2001), 97; See also: Kotva, *Case for Virtue*, 17–23; Nussbaum, *Fragility*, 6, 284. Pincoffs acknowledges the end of "human flourishing" as typical of "many contemporary writers." However, Pincoffs rejects the specific end of human flourishing as reductive on the basis that he is "a functionalist, ... not a teleologist" who does "not want to issue pronouncements about the 'end of man.'" Instead Pincoffs wants "To think of good functioning as functioning that is appropriate to the common life" in order "to leave room for different ends." Edmund L. Pincoffs, *Quandaries and Virtues: Against Reductivism in Ethics* (University Press of Kansas, 1986), 6–7, 97–99.

nature," or natural law,[26] (3) virtues are learned by observing exemplars,[27] (4) despite the fact that some of one's ability to act virtuously is controlled to some extent by Bernard Williams' "moral luck" (deterministic external factors), moral agents have some amount of free will to act virtuously (the equivalent of Christian compatibilism),[28] and (5) perfectionism, which is defined "in the sense of viewing all aspects of life as morally relevant" in the "continual growth" toward the end of human excellence.[29]

M. Slote first introduced "agent-based virtue ethics" in his 1995 essay bearing that name.[30] Slote draws on a number of sources, but particularly the nineteenth-century British ethicist James Martineau to develop his view.[31] Whereas in neo-Aristotelian virtue ethics, "the virtuous individual ... *sees* or *perceives* what is good," based on nature, agent based virtue ethics "treat the moral or ethical status of actions as entirely derivative from ... the motives, ... of the individuals who perform them. ... without making any appeal to the supposed value of the Forms," meaning there is no basis in natural law or realist metaphysics.[32] Since Slote views agent-based virtue ethics as "an agent-based *analogue* (or '*interiorization*') of utilitarianism," then his theory is deontological because it deals with duty, obligation, and rules or "standards ... [which] bind, as it were, *from within*," where the internal motive of the agent serves as a rule to make actions right.[33]

In *After Virtue*, Alasdair MacIntrye developed a third type of virtue ethics, which Smith has called "philosophical, linguistic virtue ethics."[34] Smith uses this term not only to characterize MacIntyre's ethics accurately, but also

---

26 Rosalind Hursthouse, *On Virtue Ethics* (Oxford University Press, 2001), 13, 192. See also: Foot, *Natural Goodness*, 12, 26–27.

27 Hursthouse, *Virtue Ethics*, 80–81, 130; Kotva, *Case for Virtue*, 6, 21; Nussbaum, *Fragility*, 158, 186, 220; Pincoffs, *Quandaries*, 14, 172–173. Hursthouse seems to allow for the acquisition of virtues by exemplars, but rejects exemplars as necessary for decision-making.

28 Bernard Williams, "Moral Luck," *Aristotelian Society: Supplementary Volume* 50 (1976): 115–136. See also: Foot, *Natural Goodness*, 104–105; Kotva, *Case for Virtue*, 26–29; Nussbaum, *Fragility*, 1–21, 424.

29 Kotva, *Case for Virtue*, 37–38. See also: Pincoffs, *Quandaries*, 103–114.

30 Michael A. Slote, "Agent-Based Virtue Ethics," in *Moral Concepts*, ed. Peter A. French, Theodore Edward Uehling, and Howard K. Wettstein, MSP 20 (University of Notre Dame Press, 1995), 83–101. Slote more fully develops his virtue ethics in *Morals from Motives*, but the basic characteristics of his view remain the same even with verbatim repetition from his essay. Michael A. Slote, *Morals from Motives* (Oxford University Press, 2003).

31 Slote, "Agent-Based," 84; cp. Slote, *Motives*, ch. 3, "Morality as Inner Strength."

32 Emphasis original. Slote, "Agent-Based," 83–84, 88; cp. Slote, ch. 3, "Morality as Inner Strength."

33 Emphasis original. Slote, "Agent-Based," 87, 89, 93; cp. Slote, *Motives*, ch. 4, "Morality as Universal Benevolence."

34 R. Scott Smith, *Virtue Ethics and Moral Knowledge: Philosophy of Language after MacIntyre and Hauerwas*, Ashgate New Critical Thinking in Philosophy (Ashgate, 2003), 39.

to distinguish it from S. Hauerwas' later "theological, linguistic virtue ethics" in "which he draws from MacIntrye" to develop his own system.[35] According to Smith, who analyzes and critiques MacIntyre and Hauerwas, an oversimplified but useful distinction between their linguistic virtue ethics is to view MacIntyre as having a constructive philosophical concern and Hauerwas as having a concern for theological application such that MacIntyre "justifies a narrative based virtue ethic, ... as the most rational tradition *so far*... while Hauerwas applies the theory" theologically to find that "Christ's story, ... is the true story for all people."[36] As a result of these differing emphases, MacIntrye's work has greatly influenced philosophy, religious studies, and the Christian church, while Hauerwas' studies have had tremendous impact on Christian Ethics.[37] Since there is much overlap between MacIntrye's and Hauerwas' thought, then the focus of this categorization of three types of virtue ethics is limited to characterizing the shared generalizations of the linguistic virtue ethic in MacIntrye's work.[38] One unique characteristic of MacIntrye's ethics is that he shifted from his "conclusion ...[for] a rationally defensible statement of ... the Aristotelian tradition" in *After Virtue* to a "Thomistic conclusion" or a basis in Aquinas for his ethics in *Whose Justice? Which Rationality?*.[39]

In terms of the general characteristics of linguistic virtue ethics, MacIntrye explicitly expressed his "indebtedness to ... Wittgenstein" for the philosophical and linguistic basis of his post-modern approach to virtue ethics.[40] MacIntrye's virtue ethic is post-modern in that it emphasizes narrative and community. For example, he develops a "thesis about the relationship between virtues and forms of narratives" in which "the conception and role of the virtues ... is linked to some particular notion of the narrative structure ... of human life."[41] The idea of narrative is interconnected with that of community in that "the story of my life is always embedded in the story of those com-

---

35 Ibid., 67.
36 Emphasis original. Ibid., 14, 76.
37 Ibid., 3.
38 Hauerwas is quite prolific, but many of the main features of his virtue ethics are outlined in the following works: Stanley Hauerwas, *Vision and Virtue: Essays in Christian Ethical Reflection* (Fides, 1974); idem, *Character and the Christian Life: A Study in Theological Ethics* (Trinity University Press, 1975); idem, *A Community of Character: Toward a Constructive Christian Social Ethic* (University of Notre Dame Press, 1981); Stanley Hauerwas, David B. Burrell, and Richard Bondi, *Truthfulness and Tragedy: Further Investigations in Christian Ethics* (University of Notre Dame Press, 1977).
39 Alasdair MacIntyre, *After Virtue: A Study in Moral Theory*, 2nd ed. (University of Notre Dame Press, 1984), 259; Alasdair C. MacIntyre, *Whose Justice? Which Rationality?* (University of Notre Dame Press, 1988), 403.
40 Alasdair MacIntyre, "Preface," in *Metaphysical Beliefs: Three Essays*, The Library of Philosophy and Theology (SCM Press, 1957), 9.
41 MacIntyre, *After Virtue*, 147, 174.

munities from which I derive my ... moral identity."[42] MacIntyre's reliance on Ludwig Wittgenstein's philosophy of language leads him to reject three types of realism. MacIntrye's virtue ethics deny metaphysical and moral realism, when he claims that a "'[f]act' is in modern culture a folk-concept with an aristocratic ancestry."[43] His ethics also reject epistemic realism through the claim that it is an "error ... to suppose that the observer can confront a fact face-to-face without any theoretical interpretation interposing itself."[44] Despite his claims to the contrary, MacIntyre's ethics are deontological because of his explicit rejection of Aristotle's metaphysics and his repeated emphasis on rules.[45]

Therefore, of the three theories of virtue ethics proliferated by the contemporary resurgence of virtue ethics, only the neo-Aristotelian variety is teleological and based on metaphysical realism, while the agent-based and linguistic types are deontological and consistent with metaphysical nominalism. As Christians approach the Bible to determine what kind of ethics are involved in Trinitarian progressive sanctification, they are confronted with deciding whether teleological virtue ethics or the deontological ethics of the utilitarian, Kantian, or virtue types are biblically consistent. This determination can be made by demonstrating whether metaphysical realism or nominalism is consistent with the Bible. Consequently, the criterion for de-

---

42 Ibid., 221.

43 Ibid., 79. Despite the fact that MacIntrye's comments about the nature and perception of facts are in his description section where he critiques modernity, he explicitly qualifies later in his book that his arguments, including the ones dealing with facts, are intended to lay the basis for *his* "alternative way of envisaging ... the Aristotelian tradition" and which "*presuppose* a systematic, ... account of rationality." Emphasis original. Ibid., 259–260. MacIntrye's denial of moral and metaphysical realism is evident when seen as a contradiction of Brink's definitions in which moral realism is "a special case of a global realist metaphysical view" in which the term "moral" is substituted into his definition of metaphysical realism as the two-part claim that: "(1) there are moral facts or truths, and (2) these facts or truths are independent of the evidence for them" so that "that there is a single true morality that applies to all agents." Brink, *Moral Realism*, 14, 16–18, 53.

44 MacIntyre, *After Virtue*, 79. MacIntyre's claim about the indirect perception of facts is a denial of epistemic realism because it contradicts Geisler's definition of epistemic realism: epistemic "*Realism* postulates that we are in direct contact with an independent, material, external world." Geisler and Feinberg, *Introduction*, 148. MacIntyre's comments seem to be drawing on Wittgenstein's concept that nothing exists outside of language or his claim that, *"Man glaubt, wieder und wieder der Natur nachzufahren, und fährt nur der Form entlang, durch die wir sie betrachten. En Bild hielt uns gefangen. Und heraus konnten wir nicht, denn es lag in unsrer Sprache."* [One thinks, again and again, they are navigating the nature, and they are only navigating along the trim, through which we look at it. A picture held us captive. And we are not able to get out, for it lay in our language.] Ludwig Wittgenstein, *Philosophische Untersuchungen*, 2nd ed. (Blackwell, 1958), 48.

45 MacIntyre, *After Virtue*, 151–152, 163, 169, 196.

termining the biblical consistency of ethical theories is their metaethics or metaphysics (realism versus nominalism).

Metaphysical Realism is Biblically Consistent—Nominalism is Not

This section defends the claim that virtue ethics based on metaphysical realism is the most biblically consistent ethical framework for Trinitarian progressive sanctification by arguing that realism is consistent with the Bible while nominalism is not.[46] The argument for the biblical consistency of realism proceeds in three parts: (1) historically, realism is the predominant position of historic Christianity, (2) theologically, Christian doctrine is dependent upon the existence of universals, and (3) exegetically, the Bible teaches the existence of mind independent facts/reality.

The historical argument. Historically, the majority of orthodox Christians have held to some kind of metaphysical realism including some type of universal/form and those who have held to nominalism have been charged with heterodoxy, which suggests that realism rather than nominalism is biblically consistent. As a brief selective sampling, in the Patristic era according to John Rist, Augustine was "some sort of Platonist" and as such he held to a form of realism; in medieval scholasticism, Anselm and Bonaventura represent realism in the Platonic tradition, while Aquinas represents Aristotelian realism; in the modern period, A. H. Strong, C. Hodge, and M. Erickson have defended some form of realism.[47] From the time of the medieval debates of the twelfth century onward and from one of the earliest Christian nominalists, Roscelin of Compiègne (1050–1125), some well-known figures such as Abelard, Ockham, F. D. E. Schleiermacher, and Albrecht Ritschl have followed the nominalistic path, and historically some have charged that due to this path, they have denied essential core historic Christian doctrines (e.g., the Trinity [Roscelin of Compiègne, Abelard, and Schleiermacher], penal substitutionary atonement [Abelard, Schleiermacher, and Ritschl], and salvation by grace [Ockham]). For example, Anselm of Canterbury charged that Roscelin of Compiègne's nominalism led to tritheism and similarly others accused

---

46 For a similar judgment see: Kotva, *Case for Virtue*, 153–155; Smith, *Virtue Ethics*, 5, 8, 219.

47 John Rist, "Faith and Reason," in *The Cambridge Companion to Augustine*, ed. Eleonore Stump and Norman Kretzmann (Cambridge University Press, 2001), ch. 2; Augustine, *Div. quaest. LXXXIII* 46 *De ideis* (CCSL 44A:70–73); Paul P. Enns, *The Moody Handbook of Theology* (Moody, 1989), 435; (Erickson strongly defended realism in the first edition [page 55], weakly in the seond [169, 313], and has only a hint of it in the third edition of his theology.) Millard J. Erickson, *Christian Theology*, 3rd ed. (Baker Academic, 2013), 26, 41–42, 258; Charles Hodge, *Systematic Theology* (Logos Research Systems, 1997), 1:379, 2:46; Augustus Hopkins Strong, *Systematic Theology* (American Baptist Publication Society, 1907), 1:244.

Abelard that his nominalism led to Sabellianism or modalism (the idea that the three persons of the Trinity are merely manifestations of the one divine being).[48] Furthermore, Ockham's nominalism caused him to reject all of the traditional arguments for and explanations of the Trinity, which he said must simply be accepted on faith, and led him to take a soteriological position that Thomas Bradwardine (1295–1349) and John Wycliffe (1330–1384) labeled as Pelagian (based on works).[49]

While many historic orthodox Christian thinkers have favored the realist position, this fact does not in itself demonstrate the biblical consistency of the position. It does, however, suggest consistency since it would be hard to imagine how these thinkers could remain faithful to the historic Christian faith while holding to a biblically inconsistent position. And again, Christians such as Abelard and Ockham, who have denied realism, have also deviated from the historic faith. In fact, realism is necessary in order to adhere to many, if not all, historic Christian doctrines.

The theological argument. Theologically, the biblical consistency of the realist belief in the existence of universals may be established through the analysis of Christian doctrine. If doctrines that are derived from the Bible depend upon the concept of universals/forms for their existence and explanation, then the Bible from which they are derived must be consistent with the concept of universals/forms. Since not every doctrine can be examined in this book due to space limitations, then three representative doctrines will be investigated: the dichotomous nature of human beings, the Trinity, and the hypostatic union of Christ.[50] Not only are these central and essential doctrines of Christianity, but also Hodge has argued that the first and last are "intimately connected with some of the most important doctrines of the Bible."[51]

---

48 Simo Knuuttila and Robert F. Brown, "Nominalism," in *EC*, ed. Erwin Fahlbusch and Geoffrey William Bromiley (Eerdmans, 2003), 3:767.

49 Ibid., 3:767; Jan Rohls and Robert Kolb, "Predestination," in *EC*, ed. Erwin Fahlbusch and Geoffrey William Bromiley (Eerdmans, 2005), 4:341.

50 While some have held to a multifaceted, trichotomous, or a monistic view and based their views on Scripture, here it is assumed that the dichotomous view has been the dominant view in Christian history as attested by the following sources in this footnote. No comment is being made about the veracity of these other views by setting them aside and the dichotomous view is treated merely as the view most representing historic Christianity and as an example of a central and widely held doctrine that is consistent with realism. Louis Berkhof, *Systematic Theology* (Eerdmans, 1938), 191–192; Enns, *Moody Handbook*, 306–307; Erickson, *Christian Theology*, 540; Wayne A. Grudem, *Systematic Theology: An Introduction to Biblical Doctrine* (Zondervan, 2004), 472–473.

51 This argument follows Hodge in using dichotomy as an example of realism that "stands opposed to materialism and idealism." Hodge claims realism impacts: redemption, the fall, original sin, regeneration, the final state, and the resurrection. If these doctrines depend on

The doctrine of the dichotomous nature of human beings is derived from Scripture (Gen 2:7; Eccl 12:7; Matt 10:28; James 2:26) and depends on the realist concept of the existence of universals/forms such that the Bible is consistent with the existence of universals/forms. J. P. Moreland has argued with regard to universals, "three phenomena have been most important in the debate: predication, exact similarity [resemblance] and abstract reference."[52] K. Mulligan defines the term "predication" as referring to those "sentences ... consisting only of a part which serves to pick out a particular object and a part which says something about the object picked out. ... Thus 'smokes' in 'Sam smokes' is a predicate."[53] In order to illustrate how predication is used to argue for realism, Moreland offers the example that if "Socrates is red," and if "Plato is red," then "Socrates and Plato are members of this (non-arbitrary) class [of things that are red or things that exemplify redness] because each has the same property [universal] which grounds class membership."[54] Similarly, Aquinas expressed the biblical doctrine of dichotomy (James 2:26) through the Aristotelian realist claim involving predication that "the soul, which is the form of the body."[55]

The dichotomous position is consistent with realism as further illustrated by the fact of the doctrine's inconsistency with nominalism and post-Kantian idealism. If Moreland's argument is accepted that extreme and moderate nominalism are identical with naturalism and materialism, then the nominalist-naturalist-materialist will deny the existence of the immaterial soul, which is inconsistent with the dichotomous position of the soul's existence.[56] Post-Kantian idealism will at worst completely deny the existence of the body and at best "make the body a form of the mind," both of which are in contradiction to the dichotomous view of the objective existence of the body.[57] By elimination, realism is the only position left to be consistent with the dichotomous view. Since realism is consistent with dichotomy which comes from Scripture, then realism is consistent with Scripture and nominalism is not.

Despite having been criticized in seemingly every generation, the doctrine of the Trinity has been held as a historic Christian belief originating

---

universals, then the remainder of the doctrines also depend on universals at least indirectly. Hodge, *Systematic Theology*, 2:46.

52 J. P. Moreland, *Universals*, Central Problems of Philosophy, ed. John Shand (McGill-Queen's University Press, 2001), 4.

53 Kevin Mulligan, "Predication," in *CREP*, ed. Edward Craig (Taylor & Francis, 2002), 708.

54 Moreland, *Universals*, 5.

55 "*animae, quae est forma corporis.*" Aquinas, *STh.*, I q.85 a.1 resp. (*OOII* 5:331).

56 Moreland, *Universals*, 17. The immaterial soul is itself a kind of abstract object which nominalism denies.

57 Hodge, *Systematic Theology*, 2:46.

from Scripture (Matt 3:13–17; 28:19; 2 Cor 13:14) and has depended upon the concept of universals/forms. In his *De trinitate*, when reflecting on the Bible to explain the doctrine of the Trinity, Augustine claims that "but in God nothing is said according to accident, because nothing in him is mutable; nor still is all that is said, said according to substance. For it is said according to a particular [relation]."[58] In this claim, Augustine is using the concept of predication in a realist way to distinguish those universals that apply to the substance of God (good and great) as opposed to those universals (Father and Son) that apply to the relationships of the three persons of God respectively in order to distinguish each of the three persons. If the universals of Father and Son are no longer thought of as "properties of relation" but rather as particulars, then the doctrine of the Trinity seems to collapse by logical necessity into either tritheism or Modalism, as it actually does in Schleiermacher's nominalistic view of Christianity.[59] Since the doctrine seems to require the realist concept of universals and the doctrine originates from Scripture, then Scripture is consistent with the realist concept of universals and is not consistent with nominalism.

The hypostatic union is another doctrine that originates from Scripture (Phil 2:6–7) and is explained by means of universals/forms. In the *Summa*, Aquinas explains the doctrine using predication as follows:

> "(Because certainly Christ is true God and true man), but by means of the truth of predication ... in the same way as with regard to Socrates, and Plato properly, also man is truly predicated ... truly and properly this noun *man* can be predicated with regard to this noun *God*, according to which it substitutes for the person of the Son of God."[60]

The phrase "*sed etiam propter veritatem praedicationis*" ("but even on account of/by means of the truth/fact of prediction") indicates that Aquinas sees the basis or "*propter veritatem*" ("means of validity") of the doctrine as resting on realist "*praedicationis*" ("predication"). The fact that he compares the "the

---

58 "*In deo autem nihil quidem secundum accidens dicitur quia nihil in eo mutabile est; nec tamen omne quod dicitur secundum substantiam dicitur. Dicitur enim ad aliquid.*" Augustine. *Trin.* 5.5.6 (CCSL 50:210).

59 Schleiermacher seems to endorse Modalism in his discussion of the Trinity as charged by Barth and those following in his tradition. Friedrich Schleiermacher, *The Christian Faith*, ed. H. R. Mackintosh and J. S. Steward (T&T Clark, 1999), 750; Karl Barth, *CD* 1.1:353.

60 (*quia scilicet Christus est verus Deus, et verus homo*), *sed etiam propter veritatem praedicationis. ... sicut de Socrate, et Platone proprie, et vere praedicatur homo; ... vere et proprie hoc nomen homo potest praedicari de hoc nomine Deus, secundum quod supponit pro persona Filii Dei.* Aquinas, *STh.*, III q.16 a.1 resp. (*OOII* 11: 198).

predication of the noun *man* with regard to this noun *God*" in the doctrinal formula "Christ is true God and true man" to the way in which "man predicates Socrates and Plato" indicates that Aquinas views "man," as a universal that is instantiated by the particulars Socrates and Plato.[61] Since Aquinas explicitly shows that the doctrine requires the realist concept of universals/forms and that the doctrine originates from Scripture, then Scripture is consistent with the realist concept of universals/forms.

Moreover, the consistency of the hypostatic union with realism is further illustrated by the fact of the doctrine's inconsistency with nominalism and post-Kantian idealism. The inconsistencies are similar to those of the dichotomous view. Since the hypostatic union posits the union of a divine nature, consisting of spirit (John 4:24), and a human nature, consisting of body and spirit (Gen 2:7; Eccl 12:7; Matt 10:28; James 2:26), then the nominalist-naturalist-materialist will object to the spirit aspect of the divine and human natures while the idealist will object to the bodily aspect of the human nature in the hypostatic union. By elimination, realism is the only position left to be consistent with the hypostatic union. If realism is consistent with the hypostatic union which comes from Scripture, then realism is consistent with Scripture. Since dichotomy, the Trinity, and the hypostatic union depend on realism and other doctrines depend on these three, then it seems that realism is necessary in order to adhere to many, if not all, historic Christian doctrines.

The exegetical argument. Exegetically, an argument based on value demonstrates that realism is consistent with the Bible by demonstrating that the Bible teaches the existence of mind independent facts/reality. According to Lemos, intrinsic value is that which is valued "in terms of its being correct or fitting to love or like a thing in and for itself or for its own sake" and not "as a means" to something else.[62] It is to be distinguished from extrinsic or instrumental value, which according to Chisholm, is that which is valued "as a means" for something else.[63]

The value argument for realism is structured as follows: (1) God exists (Gen 1:1) as a unique being of intrinsic value (2 Sam 7:22; Ps 57:5; Is 42:8; Rev 4:11), (2) God has made the creation order with instrumental value (Gen 1:10, 12, 18, 21, 25, 31) and to reflect his intrinsic value (Ps 19:1; Acts 14:17; Rom 1:19–20), (3) God has created people (Rom 2:14–15) such that they respond morally

---

61 "*hoc nomen homo potest praedicari de hoc nomine Deus ... Christus est verus Deus, et verus homo ... Socrate, et Platone ... praedicatur homo.*"

62 Noah M. Lemos, *Intrinsic Value: Concept and Warrant* (Cambridge University Press, 1994), 6.

63 Roderick M. Chisholm, *Brentano and Intrinsic Value* (Cambridge University Press, 1986), 57.

to the objective value in and reflected by the creation order (Rom 12:2, 9), and (4) therefore the mind-independent existence of objective value implies that objective (moral) facts exist independently of people.

First, God exists (Gen 1:1) as a unique being of intrinsic value (2 Sam 7:22; Rev 4:11). From Genesis 1:1 forward, the Bible assumes the existence of God. In a number of verses, the language used (2 Sam 7:22 [גָּדֹל]; Ps 57:5 [כָּבוֹד]; Is 42:8 [כָּבוֹד]; Rev 4:11 [τιμή]) to describe the uniqueness of God in and of himself indicates his intrinsic value.[64]

Second, God has made the creation order with instrumental value (Gen 1:10, 12, 18, 21, 25, 31) and to reflect his intrinsic value (Ps 19:1; Acts 14:17; Rom 1:19–20). In the immediate context of Gen 2:9 and 3:6, the qualifying phrase, "good for food," indicates that instrumental value is generally in view in the creation order.[65] A number of verses indicate that God's nature or character is reflected in the creation (Ps 19:1; Acts 14:17; Rom 1:19–20), which implies that his intrinsic value is also reflected.[66] Therefore, realism is consistent with the Bible because the value existing in and reflected by the creation order is a created fact (Gen 1:1), sustained by God (Col 1:17; Heb 1:3), is not dependent upon the human mind for its existence, and is an independent reality. Furthermore, the following analysis of Rom 2:14–15 and 12:2, 9 demonstrates that the value of the creation order is an objective moral fact to which people respond and do not create themselves.

Third, God has created people (Rom 2:14–15) such that they respond morally to the value in and reflected by the creation order (Rom 12:2, 9). In Rom 2:14–15, the moral idea of the law (v. 15), the focus on the ontology of people through the "doing by *nature* the things of the law" (v. 14) and the mention of the "heart," "conscience," and "thoughts" in v. 15, and the mention of the act of creation (Rom 1:20) indicate that the metaphor "the work of the law written on the heart" (v. 15) refers to God creating people in such a way that their

---

64 The following sources indicate that the original biblical languages for "great," "glory," and "honor" used in the cited verses have to do with "value" or "intrinsic worth": BDAG, s.v. "τιμή"; BDB, s.v. "גָּדֹל"; E. F. Harrison, "Glory," *ISBE* 2:479.

65 Since by definition, instrumental value is that which is valued as a means for something else and in this case the trees are valued for their ability to produce fruit for food, then instrumental value is in view. The following sources interpret טוֹב as having intrinsic value: Gordon J. Wenham, *Genesis*, WBC 1 (Word, 2002), 18; Christopher J. H. Wright, *Old Testament Ethics for the People of God* (InterVarsity, 2004), 107. The following sources argue for an instrumental value: K. A. Mathews, *Genesis*, NAC (B&H, 1995), 151; Carl Friedrich Keil and Franz Delitzsch, *Commentary on the Old Testament*, rev. ed. (Hendrickson, 1996), 1:38; John H. Sailhamer, *Genesis*, vol. 2 of *EBC*, ed. Frank E. Gaebelein and J. D. Douglas (Zondervan, 1981), 26–27.

66 Wenham, *Genesis*, 18.

heart is able to "know" morality.⁶⁷ How the heart knows morality is not explicitly stated in Rom 2:14–15, but the canonical context indicates that contrary to the contemporary culture assigning reason to the mind and emotion to the heart, the Bible has the heart handle both the emotional (John 14:1) and rational (Matt 9:4) functions.⁶⁸ Later in the argument in Rom 12:2, 9, the function of the heart in knowing morality is explained.

Romans 12:2, 9 indicate that people respond morally to the value of the creation order through their heart or their emotions, and in this way, the existence of objective value implies that objective moral facts exist independently of people.⁶⁹ In Rom 12:2, the mind, emphasizing the reasoning function of the heart, functions to "δοκιμάζειν the good" or to determine what is morally good by testing or evaluating value.⁷⁰ In Rom 12:9, the parenetic linking word "good" (Rom 12:2, 9) and the parallel concept with similar wording in 1 Thess 5:21–22 indicate that Rom 12:9 is explaining that the mind, as the rational aspect of the heart, should test or evaluate value through the emotional responses of "hating the evil" and "loving or clinging to the good."⁷¹

---

67 John Murray, *The Epistle to the Romans*, NICNT (Eerdmans, 1968), 1:75. Augustine claims that the phrase "written on the heart" refers to the image of God in people as does Harrison. Augustine, *Spir. et litt.* 28 (CSEL 60: 202); Everett F. Harrison, *Romans*, vol. 10 of *EBC*, ed. Frank E. Gaebelein and J. D. Douglas (Zondervan, 1981), 31.

68 Bruce K. Waltke, "Heart," in *EDBT*, ed. Walter A. Elwell (Baker, 1996), 331. See also: Thomas W. Ogletree, "Love, Love Command," in *DSE*, ed. Joel B. Green (Baker Academic, 2011). According to Carl Henry, the church has traditionally interpreted Romans 2:15 as support for the philosophical concept of innate ideas (ideas present in an individual from birth). The following analysis of value is not intended to deny the concept of innate ideas, but rather to complement it. Carl Ferdinand Howard Henry, *God Who Speaks and Shows*, vol. 1 of *God, Revelation, and Authority* (Crossway, 1999), 334. Furthermore, there is some controversy over whether the function of the heart and the conscience are conflated. The fact that v. 15 states that "their consciences bear witness *with*," something, perhaps the law or the heart, indicates that the function of the heart and the conscience are separate and are not to be conflated.

69 In other words, contrary to Hume's fact/value dichotomy, "ought" is derived from the "is" of the value in the creation order, which reflects God's nature.

70 Towner argues that Paul's use of the mind "corresponds closely with the Old Testament" or "overlaps in meaning" with the Hebrew concept of the heart that entails both rational and emotional aspects. Philip H. Towner, "Mind/Reason," in *EDBT*, ed. Walter A. Elwell (Baker, 1996), 527–528. In v. 2, "so that," indicates that the purpose of "the renewing of the mind," is for the mind to be able to δοκιμάζειν or "to approve the good as a result of testing the worth or value." This translation of δοκιμάζειν is valid for at least two reasons. First, the BDAG defines δοκιμάζειν as "to draw a conclusion about worth on the basis of testing, *prove, approve,* where the focus is on the result of a procedure or examination," which Morris summarizes in the concise suggested translation of "approve as a result of testing;" BDAG, s.v. "δοκιμάζω;" Leon Morris, *The Epistle to the Romans*, PNTC (Eerdmans, 1988), 436. Second, the list of three adjectives at the end of v. 2, including τὸ ἀγαθόν, "the good," are substantial and so stand in apposition to τὸ θέλημα τοῦ θεοῦ, "the will of God," with the result being the meaning is that the good or value is being tested in order to determine God's will; Douglas Moo, *The Epistle to the Romans*, NICNT (Eerdmans, 1996), 757; Murray, *Romans*, 115.

71 On the idea of linking words in this parenetic section see: Moo, *Romans*, 774. On the parallel between Rom 12:2, 9 and 1 Thess 5:21–22 see Dunn, who points out that "both exhor-

However, someone might raise the philosophical objection that the emotions are non-cognitive, irrational bodily sensations in response to external stimuli (much like an amoeba responding to light or heat) by which one projects their preferences onto the world so that the value they "discern" is not that of the objective value of the creation order, but rather the subjective value of the observer. This objection involves the metaethical debate over whether there is a cognitivist epistemology (theory of knowledge) or a non-cognitivist epistemology. In cognitivism, moral facts are discovered through judgments which express beliefs or "factual statements capable of being literally true or false."[72] In cognitivism, the emotions are considered cognitive judgments "capable of truth or falsity, depending on whether they accurately represent [the] moral reality" related to the intrinsic value of the creation order.[73] In non-cognitivism, "moral judgments are not fact-stating, ... they signal our feelings or commitments, or are imperatives of conduct."[74] In response, the fact that emotions are being commanded implies that they may be rationally chosen (Rom 12:9)[75] and the term ἀνυπόκριτος, "un-hypocritical," in the com-

---

tations follow immediately upon teaching related to charisms," where Rom 12:6–8 discusses gifts to be used in service as living sacrifices and 1 Thess 5:19–20 discusses prophecy; James D. G. Dunn, *Romans 9–16*, WBC 38B (Word, 2002), 740. The phrases following "love must be genuine" are explaining or defining this phrase so that "clinging to" defines or is contextually synonymous to love. Because Rom 12:9 is describing the function of the heart, then the meaning is not limited to the emotions but also involves reason. For this reason, the contextual-linguistic idea of the heart's function in Rom 12:9 is similar to but has significant differences from Brentano-Chisholm's idea that "the phenomena of love and hate are like judging in that they, too, involve taking a stand toward an object of presentation ... in being either affirmative or negative." The similarity is between Brentano-Chisholm's "love and hate ... taking a stand toward an object of presentation" and Rom 12:9 "hating the evil and clinging to/loving the good." The difference is that whereas Brentano claims that "here the stand is emotive rather than intellectual," and Rom 12:9 is describing the function of the heart, in which the meaning is not limited to the emotions but also involves reason. Chisholm, *Intrinsic Value*, 18. As evidence that "evil" and ἀγαθῷ "good" are referring not just to moral quality but also to worth or value see BDAG, which indicates that both πονηρόν and ἀγαθῷ entail not only a concept of morality but also of worth. BDAG, s.v. "πονηρός," "ἀγαθός."

72 Railton, "Analytic Ethics," 28.
73 Shafer-Landau, *Moral Realism: A Defence* (Oxford University Press, 2003), 2, 17.
74 Ibid., 29.
75 Although there are some dissenters, there is a long tradition of textual interpretation taking the verbal ideas in v. 9 to be imperatival despite the lack of finite verbs. Mounce notes that "there are no finite verbs in the paragraph. There are, however, ten participles that serve as imperatives." He also notes that Barrett disputes the imperatival use but despite the objection, Mounce, Dunn, Luther, Calvin, and Aquinas affirm the imperatival interpretation. Robert A. Mounce, *Romans*, NAC (B&H, 1995), 236; Dunn, *Romans*, 739; Martin Luther, *Lectures on Romans*, (LW 25:106); John Calvin, *Commentary on the Epistle of Paul the Apostle to the Romans*, trans. John Owen, Calvin's Commentaries (Logos Bible Software, 2010), 464; Aquinas, *Super Epistolam B. Pauli ad Romanos lectura* C.12 L.2.983–84, ed. J. Mortensen and E. Alarcón, trans. F. R. Larcher, Under the title *Commentary on the Letter of Saint Paul to the Romans*, Latin/English ed., Biblical Commentaries 37 (The Aquinas Institute, 2012), 332, 335. If emotions are chosen, then reason drives the emotions similar to Augustine's claim, "*Ratio ista ergo uel mens uel spir-*

mand stresses the true-false contrast of hypocrisy verses genuineness in the emotions, implying that emotions can be true or false (Rom 12:9), so that both of these textual features indicate that the Bible is taking a cognitivist view of the emotions and implies that the value the emotions are judging is objective.

Fourth, therefore, Gen 1 and Rom 2:14–15; 12:2, 9 demonstrate that God created people's "hearts" to function so as "to approve the good as a result of testing the worth or value" of the creation order through the use of cognitive emotions, which indicates that the Bible teaches that objective or mind independent moral facts exist so that the claims of metaphysical realism are consistent with the Bible. However, since the above exegetical argument based on objective value has a philosophical and a detailed exegetical basis, then further objections might arise from either of these fields of study. Philosophical discussions detailing specific objections and responses to value, cognitivism, and the emotions are available in the literature of the field.[76] More importantly, the above argument has demonstrated the biblical consistency of the respective positions defended: intrinsic over extrinsic value, cognitivism over non-cognitivism, and the emotions as rational rather than irrational. With respect to the exegesis, while some objections have been addressed, readers may still have a wide range of reactions to the details in the analysis. Those reactions, however, may not impact the overall argument significantly.[77]

Therefore, the arguments based on history, theology, and exegesis demonstrate that metaphysical realism and teleology are consistent with the Bible, whereas by implication, metaphysical nominalism and deontology are biblically inconsistent. Since deontological ethical theories are biblically inconsistent, then teleological virtue ethics based on metaphysical realism is the

---

itus ... inrationales animi motus regit," [Such reason, therefore, either mind or spirit, rules the movement of irrational emotions.] rather than the emotions driving reason as in Hume, "reason is, and ought only to be, the slave of the passions," so that the emotions are cognitive rather than non-cognitive, or involuntary bodily sensations dependent upon the autonomic nervous system as in the James-Lang hydraulic theory of emotions. Augustine, *Lib.* 1.8.65 (CCSL 29:223); David Hume *Treatise of Human Nature* 2.3.3 L. A. Selby-Bigge, ed., *A Treatise of Human Nature* (Clarendon, 1888), 415. This interpretation is consistent with Nussbaum and Solomon's claims regarding emotions; Nussbaum, *Upheavals*, 23; Robert C. Solomon, *Not Passion's Slave: Emotions and Choice*, The Passionate Life (Oxford University Press, 2003), (cognitive) 26, 92–114, (chosen) 195–232.

76 Some helpful works dealing with these discussions include: Paul Bloomfield, *Moral Reality* (Oxford University Press, 2001); Brink, *Moral Realism*; Chisholm, *Intrinsic Value*; Lemos, *Intrinsic Value*; Nussbaum, *Upheavals*; Shafer-Landau, *Moral Realism*; Solomon, *Not Passion's Slave*.

77 Other arguments in support of the consistency of realism with the Bible can be found in the following sources: Ronald M. Rothenberg, "A Biblically Consistent Metaethic: The Consistency of Moral Realism with the Bible" (paper presented at the regional meeting of the Evangelical Theological Society, New Orleans, LA, 27 February 2010); Wright, *Old Testament Ethics*, 107.

most biblically consistent ethical framework for Trinitarian progressive sanctification.[78] By demonstrating the biblical consistency of metaphysical/moral realism, this book does not claim that realism is the only correct position, but only that the particular position being considered seems to be the most consistent of the positions extant to date. It is possible that someone may develop another metaphysical/metaethical position in the future which is more biblically consistent than those currently extant. Although defining virtue ethics as teleological and based on metaphysical realism is important because it narrows down the options, this is still a very broad definition of virtue ethics and a more precise definition is needed.

THREE HISTORIC SOURCES OF VIRTUE ETHICS: ARISTOTLE, AUGUSTINE, AQUINAS

In order to construct a more precise definition of virtue ethics, this book selectively draws on the teleological virtue ethics of the Aristotelian-Augustinian-Thomistic tradition. While the three characteristics of *eudiamonia*, virtue, and moral exemplars of the neo-Aristotelian virtue ethics of the contemporary resurgence of virtue ethics are helpful, this section constructs a more complete definition by characterizing the virtue ethics of Aristotle, Augustine, and Aquinas through selective sketches which emphasize the elements relevant for this book.[79] After providing these sketches in the next section, an analysis explains how these characterizations are critically appropriated to support the definition of virtue ethics from chapter 2.

Aristotle's Virtue Ethics

Aristotle's virtue ethics are focused on character with a basis in natural law and a theistic framework.[80] Aristotle claims that "the virtue of a thing is in

---

78 For a similar judgment see: Kotva, *Case for Virtue*, 167, 176; Smith, *Virtue Ethics*, 5, 8, 219.

79 For an overview of each writer's ethics see: Frederick S. Carney, "The Structure of Augustine's Ethic," in *The Ethics of St. Augustine*, ed. William S. Babcock, JRESR 3 (Scholars Press, 1991), 11–37; Gerard J. Hughes, *Routledge Philosophy Guidebook to Aristotle on Ethics*, Routledge Philosophy Guidebooks (Routledge, 2001); Stephen J. Pope, "Overview of the Ethics of Thomas Aquinas," in *The Ethics of Aquinas*, Moral Traditions Series (Georgetown University Press, 2002), 30–53.

80 Aristotle, *Eth. nic.* 1.9.1099b.10–15, 29–32; 5.7.1134b.20–30 (*AO* 9:14–15, 102); idem, *Rhet.* 1.13.1373b.2–8 (*AO* 11:50). Among others, Jaffa disputes the presence of natural law in Aristotle. However, the passages in this note cited from Aristotle's *Ethics* and *Rhetoric* are the traditional evidence originating with Aquinas. Furthermore, Aristotle speaks of many things being "by nature." Harry V. Jaffa, *Thomism and Aristotelianism* (University of Chicago Press, 1952), 174–182.

accord with its purpose ... [and] accordance with its nature."⁸¹ Aristotle also claims that, "it seems reasonable that *eudiamonia* [happiness] is given by the gods ... but (it) comes by virtue and some learning or practice," meaning self-effort.⁸² In Aristotle's system, virtue is learned by observing, associating with, reading stories or narratives about, and "imitating the best" moral exemplars.⁸³ Likewise, virtue is practiced by the principles of habituation (repeated action to form a habit) and reciprocity (action leads to being, but being also leads to action).⁸⁴ His ethic is concerned with the cardinal virtues of justice, prudence, courage, and temperance.⁸⁵ Aristotle holds that people act viciously due to lack of knowledge and/or power.⁸⁶

Augustine's Virtue Ethics

Augustine's (354–430 A.D.) virtue ethics combine the Greek (the neo-Platonic thought of Plotinus particularly but not exclusively) virtue tradition with the Bible, such that he has great continuity as well as some significant differences with Aristotle.⁸⁷ Like Aristotle, Augustine holds that people act viciously due to lack of knowledge and power, but unlike Aristotle who does not deal with sin, Augustine claims that people need God's help to act virtuously or righteously.⁸⁸ As a result, Augustine claims that the unbeliever's "virtues ... if not counted in relation to God, are really vices rather than virtues" apart from God, and at best the unbeliever can only act out of a self-love such that

---

Hare has demonstrated that theism is an inextricable part of Aristotle's ethics. John E. Hare, *God and Morality: A Philosophical History* (Wiley-Blackwell, 2009), 3, 65–66.

81 "ἡ δ' ἀρετὴ πρὸς τὸ ἔργον τὸ οἰκεῖον ... [καὶ] παρὰ φύσιν." Aristotle, *Eth. nic.* 6.2.1139a.15–19; 9.9.1170a.24–25 (*AO* 9:113, 191); idem, *Phys.* 7.3.247a.2–3 (*AO* 2:158).

82 "εὔλογον καὶ τὴν εὐδαιμονίαν θεόσδοτον εἶναι, ... ἀλλὰ δι' ἀρετὴν καί τινα μάθησιν ἢ ἄσκησιν παραγίνεται". Aristotle, *Eth. nic.* 1.9.1099b.15–19 (*AO* 9:15).

83 Observing: Aristotle, *An. post.* 1.33.89b5–11; 2.13.97b5–25 (*AO* 1:229, 250–251); Associating: idem, *Eth. nic.* 9.9.1170a.10–12; 9.12.1172a.1–15 (*AO* 9:190, 195); Reading: idem, *Pol.* 7.17.1336a.30–35; 8.3.1337a.20–23; 8.3.1337a.35–1337b.11; 8.3.1337b.24–28 (*AO* 10:216, 218–219); Imitating: "imitating the best" (τὰ κάλλιστα μιμεῖσθαι), idem, *Mag. mor.* 1.19.1190a30–34 (*AO* 9:241–242). Although some dispute whether or not Aristotle wrote the *Magna moralia*, it at least seems to contain Aristotle's thought. Aristotle, "Magna Moralia," in *The Works of Aristotle* ed. W. D. Ross, trans. George Stock (Clarendon, 1925), 9:v.

84 Aristotle, *Eth. nic.* 2.1.1103a.18–b25; 2.2.1104a.34–b.3 (*AO* 9:23–26).

85 Aristotle, *Eth. nic.* 3.6.1115a.7ff.; 3.10.117b.24ff.; 5.1.1129a.1ff.; 6.7.1141a.9ff. (*AO* 9:52, 59, 87, 118).

86 Aristotle, *Eth. nic.* 3.1.1109b.29–1110.b.1, 3.1.1110b.25–30; 7.3.1147a.10–1147b.19 (*AO* 9:39–40, 42, 133–134); idem, *Ethica eudemia* 2.8.17.1225.a1–2.9.4.1225b.16 (*AO* 9:330–231).

87 Augustine, *Civ.* 8.11.1; 8.12.1; 9.10.1; 19.1.1; 19.4.5 (CSEL 40/1: 371–374, 422; 40/2: 362–367, 377–380). Incredibly, Carney's revisionist effort depicts Augustine as integrating teleology and deontology. Carney, "Structure," 11, 17, 25–27.

88 Augustine, *Enchir.* 22.81 (CCSL 46:94–95); idem, *Civ.* 4.20.1; 19.4.1 (CSEL 40/1:186–87; 40/2:373).

"love ... delights in itself ... not on account of God."[89] He denies that happiness comes by virtue or self-effort, but instead affirms that it comes from God, who is the chief end or good.[90] According to Augustine, the theological virtues (faith, hope, and love), gained before the cardinal virtues, are infused as a supernatural gift of the Spirit to empower the believer to live righteously.[91] The theological virtues empower people to act out of *caritas* (love of God and love of neighbor for God's sake) to gain *beati* (equivalent of Aristotle's *eudiamonia*) and ultimately *beatitudo/makarios* (the blessedness that comes from God).[92] Furthermore, Augustine connects both the cardinal and theological virtues to sanctification through his explicit claim that: "For having been sanctified, we burn with full and complete love ... I assert that virtue is entirely nothing except the highest love of God" and through his use of Scripture citations (Rom 8:29; 2 Cor 4:16; Col 3:9–10).[93] On the basis of *De Civitate Dei* 11.28, Frederick Carney argues that Augustine's virtue ethic has a Trinitarian element in which believers are being restored into the Creator's image of eternity (Father), truth (Son), and love (Spirit) from which they have fallen due to sin.[94] In order to recognize the Trinitarian character in *De Civitate Dei* 11.28, Carney claims one must realize that often in Augustine's writings the Father is associated with eternity (*Trin.* 6.10.11), the Son with truth (*Trin.* 4.18.24), and the Spirit with love (*Trin.* 15.17.27).[95]

---

89 "*uirtutes, ... retulerit nisi ad Deum, etiam ipsae uitia sunt potius qum uirtutes.*" Augustine, *Civ.* 19.25.1 (CSEL 40/2:420); cp. idem, *Civ.* 5.19.1; 19.4.5 (40/1:251–254; 40/2:379–380); idem, *Enchir.* 32.121 (CCSL 46:113–114); "*cupiditatem ... ad fruendum se et ... non propter deum*"; idem, *Doct. chr.* 3.10.16 (CCSL 32:87).

90 Augustine, *Civ.* 19.20.1; 19.25.1 cp. 19.1.3; 19.11.1 (CSEL 40/2:407, 420 cp. 366, 388–390); idem, *Mor. Eccl.* 1.3.5; 1.4.6; 1.6.10; 1.25.46 (CSEL 90:7–9, 12–13, 51).

91 For chronological priority of the theological virtues see: Augustine, *Civ.* 5.19.1; 5.20.1; 19.4.5 (CSEL 40/1:251–255; 40/2: 379–380), idem, *Mor. eccl.* 1.15.25 (CSEL 90:29–30). On the attainment of *talis*, "excellence (of character)," by infusion of the Spirit see: idem, *Spir. et litt.* 36.66 (CSEL 60:199–200); On infusion of the virtues see: idem, *Conf.* 8.12.29 (CSEL 33:195); idem, *Civ.* 4.20; 5.19 (CSEL 40/1:186–187, 252); idem, *C. du. ep. Pelag.* 1.8.13 (CSEL 60:435). On love of God enabling righteousness living, see: idem, *Civ.* 10.6 (CSEL 40/1:454–455).

92 "*Caritatem uoco motum animi ad fruendum deo propter ipsum et se atque proximo propter deum*" [*Caritas*/Love is called an emotion of the mind according to delight in God for himself and also one's neighbor on account of God]. Augustine, *Doctr. chr.* 3.10.16 (CCSL 32:87); idem, *Civ.* 8.8.1; 10.6.1; 19.10.1 (CSEL 40/1:366–368, 454–456; 40/2:388–390).

93 "*Sanctificati enim plena et integra caritate flagramus ... nihil omnino esse uirtutem affirmauerim nisi summum amorem dei.*" Augustine, *Mor. eccl.* 13.22; 15.25 (see also: 13.23; 19.36; 25.46) (CSEL 90: 27, 29, see also: 26–29, 40–41, 51).

94 Augustine, *Civ.* 11.28 (CSEL 40/1:554–556); Carney, "Structure," 11, 15, 33.

95 Augustine, *Civ.* 11.28 (CSEL 40/1: 554–556; idem, *Trin.* 4.18.24; 6.10.11 (CCSL 50:191–193, 241–242); idem, *Trin.* 15.17.27 (CCSL 50A:501–502); Carney, "Structure," 11, 15, 33.

Aquinas' Virtue Ethics

Aquinas (1225–1274) is well known for his synthesis of the philosophy of Aristotle and the theology of Augustine with the result that his virtue ethics have much in common with both of them.[96] Aquinas follows Aristotle by defining virtue as that which is in accord with the nature of a thing and the natural law.[97] Similar to Augustine, Aquinas contradicts Aristotle by claiming that "man's greatest end is the uncreated good, certainly God, ... moreover the greatest end is called *beatitudo*. ... which is discovered ... in God alone."[98] Along with Augustine, in order to heal the viciousness resulting from sin and to overcome the metaphysical gap between people's natural ability and the supernatural end of *beatitudo*, Aquinas claims that it is necessary for God to infuse people with grace.[99] Infused grace results in the infusion of the theological virtues and supernaturally "proportional" cardinal virtues, which enable people to abstain from sin/viciousness, live righteously, and attain the supernatural end of *beatitudo*.[100] Aquinas argued for a progress of infused virtue as a part of sanctification: "according to Augustine ... the invisible mission happens for the sanctification of the creature ... according to the progress of virtue, or an increase of grace, the invisible mission happens."[101] Similar to Aristotle's view of the emotions as immediate fallible cognitive judgments of value, Aquinas views the emotions as cognitive perceptions of intentional objects which detect "moral good and evil."[102]

---

96 MacIntyre, *Justice*, 402; Servais-Théodore Pinckaers, "The Sources of the Ethics of St. Thomas Aquinas," in *The Ethics of Aquinas*, Moral Traditions Series (Georgetown University Press, 2002), 20; Smith, *Virtue Ethics*, 52, 60–61, 106.

97 Aquinas, *STh.*, I–II q.94 a.3 resp.; II–II q.17 a.1 resp.; II–II q.34 a.5 ad.1 (*OOII* 7:170; 8:124, 280).

98 "*ultimus hominis finis est bonum increatum, scilicet Deus, ... Ultimus autem finis vocatur beatitudo... quod non invenitur in aliquo creato, sed solum in Deo.*" Aquinas, *STh.*, I–II q.3 a.1 resp.; I–II q.2 a.8 resp. (*OOII* 6:24, 26).

99 Aquinas, *STh.*, I–II q.62 a.1 resp.; I–II q.109 a.1 resp.; I–II q.109 a.2 resp.; I–II q.109 a.7 resp.; I–II q.109 a.7 ad.2 (*OOII* 6:401; 7:289–291, 301–302).

100 Aquinas, *STh.*, I–II q.62 a.1 resp.; I–II q.63 a.3 ad.1.; I–II q.109 a.8 resp.; I–II q.109 a.9 resp.; I–II q.110 a.3 resp. (*OOII* 6:401, 409; 7:303, 307–308, 313–314).

101 "*secundum August. ... missio invisibilis fit ad sanctificandam creaturam ... secundum profectum virtutis, aut augmentum gratiae fit missio invisibilis.*" Aquinas, *STh.*, I q.43 a.6 s.c.; I q.43 a.6 ad.2 (*OOII* 4:451). For the infusion of virtues see: idem, *STh.*, I–II q.110 a.3 resp. (*OOII* 7:313). Aquinas also connects sanctification and virtue in his discussion of the sacraments: "*et forma nostrae sanctificationis, quae consistit in gratia, et virtutibus*" [and the form of our sanctification, which consists in grace and the virtues]. Idem., *STh.*, III q.60 a.3 resp.; III q.79 a.4 ad.1; III q.79 a.6 (*OOII* 12:12:6, 223, 225).

102 Aristotle, *Rhet.* 2.1.1378a.20–2.2.1378b.10 (*AO* 11:62–63); idem, *Eth. nic.* 2.5.1105b.20–1106a.13 (*AO* 9:29–30); Aquinas, *STh.*, I–II q.22 a.2 resp.; I–II q.22 a.3 s.c.; I–II q.23 a.1 resp.; I–II q.24 a.1 resp. (*OOII* 6:169, 171, 173, 179). King claims that "Aquinas is therefore a cognitivist about emotion, since cognitive acts are not only causal preconditions of emotion, but contribute

Definition by Biblical-Theological-Historical Synthesis

A comparison of the three sketches of Aristotle's, Augustine's, and Aquinas' virtue ethics to the definition given in chapter 2 demonstrates how these characterizations are being critically appropriated to construct a working definition of virtue ethics in this book. In chapter 2, virtue ethics was defined as a partial synonym to Trinitarian progressive sanctification and, by broadly following the Aristotelian-Augustinian-Thomistic tradition, it was construed as the teleological process based on natural law and requiring metaphysical realism in which the believer actualizes their positional holiness (Rom 6:22) by imitating (Matt 4:19; 1 Cor 11:1) the nature/character of the Father as expressed in the creation (Ps 19:1; Acts 14:17; Rom 1:20) and the Son (John 8:38; 14:9–10) by habitually (Luke 6:40; 1 Tim 4:7; Heb 5:14) acting in accordance with created purposes through the power of the Holy Spirit (Rom 5:6; 8:3), prayer-help of Christ (Luke 22:31; Rom 8:34; Heb 2:14–18), and motivation of Spirit-empowered virtues (Luke 8:1–15; Rom 12:1–2, 9), to be transformed (Rom 12:1–1; Col 3:10) into the *telos* or end of the good, the image of Christ (Mark 10:18; Rom 8:29).

Comparing Aristotle's virtue ethics to this definition indicates that nearly all of his concepts regarding virtue ethics in the sketch are appropriated including: teleology, natural law, virtues as being in accord with the nature and the purpose of a thing, imitation of moral exemplars (Matt 4:19; 1 Cor 11:1), habituation (Luke 6:40; 1 Tim 4:7; Heb 5:14), reciprocity (Matt 7:15–26), and vicious actions being based, in part, on lack of knowledge and power (Lev 4:27–28; Luke 12:48; Rom 5:6; 8:3). The teleological, realistic, and natural law elements have been given some biblical support in the previous arguments based on history, theology, and exegesis (Gen 1; Rom 2:14–15; 12:2, 9). Some of the other elements such as imitation, habituation, and reciprocity are biblically supported by exegesis in chapter 4.

Comparing Augustine and Aquinas' virtue ethics to the definition offered by this book indicates that nearly all of their concepts regarding virtue ethics in the sketch are appropriated including: the rejection of Aristotle's emphasis on self-effort in favor of an explicit emphasis on the gracious work of the Trinity, a supplementing of Aristotle's emphasis on vicious actions being due to lack of knowledge and power by a human inability due to sin (Rom 7:18; Gal 5:16–18), an emphasis on the theological virtues (1 Cor 13:13) over Aristot-

---

their formal causes as well. ... Aquinas' account of the emotions is ... like contemporary 'perception theories' ... in taking the evaluative element ... not to be a judgment, ... but rather a perception. Peter King, "Emotions," in *The Oxford Handbook of Aquinas*, ed. Brian Davies and Eleanore Stump (Oxford University Press, 2012), 215, 222.

le's cardinal virtues (Josh 1:6–18; Prov 1:1–3, 7; 2:6; Mic 6:8; Lev 18:7–24), a view of the emotions as immediate fallible cognitive judgments of value (Rom 12:2, 9), the idea that virtue ethics has a significant function in sanctification where progress in exemplifying the virtues is a key aspect of sanctification (1 Thess 3:12; 2 Thess 1:3; 1 Pet 1:13–16; 2 Pet 1:5–9), and the Trinitarian interpretation of sanctification (1 Cor 6:11; 1 Thess 5:23).[103] Aristotle and Aquinas' cognitive view of the emotions received some support from the previous exegetical argument based on value and Augustine and Aquinas' emphasis on the theological virtues receives some biblical support in chapter 4.

One major element requiring modification in Augustine and Aquinas' virtue ethics is their doctrine that the virtues are supernaturally infused by the Spirit. If the virtues are possessed by the believer as an ontological attribute, then they would represent a self-merit or inherent righteousness that would compromise salvation by grace through faith alone (Eph 2:8–10). Instead, this book (in chapter 4) follows John Owen in viewing the virtues as being due to the immediate operation of the indwelling Spirit (Rom 8:9–11; 1 Cor 3:16) in cooperation with the Father and the Son (Phil 2:13) so that they are not something possessed by the believer.[104] Other aspects of the definition and of Aristotle's, Augustine's, and Aquinas' virtue ethics receive some biblical support in chapter 5.

Conclusion

The preceding arguments have defined the nature and function of virtue ethics in Trinitarian progressive sanctification. The nature of virtue ethics is that it is a biblically consistent teleological ethical theory based on metaphysical realism. This claim was defended by demonstrating that the popular distinction between teleological and deontological ethics based on ends is inadequate, because it fails to account for the different meaning of the term "ends" in virtue ethics (final cause) and utilitarianism or consequentialism (consequence of an action). A more helpful distinction comes from the historic definitions of the terms in which teleology is based on metaphysical realism and deontology is based on a conception of duty, obligation, and utility that is

---

103 The modification of Aristotle's view of self-effort by grace by Augustine and Aquinas was also suggested by Kotva and noted in chapter 1. Kotva, *Case for Virtue*, 76.

104 John Owen, Πνευματολογια· or, a Discourse Concerning the Holy Spirit (Works 3:383–384, 405, 472, 536, 553–554). Owen does have "a principle of grace implanted in us by the Holy Ghost" and "a principle of spiritual life and grace, wrought, created, infused into our souls," but this book is only following him on the immediate operation of the indwelling Spirit and not the idea of implantation of a principle (ibid., 3:475, 551).

consistent with metaphysical nominalism. This metaethical or metaphysical distinction between realism and nominalism becomes the criterion for determining the biblical consistency of ethical theories. Since arguments based on history, theology, and exegesis demonstrated that realism is consistent with the Bible and nominalism is not, then teleological virtue ethics rather than any deontological type of ethics, including the agent based and linguistic virtue ethics of the resurgence of virtue ethics, is the type of ethics consistent with Trinitarian progressive sanctification.

The nature of virtue ethics was further defined by demonstrating how aspects of Aristotle, Augustine, and Aquinas' virtue ethics are critically incorporated into the definition of virtue ethics provided in chapter 2. Some of these aspects have already been supported biblically, while others receive Scriptural support in the following chapters. Two main aspects from the thought of Augustine and Aquinas are that virtue ethics are involved in sanctification (1 Pet 1:13–16; 2 Pet 1:5–9) and have a Trinitarian aspect (1 Cor 6:11; 1 Thess 5:23). Another important aspect is that of emphasizing the theological virtues over the cardinal virtues.

The function of virtue ethics in sanctification discovered so far is that progress in exemplifying the virtues is a key aspect of sanctification (1 Thess 3:12; 2 Thess 1:3; 1 Pet 1:13–16; 2 Pet 1:5–9). The argument for realism based on intrinsic value has laid the foundation for developing other functions of virtue ethics in sanctification in the following chapters. Chapter 4 builds on the ideas of value and the emotions as cognitive judgments to demonstrate how the theological virtues function as moral motivation in sanctification (Luke 8:1–15; 18:1–8; John 14:15, 23). Both chapters 4 and 5 use virtue ethics as a tool to demonstrate how progressive sanctification is a Trinitarian act.

Therefore, virtue ethics is key to understanding Trinitarian progressive sanctification, because virtue ethics based on metaphysical realism is the most biblically consistent ethical framework for Trinitarian progressive sanctification.

CHAPTER 3

JESUS' ROLES AS TEACHER AND EXAMPLE

The main claim of this chapter is that virtue ethics is key to understanding Trinitarian progressive sanctification because Jesus' active roles as a teacher and example of virtue are crucial to understanding how the Trinity progressively sanctifies believers. In this chapter, this claim is supported by following the method given in the introduction of determining which philosophies are biblically consistent (rather than shunning philosophy) by demonstrating that many, but not all, of the assertions of virtue ethics are consistent with Jesus' teaching on the virtues and particularly his teaching on the theological virtues in the Gospels. After establishing the virtue content of Jesus' teaching, exegesis of select passages shows that Jesus taught that the theological virtues provide moral motivation for ethical action. Furthermore, exegesis of other select passages reveals that the Aristotelian principles of habituation and reciprocity are similar to but have significant differences from how Jesus taught that his own example should be imitated through a process of discipleship involving sanctification. In keeping with the emphasis of the contemporary Trinitarian proponents in highlighting the applicability of the Trinity to Christian living, these insights regarding Jesus' teaching on and example of virtue are briefly applied to the Christian life.[1] Subsequently, the active sense of Jesus' teaching and example is evinced. Finally, these observations concerning Jesus' active role in sanctification through virtue ethics are combined with those from the earlier chapters to give a Trinitarian formulation of sanctification in accord with the Triune premise.

---

1 Robert W. Jenson, *The Triune God*, vol. 1 of *Systematic Theology* (Oxford University Press, 1997), 154; Catherine Mowry LaCugna, *God for Us: The Trinity and Christian Life* (HarperSanFrancisco, 1991), 1; Karl Rahner, *The Trinity*, trans. Joseph Donceel (Crossroad, 1970), 9–15.

Before proceeding with the argument, the method in this chapter requires at least two further qualifications in order to safeguard the divine authority, sufficiency, and inerrancy of Scripture and Jesus. First, in using the method of determining the biblical consistency of the philosophical concepts in virtue ethics, it is necessary to make comparisons. In a comparison, typically the thing being compared is named first while the thing that serves as the standard of comparison is named second. For example, when one says "This food tastes like chicken," the "food" is the thing being compared and "chicken" is the standard to which it is being compared. In the present case, the virtue tradition and particularly Aristotle is being compared to the standard of the Bible and the sayings of Jesus. However, in the process of making the argument, it is necessary to first exegete the biblical text in order to determine its meaning and then see how the virtue tradition (that has already been described in chapter two) compares to the meaning of the text. This reversal of the order of comparison at some points in the argument is not intended to relativize the Bible, which is the inerrant standard for Christian faith and life. The argument shows the comparisons of virtue ethics to the Bible so that the Bible is recognized as the standard that it is.

Second, the argument's use of source criticism ("an attempt to uncover written documents lying behind a given text") in the exegesis of the biblical text is not intended to undermine the doctrines of Scripture's authority and Jesus' divinity.[2] It is well known and has been argued by others that the Bible's use of sources does not necessarily validate those sources and the Bible's view of its sources must be determined as best as possible by the context in which the sources appear.[3] The intent in using source criticism is *not* to argue that the divine Jesus is a good student of or drew upon Aristotle for his ideas, but rather it is to acknowledge the cultural milieu in which Jesus spoke and the Bible was written and to demonstrate that perhaps at times Jesus and the Bible interacted with the Greek virtue tradition familiar to their audience in order to make unique theological points.[4] The point of the argument is to demonstrate that sometimes the virtue tradition agrees with the Bible and at other times the virtue tradition must be modified to conform to the type of virtue ethics presented in Scripture. However, the emphasis of the argument

---

2 Paul L. Redditt, "Source Criticism," in *Dictionary for Theological Interpretation of the Bible*, ed. Kevin J. Vanhoozer et al. (Baker Academic, 2005), 761.

3 For example see: D. A. Carson and Douglas J. Moo, *An Introduction to the New Testament*, 2nd ed. (Zondervan, 2005), 67–69, 694–695.

4 Scholarship currently acknowledges that it is possible that Jewish, Greco-Roman, or a combination of these two civilizations may be the cultural context for the NT and the sayings of Jesus. Ibid., 67.

is on demonstrating the similarity of the virtue ethic tradition to the Bible, which itself teaches a type of virtue ethic.

THE EXISTENCE OF THE THEOLOGICAL VIRTUES IN THE TEACHING OF JESUS

In order to demonstrate that the theological virtues are present in the teaching of Jesus, it is important to establish that many of the principles of virtue ethics are consistent with Jesus' teaching. To accomplish this task, a number of evidences selected from the characteristics of virtue ethics in the previous chapters and which seem to have become routine or standard in the field of ethics for identifying the presence of virtue ethics in the Bible are introduced. These evidences play a twofold role: they establish that the characteristics of virtue ethics introduced in the earlier chapters are consistent with the Bible generally and specifically with the teaching of Jesus. There are several standard evidences: (1) the Greek philosophical term ἀρετή may indicate virtue in Philippians 4:8 and 2 Peter 1:5,[5] (2) the Bible uses a variety of terms including Aristotle's ἦθος to discuss character,[6] (3) both the OT and the NT emphasize the idea of moral formation through instruction/discipleship and the imitation of moral exemplars,[7] and (4) the NT uses numerous virtue and vice lists similar to those found in the extra-biblical writers on virtue ethics of the time.[8] Overlapping with and in addition to these standard evidences, chapter

---

5 The term "virtue" does not occur in the OT and the Greek term for virtue, ἀρετή, is only used with respect to God in the Septuagint, it does occur several times in the NT (Phil 4:8; 1 Pet 2:9; 2 Pet 1:3, 5) and BDAG suggests the term "virtue" as one of the translation options (Phil 4:8; 2 Pet 1:5). BDAG, s.v. "ἀρετή;" Johan Lust, Erik Eynikel, and Katrin Hauspie, eds., *A Greek-English Lexicon of the Septuagint*, rev. ed. (Deutsche Bibelgesellschaft, 2003), s.v. "ἀρετή;" Nikki Coffey Tousley and Brad J. Kallenberg, "Virtue Ethics," in *DSE*, ed. Joel B. Green (Baker Academic, 2011); Jonathan R. Wilson, "Virtue(s)," in *DSE*, ed. Green.

6 "Although "ēthos [ἦθος], the technical Aristotelian term for character, occurs only once in the NT" (1 Cor 15:33), both the OT and the NT use "a variety of related terms" to communicate the concept; *in the OT*: "'ĕmûnâ [אֱמוּנָה], 'integrity' (1 Sam 26: 23); 'ōraḥ [אֹרַח], 'way of living' (Job 34:11; Ps 119:9); tām [תֹּם], 'integrity' (Ps 26:1); 'ăšûr [אָשֻׁר], 'step' (Ps 44:18; Prov 14:15); 'ĕmet [אֱמֶת], 'faithfulness, reliability' (Neh 7:2); derek [דֶּרֶךְ], 'way' (Ps 50:23; 2 Kgs 22:2; cf. Deut 5:33); 'šēm [שֵׁם], 'name' (Ps 41:5; Prov 22:1)" and *in the NT*: "dokimē [δοκιμή], 'character' (Rom 5:4; Phil 2:22); tropos [τρόπος], 'way of life' (Heb 13:5); katastēma [κατάστημα], 'behavior' (Titus 2:3); semnos [σεμνός], 'honorable, of good character' (Phil 4:8; 1 Tim 3:8, 11; Titus 2:2)." D. Michael Cox and Brad J. Kallenberg, "Character," in *DSE*, ed. Green.

7 Charles H. Cosgrove, "Moral Formation," in *DSE*, ed. Green. Instruction/discipleship (Prov 1:8; 4:1; 1 Sam 10:5, 10; 1 Kgs 20:35; 2 Kgs 2:3, 5, 7, 15; 4:1, 38; Is 8:16; 50:4; Matt 9:14; 11:1; 28:19; Mark 9:31; John 1:35; 4:1–2; 15:7–8; Acts 6:2). Imitation of moral exemplars (2 Kgs 14:3; Eccl 9:13; John 13:34–35; 1 Cor 4:16; 10:6, 11; 11:1; Gal 4:12; Phil 3:17; 4:9; 1 Thess 1:6; 2:14; Heb 6:12, 13:7; 1 Pet 2:21).

8 Downs claims that "Although some would include more and some fewer passages, the following texts generally are seen as representatives of this literary form in the NT: *Virtue Lists*: 2 Cor 6:6–7a; Gal 5:22– 23; Eph 4: 2– 3, 31–5:2, 9; Phil 4:8; Col 3:12; 1 Tim 3:2–4, 8–10, 11–12; 4: 12;

2 discussed J. Kotva's argument that virtue ethics and Matthew and Paul agree in focusing on "internal qualities" (virtues), reciprocity, a *telos*, and discipleship/training (habituation).[9]

Several of these characteristics of or evidences for virtue ethics in the Bible may be found in the teaching of Jesus. For example, some of the previously mentioned virtue ethical elements that are found in the teaching of Jesus include: (1) the *telos* of the kingdom of God is present (Matt 13:44–50),[10] (2) the use of reciprocity to build character is extant (Matt 7:15–23, 12:33–35; Luke 6:43–45),[11] (3) in Jesus' concept of and teaching on discipleship, the imitation of Jesus as a moral exemplar involving habituation and reciprocity is found (Matt 4:19; Luke 6:40; John 13:34–35),[12] and (4) the presence of virtue (the beatitudes, Matt 5:3–12; Luke 6:20–23) and vice (Matt 15:19; Mark 7:21–22) lists in the teaching of Jesus is evident.[13] While some of these ideas will be discussed in further detail as the chapter progresses, for now they serve as evidence that many of the characteristics of virtue ethics presented in the previous chapters are found in Jesus' teaching. Therefore, when the theological virtues are

---

6:11, 18; 2 Tim 2:22–25; 3:10; Titus 1: 8; 2:2–10; Heb 7:26; 1 Pet 3:8; 2 Pet 1:5–7 (cf. Matt 5:3–11; 1 Cor 13:4–7; Jas 3:17) *Vice Lists*: Matt 15:19; Mark 7:21–22; Luke 18:11; Rom 1:29–31; 13:13; 1 Cor 5:10–11; 6: 9–10; 2 Cor 12:20–21; Gal 5:19–21; Eph 4:31; 5:3–5; Col 3:5–9; 1 Tim 1:9–10; 6:4–5; 2 Tim 3:2–4; Titus 1:7; 3:3; 1 Pet 2:1; 4:3, 15; Rev 9:21; 21:8; 22:15 (cf. Luke 18:11)." David J. Downs, "Vices and Virtues, Lists Of," in *DSE*, ed. Green.

9 Ibid., 28, 104–108, 120–121, 126–129, 131.

10 Daniel J. Harrington and James F. Keenan, *Jesus and Virtue Ethics: Building Bridges between New Testament Studies and Moral Theology* (Sheed & Ward, 2002), 35–47, 49; Joseph J. Kotva, Jr., *The Christian Case for Virtue Ethics* (Georgetown University Press, 1996), 17–23.

11 Cox and Kallenberg, "Character"; Kotva, *Case for Virtue*, 104–106; Dennis P. Hollinger, *Choosing the Good: Christian Ethics in a Complex World* (Baker Academic, 2002), 87–90; Arthur Walkington Pink, *The Doctrine of Sanctification* (Logos Research Systems, 2005), 23, 41.

12 Cox and Kallenberg, "Character"; Harrington and Keenan, *Jesus and Virtue*, 53; Kotva, *Case for Virtue*, 107–108.

13 Burton Scott Easton, "New Testament Ethical Lists," *JBL* 51 (1932): 8; James A. Brooks, *Mark*, NAC (B&H, 1991), 118; R. T. France, *The Gospel of Mark: A Commentary on the Greek Text*, NIGTC (Eerdmans, 2002), 292; Donald A. Hagner, *Matthew 14–28*, WBC 33B (Word, 2002), 437. As evidence that the list (Matthew 15:19; Mark 7:21–22) really is a series of vices, there seems to be a consensus that the terms in the list are commonly found in the vice lists of both the NT and Jewish-Hellenistic sources. Easton, "Ethical Lists," 8; Robert Guelich, *Mark 1–8:26*, WBC 34A (Word, 1998), 379; Brooks, *Mark*, 118; France, *Mark*, 293. For this reason, Easton seems to deny and Brooks claims that others have denied the authenticity of the list, viewing it as a later tradition placed in the mouth of Jesus. Assuming the authenticity of the list, Brooks is correct to claim "the list may well be a summary rather than a verbatim report of what Jesus said, but doubtless Jesus set forth a list of similar vices." Easton, "Ethical Lists," 8; Brooks, *Mark*, 118. Scholars who think that the beatitudes are a virtue list or at least something like one that deals with internal qualities or goods include: Kotva, *Case for Virtue*, 104–106; Harrington and James, *Jesus and Virtue*, 62; Benjamin W. Farley, *In Praise of Virtue: An Exploration of the Biblical Virtues in a Christian Context* (Eerdmans, 1995), 103, 112; Glen H. Stassen and David P. Gushee, *Kingdom Ethics: Following Jesus in Contemporary Context* (InterVarsity, 2003), 33–48; Jonathan R. Wilson, *Gospel Virtues: Practicing Faith, Hope, and Love in Uncertain Times* (InterVarsity, 1998), 90.

encountered in the teaching of Jesus, they may be considered actual virtues rather than some other concept.

Since the occurrences of the theological virtues in the teaching of Jesus do not match the lists in later authors including the Pauline epistles, then the list of theological virtues may have been clarified over time as an aspect of progressive revelation.[14] The traditional triad of theological virtues of faith, hope, and love, identified as such by Aquinas and emphasized by Augustine, are themselves a virtue list in 1 Cor 13:13 and are grouped closely together in several passages (Col 1:4–5; 1 Thess 1:3; 5:8) as well as being part of other virtue lists and being grouped more loosely in a number of other passages (see Table A2 in Appendix 2).[15] However, Table A3 in Appendix 3 indicates that while Jesus taught on and associated together faith and love, he only taught on hope as an isolated virtue a few times after resurrection, and that the only possible triad of virtues occurring in the Gospels is faith, love, and endurance (Matt 24:10–13). Since the traditional theological virtues do not occur in the teaching of Jesus, then some have suggested that Paul coined the triad, but a strong scholarly consensus seems to exist that the theological virtues predate Paul.[16] As part of the debate over the sources of the NT ethical lists, there

---

14 If there is development within the Bible, then this suggests a *change* of ideas which would contradict the doctrine of inerrancy. The idea of progressive revelation implies the idea of *clarification* of earlier ideas by later ones rather than a strict change of ideas and so preserves the doctrine of inerrancy.

15 Augustine, *Enchir.* 1.3; 1 6; 122.33 (CCSL 46:49, 51, 114); Thomas Aquinas *STh.*, I–II q.62 (*OOII* 6:401–405).

16 Harrison seems to represent the opinion that Paul coined the triad. R. K. Harrison, ed. *Encyclopedia of Biblical and Christian Ethics* (Thomas Nelson, 1987), 411. Since the triad is used in numerous non-Pauline Scripture passages (see Table A2 in Appendix 2), occurs throughout the early church Fathers, and Conzelmann and Hunter have respectively argued that Paul's descriptive phrase τὰ τρία ταῦτα, "these, the three," used to introduce the triad (1 Cor 13:13) "appeals to the presupposed knowledge of the formula by the readers" (Conzelmann) and might be translated "the well-known three" (Hunter), then most scholars follow the respective conclusions of Weiss, Lang, and Hunter: "*P. habe. ... nicht selbest gepragt ... die Trias Glaube, Liebe, hoffnung*" [Paul has not coined ... the triad faith, love, and hope] (Weiss), "*Paulus nimmt hier vorpaulinische Begriffe*" [Paul refers here to pre-Pauline concepts] (Lang), and "that the triad is not Paul's own coinage, but a piece of pre-Pauline Christianity" (Hunter). Hans Conzelmann, *1 Corinthians: A Commentary on the First Epistle to the Corinthians*, ed. George W. McRae, trans. James W. Dunkly, Hermeneia: A Critical and Historical Commentary on the Bible (Fortress Press, 1975), 230; Archibald M. Hunter, *Paul and His Predecessors*, rev. ed. (The Westminster Press, 1961), 33–34; Friedrich Lang, *Die Briefe an die Korinther*, 16th ed. NTD 7 (Vandenhoeck and Ruprecht, 1986), 188–189; Johannes Weiss, *Der erste Korintherbrief* (1910; repr. Vandenhoeck & Ruprecht, 1977), 320–321. For authors who follow the conclusion of Hunter, Lang, and Weiss and provide various lists of Scriptural and Patristic triad occurrences see: Gordon Fee, *The First Epistle to the Corinthians*, NICNT (Eerdmans, 1988), 650; Charles A. Wanamaker, *The Epistles to the Thessalonians: A Commentary on the Greek Text*, NIGCT (Eerdmans, 1990), 75; F. F. Bruce, *1 and 2 Thessalonians*, WBC 45 (Word, 1998), 112; Günther Bornkamm, *Paul*, trans. D. M. G. Stalker (Harper and Row, 1971), 219; James D. G. Dunn, *The Epistles to the Colossians and to Philemon: A*

are several possibilities for pre-Pauline sources of the theological virtues including but not limited to (1) the Qumran sectarian manuscripts (1QS 2.24–25; 4.3; 5.3–4, 25), (2) Apocrypha-Septuagint (1 Macc 2:59–61; Sirach 2:6, 8–9), (3) OT Pseudepigrapha (4 Macc 17:2–4), and (4) Porphyrius of Tyre's "quartet" of "τέσσαρα στοιχεῖα ... περὶ θεοῦ· πίστις, ἀλήθεια, ἔρως, ἐλπίς."[17] However, NT scholarship seems to follow the opinion of Macarius the Egyptian that the triad originated with Jesus.[18]

Commentary on the Greek Text, NIGTC (Eerdmans, 1996), 58; William O. Walker, *Interpolations in the Pauline Letters*, JSNTSup 213 (Sheffield Academic Press, 2001), 159–160.

17 With the rise of source criticism in NT studies, numerous theories have arisen which have postulated either multiple sources or a primary source mediated through one or more secondary sources as the origin of the NT ethical lists. Perhaps some of the main theories may be summarized as proposing the following sources for the NT ethical lists: (1) Iranian-Hellenistic syncretism (Kamlah), (2) Iranian-Qumran (Wibbing), (3) Stoic-Greek (Easton and Vogtle), (4) OT Judaism-Christian (apodictic law; Schroeder), and (5) OT-Jewish tradition (Jewish proselyte catechism, Noachian laws, and Qumran; Martin). However, it seems that many conservative Christian scholars hold that the *form* of the NT ethical lists, including the theological virtues, comes from Hellenistic ethical lists, but the *content* was adapted so that it has Jewish and Christian origins. C. G. Kruse, "Virtues and Vices" in *Dictionary of Paul and His Letters*, Gerald F. Hawthorne, Ralph P. Martin and Daniel G. Reid eds. (InterVarsity, 1993), 962–963; Easton, "Ethical Lists," 1; H. G. Link and A. Ringwald, "Virtue, Blameless," in *NIDNTT*, ed. Colin Brown (Zondervan, 1986), 3.927; R. P. Martin, "Virtue, Haustafeln," in *NIDNTT*, ed. Brown, 3.928–930; D. Schroeder, "Lists, Ethical," in *Supplementary Volume*, vol. 5 of *IDB*, ed. Keith Crim (Abingdon, 1962) 546–547. Conzelmann has argued that 4 Maccabees 17:2–4 may indicate "the emergence of a version of the triad in Judaism before Paul" but with ὑπομονή, "endurance," rather than ἀγάπη, "love:" "Ὦ μῆτηρ ... δείξασα τὴν τῆς πίστεως γενναιότητα. ... θάρρει τοιγαροῦν, ὦ μῆτηρ ἱερόψυχε, τὴν ἐλπίδα τῆς ὑπομονῆς βεβαίαν ἔχουσα πρὸς τὸν θεόν." [O mother ... having displayed the nobility of *faith*. ... Take courage, therefore, holy-souled mother, having the *hope* of *endurance*, certain from God.] Conzelmann, *1 Corinthians*, 229. Emphasis added. Alfred Rahlfs, ed. *Septuaginta: With Moorphology* (Deutsche Bibelgesellschaft, 1996), s.v. "4 Macc. 17:2–4." Reitzenstein argued that Paul developed the theological virtues as an anti-Gnostic polemic against Porphyrius of Tyre's "quartet" of τέσσαρα στοιχεῖα ... περὶ θεοῦ· πίστις, ἀλήθεια, ἔρως, ἐλπίς. Richard Reitzenstein, *Historia monachorum und Historia lausiaca*, FRLANTNF 7 (Vandenhoeck und Ruprecht, 1916), 101–102, 242–255. "four principles ... concerning God: faith, truth, love, and hope." Porphyry *Ad Marcella* 24.376–378 Kathleen O'Brien Wicker, ed., *Porphyry the Philosopher to Marcella: Text and Translation with Introduction and Notes*, SBLTT 28/SBLGRRS 10 (Scholars Press, 1987). 66. However, there seems to be a general consensus among the relatively recent sources discussing Reitzenstein's proposal that Porphyry (AD 232–304) is far too late to have influenced Paul or Jesus. Furthermore, it has already been demonstrated that source critical scholarship generally opposes a Pauline origin for the triad of virtues. Conzelmann, *1 Corinthians*, 229; C. T. Craig, *The First Epistle to the Corinthians*, vol. 10 of *IB*, ed. George Arthur Buttrick (Abingdon, 1953), 194–195; Anthony C. Thiselton, *The First Epistle to the Corinthians: A Commentary on the Greek Text*, NIGTC (Eerdmans, 2000), 1072; O'Brien Wicker, *Porphyry*, 110. The theological virtues also occur in other gnostic texts such as those in the *Nag Hammadi Library*, i.e. the Gospel of Philip 79:18–33 (AD 250–300), but these are also too late to have been sources for the NT.

18 At the beginning of Homily XXXVII, Macarius the Egyptian claims that Jesus taught on the triad and even gives a supposed Jesus *logion*: "ἀλλ' ἀκούων τοῦ κυρίου κελεύοντος ἐπιμελεῖσθαι πίστεως καὶ ἐλπίδος, δι' ὧν γεννᾶται ἡ φιλόθεος καὶ φιλάνθρωπος ἀγάπη, τὴν αἰώνιον ζωὴν παρέχουσα." [but hearing the Lord commanding, 'be diligent in faith and hope, through which is produced

What seems most likely is that as part of progressive revelation, Jesus intentionally saved his instructions on hope for his post-resurrection appearances (Luke 24:27; Acts 1:3), when hope would have new meaning.[19] If so, then the occurrences of the theological virtues in the teaching of Jesus do not match the lists in later authors including the Pauline epistles, because the list of theological virtues may have been clarified over time as an aspect of progressive revelation, due in large part to the resurrection. The later revelation in the NT given after the teaching of Jesus recorded in the Gospels then preserves the virtue of endurance, while placing new emphasis on the hope of the resurrection. Consequently, the theological virtues Jesus taught about are not the traditional theological virtues (faith, hope, and love, 1 Cor 13:13), but rather faith, love, and endurance (Matt 24:10–13).

JESUS' TEACHING AS MORAL MOTIVATION

Having demonstrated that Jesus taught on the theological virtues of faith, love, and endurance (Matt 24:10–13), this section defends the claim that Jesus taught the disciples about these virtues, in part, for the purpose of moral motivation. Later, the significance of Jesus' teaching on the theological virtues for moral motivation with respect to Trinitarian sanctification is explained. In ethics, there is much technical debate over how moral agents are motivated to act ethically. The issue of how agents are motivated is important for establishing how the persons of the Trinity work together in sanctification and is handled after demonstrating that Jesus taught that the theological virtues provide moral motivation.

Faith as a Motive in Luke 18:1–8

In the Parable of the Persistent Widow (Luke 18:1–8), Jesus teaches the disciples about faith as a moral motive which causes moral action. In Luke 18:1, the explicit purpose that Jesus taught the disciples the parable was "that it

---

love of God and man, which grants eternal life.'] Macarius, *Homily* 37 (GCS 2:46). While the extrabiblical source of Macarius' claim is certainly neither authoritative nor definitive, it does show that someone early in church history either thought that the theological virtues actually were attributed to Jesus or wanted to attribute the theological virtues to Jesus. Hunter (*Paul*, 35) is one of the scholars who hold that the triad likely originated with Jesus.

19 The NT emphasis on hope takes on particular significance in contrast to the OT in which love (Deut 6:5; Lev 19:18) and faith (Gen 15:6; Hab 2:4) play a large role, but hope is not highlighted as a characteristic believers are to possess with the possible exceptions by implication in a few passages (Ps 71:5; Jer 14:8; 17:13).

is necessary to always pray and not to lose heart."²⁰ BDAG indicates that the term, ἐγκακεῖν, translated as "lose heart" (NAS) means, "to lose one's *motivation* in continuing a desirable pattern of conduct or activity."²¹ In Luke 18:1, the "desirable pattern of conduct or activity" to be continued is the ethical act of prayer.²² In the context, the μὴ ἐγκακεῖν, "motivation not to be lost," in Luke 18:1 is the faith, which may or may not be found at the Son's return in Luke 18:8. That faith is the motivation for prayer is evidenced in at least two ways by the passage. First, there is no other candidate that may stand as a motivation in the context. While persistence may be implied (Luke 18:5), it is not explicitly mentioned and the form of the parable is a saying narrative in which the main point comes at the end, where faith is found. Second, against Stein who seems to see the prayer as motivating perseverance and perhaps faith (thoughts contradictory to v. 1), I. H. Marshall, John A. Martin, and Calvin all take the point of the closing question in Luke 18:8 as a challenge to the disciples to maintain their faith, which will be evidenced by their continued prayer.²³ Therefore, in Luke 18:1–8, Jesus teaches that the theological virtue of faith serves as a moral motive which causes the moral action of prayer.

Love as a Motive in John 14:15, 23

In the first Paraclete passage in the upper room discourses (John 14:15, 23), Jesus teaches the disciples about love as a moral motive which causes moral ac-

---

20 Craig S. Keener, *The IVP Bible Background Commentary: New Testament* (InterVarsity, 1993), s.v. "Luke 18:8;" John Nolland, *Luke 9:21–18:34*, WBC 35B (Word, 2002), 857; Robert H. Stein, *Luke*, NAC (B&H, 1992), 443; I. Howard Marshall, *The Gospel of Luke: A Commentary on the Greek Text*, NIGTC (Paternoster, 1978), 676.

21 BDAG, s.v. "ἐγκακέω," emphasis added.

22 Prayer may not be immediately considered an ethical action that has a good or bad value in the same way that lying might be instantly recognized as a bad ethical act. However, prayer may be considered an ethical act in Luke 18:1 in at least three respects. First, the term ἐγκακεῖν, or "to lose one's motivation," is used with an explicit ethical sense elsewhere in the NT (Gal 6:9; 2 Thess 3:13) and the use of this term may indicate that prayer is being given an ethical sense in Luke 18:1. Second, prayer is an ethical act in the relative sense that when compared to the contrasting ethically good acts of life preserving, truth-telling, and protection of property and the ethically bad acts of murder, lying, and stealing, and assuming prayer is not deemed an ethically neutral act, then it seems to fit better with the good rather than the bad acts. Third, the content of prayer may be good or bad. In the case of Luke 18, since the content of the prayer is likely for the return of Christ (Luke 17:22; 18:8) so that he may meet out eschatological justice, then the prayer is ethically good. So there is good reason to consider prayer to be a moral act in Luke 18:1. Nolland, *Luke 9:21–18:34*, 866; Stein, *Luke*, 443; Marshall, *Luke*, 674.

23 John Calvin, *Commentary on a Harmony of the Evangelists, Matthew, Mark, and Luke*, trans. William Pringle (Logos Research Systems, 2010), 2:198; Marshall, *Luke*, 669–670; John A. Martin, *Luke*, in *BKC*, ed. John F. Walvoord and Roy B. Zuck (Victor Books, 1985), 2:250; Stein, *Luke*, 446–447.

tion. In John 14:15, 23, both verses contain the structure, ἐάν + verb in the subjunctive mood (ἀγαπᾶτέ/ἀγαπᾷ), followed by a verb in the future indicative (τηρήσετε/τηρήσει) signaling a third class condition, which indicates "a *logical connection* (if A, then B)" or "cause and effect" such that love is the cause or motive of obedience.[24] In John 14:15, while commentators routinely insist that τὰς ἐντολάς, "the commands," include *more* than just what G. L. Borchert calls "ethical precepts or rules of morality," they seem to be in agreement that this term includes ethical commands.[25] Therefore, in John 14:15, 23, Jesus teaches that love motivates obedience to ethical commands.

Endurance as a Motive in Luke 8:1–15

In the Parable of the Sower (Luke 8:1–15), Jesus teaches the disciples about endurance as a moral motive which causes moral action. In the explanation of the parable in Luke 8:15, Jesus describes the fourth kind of soil or hearer of the word, as "by endurance bearing fruit." The phrase ἐν ὑπομονῇ, "by endurance," functions as an instrumental dative which indicates that endurance is the means by which the fruit is produced.[26] Although the context does not explicitly state what the content is of the fruit that is produced, the phrase describing the hearers as οἵτινες ἐν καρδίᾳ καλῇ καὶ ἀγαθῇ, "the ones being noble and good in heart," may be borrowed, as J. Nolland claims, from "the ethical language of Greek humanism," and if so, then it contextually gives the

---

24 D. A. Carson, *The Gospel According to John*, PNTC (Eerdmans, 1991), 498; Andrew T. Lincoln, *The Gospel According to Saint John*, BNTC (Continuum, 2005), 393; George R. Beasley-Murray, *John*, 2nd ed., WBC 36 (Word, 2002), 256; Daniel B. Wallace, *Greek Grammar Beyond the Basics: Exegetical Syntax of the New Testament* (Zondervan, 1999), 682, 689, 691, 696, emphasis original.

25 Gerald L. Borchert, *John 12–21*, NAC (B&H, 2002), 121. See also: Beasley-Murray, *John*, 256; Carson, *John*, 498; Lincoln, *John*, 393.

26 Wallace, *Greek Grammar*, 162–163. Only the NIV translates the phrase "ἐν ὑπομονῇ" with the preposition "by" and so explicitly indicates means. Herr seems to accept the idea of "means." The NAS, Nolland, and Stein, all ambiguously use "with," which might indicate "manner" or "means." Reiling and Swellengrebel seem to argue for "manner." However, two factors seem decisive. First, the verb καρποφοροῦσιν "bear or produce," naturally carries the idea of the means or instrument by which the production is accomplished—things are usually produced by something, not in a certain way, i.e. joyfully, sorrowfully, or with perseverance. Second, in v. 12–14, each of the other types of soil is described in terms of the means by which they are unproductive, so in a parallel manner in v. 15, it is expected that the means by which the soil is productive would be explained. Ken Heer, *Luke: A Commentary for Bible Students* (Wesleyan, 2007), 127; John Nolland, *Luke 1:1–9:20*, WBC 35A (Word, 2002), 387; J. Reiling and J. L. Swellengrebel, *A Handbook on the Gospel of Luke*, UBS Handbook Series (United Bible Societies, 1993), 336; Stein, *Luke*, 247.

fruit produced an ethical sense.[27] Therefore, endurance is used as an ethical motive in producing ethical character in the teaching of Jesus.

An Objection and Conclusion

For Luke 8:15 and John 14:15, 23, someone might object that "means" and "cause" are not the same things as "motive," so that love and endurance are the "basis" rather than the motive of ethical behavior.[28] For example, Daniel Wallace argues that in Eph 2:8, the dative χάριτί, "grace," indicates not only God's motive, but also the basis of salvation.[29] However, in analyzing the source of ethical actions, faith, love, and endurance, (as well as hope) serve as means or motivations rather than the bases or powers upon which actions take place. The basis of the ethical action of believers is the Trinity moving the will (Phil 2:13) through the divinely inspired or generated motivations of the virtues (Gal 5:22–23). If the virtues themselves are the basis rather than the means or motivation of ethical behavior, then the source of action begins to look like something within people and a works based salvation may result.

Therefore, in the Gospels, Jesus teaches that the theological virtues of faith, love, and endurance (Matt 24:10–13) function as moral motivations for ethical actions. In a similar way, in 1 Thess 1:3, Paul describes the church's service as being motivated by faith, hope, and love through a series of genitives which might be taken as either a series of subjective constructions, through use of the preposition "by" and indicating that the love is producing the labor, or as a series of ablative constructions, through "of" and indicating that love is the source of the labor.[30] Under either interpretation, the point seems to be similar to that made by Jesus, which is that the theological virtues function as the motives of actions. Consequently, not only do faith, love, and endurance function as moral motivations, but so do the traditional theological virtues, including hope.

---

27 Nolland, *Luke 1:1–9:20*, 387. Marshall is against the phrase as an ethical Hellenism and Nolland for it, but all three (Marshall, Nolland, and Stein) seem to agree that the fruit is "ethical in character." Ibid., 387; Marshall, *Luke*, 327; Stein, *Luke*, 247. If Jesus cited a phrase from Greek humanism, then it is likely that it was an expression familiar to his audience and he used it because *their* familiarity with it helped to communicate *his* message.

28 Wallace, *Greek Grammar*, 167.

29 Ibid., 167–168.

30 Wanamaker and the NIV favor the subjective construction, while the NAS favors the ablative. Wanamaker, *Thessalonians*, 75.

Motivational Internalism

In ethics, there is a debate over how moral agents are motivated to act ethically. This debate is important because which position one takes with respect to how agents are motivated morally impacts one's view of how the Trinity works in sanctification. The debate over moral motivation takes place within the metaethical discipline of moral psychology, which is "concerned with psychological issues that arise in connection with the moral evaluation of actions" according to M. Slote such as "the way humans think about morality, make moral judgments, and behave in moral situations" according to Thomas Nadelhoffer or moral development, motivation, and health as aptly summarized by Carig V. Mitchell.[31]

Within the discipline of moral psychology and in the sub-discipline of moral motivation, there are two main positions of concern for the argument of this book: internalism and externalism. Internalism has two positions: weak internalism is the position that recognition of "moral considerations [facts] provide *some* motivation ... for action" and it is to be distinguished from strong internalism which is the position that recognition of moral facts "provide *sufficient* motive for action."[32] "Externalism is the denial of internalism; externalism claims that the motivational force and rationality of moral considerations ... depends on things other than the concept of morality [moral facts], such as ... facts about agents such as their interests or desires."[33] This sub-section argues that since motivational weak internalism is biblically consistent, then by the law of non-contradiction, both motivational strong internalism and externalism are not biblically consistent.

Exegesis of John 14:15, 21, 23–24 demonstrates that motivational weak internalism is consistent with Jesus' teaching. It has already been demonstrated in these verses that even if Jesus' commands (v. 15, 21) and words (v. 23–24) involve more than moral facts, they still include basic ethical precepts.[34] In these verses, there are *two* conditions, both of which must be met, for obedience: having the commands of Jesus and loving Jesus. Virtue ethics is con-

---

31 Thomas Nadelhoffer, Eddy Nahmias, and Shaun Nichols, "Introduction," in *Moral Psychology: Historical and Contemporary Readings*, ed. Thomas Nadelhoffer, Eddy Nahmias, and Shaun Nichols (Blackwell, 2010), 1; Craig Mitchell, "Moral Psychology and Biblical Counseling" (Classroom lecture notes, Cneth 4323—The Bible and Moral Issues, Spring 2007), Electronic PowerPoint Presentation, 3; Michael Slote, "Moral Psychology," in *CREP*, ed. Edward Craig (Taylor & Francis, 2002), 596.

32 Emphasis original. David O. Brink, *Moral Realism and the Foundations of Ethics* (Cambridge University Press, 1989), 41.

33 Emphasis removed. Ibid., 42–43.

34 Beasley-Murray, *John*, 256; Borchert, *John 12–21*, 121; Carson, *John*, 498; Lincoln, *John*, 393.

sistent with these two conditions in its claim that lack of knowledge (commands of Jesus) or power (love of Jesus empowered by the Spirit) results in vice.[35] In John 14:21, the first condition of having or possessing the commands of Jesus seems to imply strongly recognition of moral facts. However, D. O. Brink objects that, "it seems all too possible to have a moral obligation and remain unmoved if only because one does not recognize the obligation as an obligation."[36] In response, in the context of the Bible, possession of divine commands implies sufficient understanding to carry out those commands as when Moses taught that possession of God's commands enabled the people to obey them (Deut 30:11–14). Thus, the point in John 14:21 is that possession or recognition of moral facts is *one* condition necessary for obedience. Hence, internalism or the idea that recognition of moral facts motivates obedience or moral action seems to be consistent with John 14:21. However, the fact that there is a second condition necessary for obedience in John 14:15, 23–24 indicates that having Jesus' commands or recognition of moral facts provides only *some* (weak internalism) and not *sufficient* (strong internalism) motivation for moral action.

In John 14:15, 23–24, love of Jesus is a second condition for obedience. This second condition is necessary not because some external factor to moral facts, such as externalism's agent's interests or desires, is necessary to motivate moral action, but rather because people biblically do not function properly due to sin (2 Chr 6:36; Ecc 7:20; Rom 3:23), which overrules or perhaps short circuits their motivation to do the good they recognize (Rom 7:18–20) and may even cause people to suppress what they know to be true (Rom 1:18). As Micah 3:2 states and Augustine pointed out, due to sin, people love and hate or value the wrong things, and as a result, they are motivated by the wrong things.[37] Since love of Jesus is only possible by the saving power of the Spirit (1 Cor 12:3), then in John 14:15, 23–24, love of Jesus indicates that a person has been freed from the power of sin (Rom 6:18; 7:4–6; 1 Cor 15:56–57). The later section in this chapter, "Statement of Virtue Ethical Trinitarian Sanctification Ordered by the Triune Premise," providing a theological synthesis, develops this idea of moral motivation to demonstrate that by the working of the Trinity, people are enabled to function properly (Phil 2:13) so that they can love and hate the right things or be motivated to act morally by recognition of moral facts or the identification of value (Rom 2:14–15; 12:2, 9).

---

35 Aristotle, *Eth. nic.* 3.1.1109b.29–1110.b.1, 3.1.1110b.25–30; 7.3.1147a.10–1147b.19 (*AO* 9:39–40, 42, 133–134); idem, *Eth. Eud.* 2.8.17.1225.a1–2.9.4.1225b.16 (*AO* 9:330–331); Augustine, *Enchir.* 22.81 (CCSL 46:94–95); idem, *Civ.* 4.20.1; 19.4.1 (40/1:186–187; 40/2:373).

36 Brink, *Moral Realism*, 41.

37 Augustine, *Doct. chr.* 1.27.28 (CCSL 32:22).

Objections and Responses

Someone might object that love of Jesus seems like an agent's interest or desire as in externalism.[38] In response, in externalism generally, the moral agent's interests and desires are the source of motivation and are subjectively determined or dependent upon the agent, and the emotions are considered irrational.[39] In this case, loving Jesus or being interested in doing anything would be a result of bodily sensations or an arbitrary determination by the agent. However, as argued in chapter 3, the emotions biblically are cognitive judgments of objective, independent value/moral facts (Gen 1; Rom 2:14–15; 12:2, 9), and these judgments or recognition of value motivate action. Consequently, Jesus is loved because by the Spirit (Eph 1:17–19; 1 Cor 2:14; 12:3), the believer recognizes his value (Rev 5:12) and so the motivation is from this objective value (internalism) rather than the believer's interests or desires (externalism).

Someone may object that virtues are not emotions and so while emotions may motivate, virtues do not. In responding to this philosophical objection and in keeping with the method from the introduction, the strategy is to respond philosophically and then demonstrate that the philosophical response is biblically consistent. Philosophically, although Aristotle claims that the virtues are dispositions ("the virtues ... they are dispositions"), he links the virtues to the emotions by claiming, "virtue is concerned with feelings and actions."[40] Moreover, in an early article, Robert C. Roberts builds on Aristotle by defining five distinctions as a non-exhaustive classification of the connections between virtues and emotions.[41] The most relevant distinction he coins is that of the *"emotion-virtues,"* which he defines as "dispositions to have the emotion from which they get their name."[42] In a later essay, Roberts seems to indicate that emotions and dispositions/virtues that share a name are fluid or flexible in use so that the names sometimes refer to an emotion

---

38 More objections and responses in the debate between internalism and externalism can be found in the following sources: Brink, *Moral Realism*, 37–80; Paul Bloomfield, *Moral Reality* (Oxford University Press, 2001), 153–194; Russ Shafer-Landau, *Moral Realism: A Defence* (Oxford University Press, 2003), 119–161.

39 Brink, *Moral Realism*, 10, 21, 68–69.

40 "αἱ ἀρεταί ... ἕξεις αὐτὰς εἶναι ... ἡ δ' ἀρετὴ περὶ πάθη καὶ πράξεις ἐστίν." Aristotle, *Ethic. nic.* 2.5.1106a.10–14; 2.6.1106b.24–25 (*AO* 9:30, 32).

41 Robert C. Roberts, "Aristotle on Virtues and Emotions," *Philosophical Studies* 56, no. 3 (1989): 293–294. Among others, Solomon also follows Aristotle in distinguishing emotions from dispositions. Robert C. Solomon, *Not Passion's Slave: Emotions and Choice*, The Passionate Life (Oxford University Press, 2003), 32, 184, 203.

42 Emphasis original. Roberts, "Aristotle on Virtues and Emotions," 293.

and sometimes to a disposition as determined by the context.[43] In terms of biblical consistency, this philosophical claim about emotion-virtues seems to be consistent with some biblical texts in which faith, hope, and love seem to be virtues (1 Cor 13:13) and others in which they seem to be emotions (Ps 42:5; Mark 11:22; Rom 13:8).

Since the concept of emotion-virtues is key to responding to the present philosophical objection and the theological virtues are the focus of this argument, then it is important to consider whether or not the theological virtues are emotion-virtues. In his latest book to date, *Spiritual Emotions*, Roberts classifies the virtue of hope as one of the emotion-virtues because it goes "by the name of [an] emotion [sic]," he does not mention faith, and he refers to his previous essay, *Emotions*, in which he classifies love as a special case in which much of it "is not an emotion but a concern on which a range of emotions are based."[44] Faith might also be included as an emotion-virtue in the qualified sense that it has historically been interpreted to have at least an emotional component.[45] Since Robert's analysis of love is heavily based on his understanding of emotions as "concerned-based construals" with which he has explicitly replaced the idea of emotions as judgments, then his analysis of love may be rejected as stemming from a faulty definition which makes emotions tied to the internal subjective concerns of agents rather than the objective external reality.[46] As the virtue of love, like hope, goes by the name of an emotion, it may be construed as an emotion-virtue. Since some virtues and particularly the theological virtues may be construed as Roberts' emotion-virtues, then they can provide moral motivation by generating the necessary emotions which motivate moral action. In terms of biblical consistency, these further claims about the theological virtues as emotion-virtues also seem to be consistent with the biblical texts in which faith, hope, and love

---

43 Robert C. Roberts, *Emotions: An Essay in Aid of Moral Psychology* (Cambridge University Press, 2003), 295.

44 Robert Campbell Roberts, *Spiritual Emotions: A Psychology of Christian Virtues* (Eerdmans, 2007), 9; Roberts, *Emotions: An Essay*, 293. In his earlier article, Roberts classified love as one of the *"virtues of willpower"* and defined these as those virtues that "are strongly determining, long-term concerns, loves, or passions for some class of states of affairs." Roberts, "Virtues and Emotions," 294.

45 John Calvin, *Inst.*1.7.4–5 (CR 30:58–61); Jonathan Edwards, "A Treatise Concerning Religious Affections: In Three Parts," (Works 1:288–289).

46 Roberts claims that the virtues as emotions "are concern-based construals ... that they are states in which the subject grasps, with a kind of perceptual immediacy, a significance of his or her situation ... [that] can be right or wrong ... And they are motivational ... The understanding of emotions as concern-based construals makes it possible for the Christian psychologist/ethicist to make sense of the idea that emotions can be expressions of character traits: emotions are based on concerns, some concerns are passions, and passions are character traits." Roberts, *Spiritual Emotions*, 11, 20.

seem to be virtues (1 Cor 13:13) and others in which they seem to be emotions (Mark 11:22; Ps 42:5; Rom 13:8).

Therefore, motivational weak internalism is consistent with Jesus' teaching in John 14:15, 21, 23–24, which implies that motivational strong internalism and externalism are not biblically consistent. Moreover, the virtues and namely the theological virtues provide moral motivation by generating the necessary emotions which motivate moral action.

APPLICATION: THE PROCESS OF SANCTIFICATION
(VIRTUES AS COGNITION AND MOTIVATION)

If believers recognize that Aristotelian cognitive emotions (reason drives the emotions) rather than Humean irrational senses (reason is a slave to the passions) are consistent with the biblical teaching on *how* the Trinity uses the emotion-virtues to sanctify, both to motivate and guide believers into realized holiness, then they may be able to cultivate the emotion-virtues and progress more effectively in sanctification. Until the recent resurgence of virtue ethics, emotions were largely neglected in ethics and the Enlightenment left the popular culture thinking that reason is superior to the emotions, which are unreliable as a moral guide.[47] With the return of the emotions in the resurgence of virtue ethics, Brian Borgman notes there are at least four common Christian misconceptions about the emotions that still persist on the popular level: (1) "emotions are bad and need to be suppressed," (2) "emotions are irrelevant and unnecessary," (3) "emotions are so powerful that they govern and control us," and (4) "emotions are the most important thing about us."[48]

In the midst of this cultural history with its misconceptions, there is a great need for believers to recognize the place and role of the emotion-vir-

---

[47] The popular contemporary understanding of a division between reason and emotion in which emotion is rejected as subjective in favor of the objectivity of reason has its origin in Hume's "fact/value dichotomy" in which ought (values) cannot be derived from "is" (facts), which has its basis in "Hume's fork" where "Reason is the discovery of truth or falsehood" and "our passions ... are not" so that they merely deal with values. Hume's dichotomy was popularized in modern philosophy by G. E. Moore's naturalistic fallacy (moral goodness can be defined in terms of a natural object) and remains a central tanent of popular thought in the contemporary culture, despite its repudiation by W. V. O. Quine. With the resurgence of virtue ethics, authors such as Solomon have followed Quine in repudiating Hume's view of the emotions in favor of Aristotle's view. David Hume *Treatise of Human Nature* 3.1.1 L. A. Selby-Bigge, ed., *A Treatise of Human Nature* (Clarendon, 1888), 458, 469–470; G. E. Moore, *Principia Ethica*, ed. Thomas Baldwin, rev. ed. (Cambridge University Press, 1993), 62–63, 66–68, 89–91, 95; W. V. O. Quine, "The Two Dogmas of Empiricism," *The Journal of Symbolic Logic* 17, no. 4 (1952): 20–43; Solomon, *Not Passion's Slave*, 3–7, 48–55, 76–95.

[48] Brian S. Borgman, *Feelings and Faith: Cultivating Godly Emotions in the Christian Life* (Crossway, 2009), 24–25.

tues in order to progress more effectively in sanctification. In considering the place of the emotions in sanctification, it is likely that Borgman's four misconceptions generally split down the middle with many traditional denominations having little place for the emotions in their pursuit of knowledge (misconceptions 1–2) and the Pentecostal-Charismatic denominations overemphasizing the emotions in their pursuit of gifts and experiences (misconceptions 3–4). Furthermore, many believers in both groups seem to be seeking service rather than the underlying virtues that produce the sanctifying emotions, which make their knowledge, gifts, and service effective (1 Cor 13:1-3).

One of the roles of the emotions as cognitive judgments of value (Rom 12:2, 9) that are fallible (Micah 3:2) is to motivate sanctified behavior.[49] As has been demonstrated, love motivates ethical obedience (John 14:15, 23) and service (John 21:15–17; 1 Thess 1:3), although many obey out of legalism and serve out of obligation, pride, or a quest for approval. Whereas endurance also motivates ethical behavior (Luke 8:1–15), hope motivates believers to endure trials and suffering (Rom 5:4; 8:18–25). However, it is likely that many falter in temptation and trial because they do not have sufficient faith and hope in the surpassing glory of the next age compared to the present sufferings of this age (Rom 8:18). Faith motivates prayer (Luke 18:1–8), but most likely many fail to believe that their prayers can move molehills much less mountains because they either doubt the power and/or passion of God to overcome their circumstances and/or care about their needs and so they are prayerless (Matt 17:20). Others perhaps give up on prayer, practically but unconsciously, because they have placed their faith in promises never made in Scripture and so were not realized (Prov 3:5–6). Moreover, as fallible cognitive judgments, the emotions can signal the importance of something to the appraiser even if their evaluation is incorrect due to sin in either its content or its magnitude (Matt 8:26). For example, if believers fail to recognize an actual offense, imagine an offense that is not real, or if they either under or overreact emotionally to such an offense, then the content and/or magnitude of the emotions tells them something about their spiritual state (Gen 4:6–7; Jonah 4:1–11; Matt 26:6–13).[50]

If believers recognize the place and role of the emotion-virtues to sanctify, then they may be able to cultivate them and progress more effectively in sanctification. Some methods of cultivation include traditional spiritual disciplines such as praying for virtue (James 1:5) and self-examination to test

---

49 Borgman also affirms the emotions as fallible cognitive judgments of value. Borgman, *Feelings and Faith*, 25–26.

50 For a similar judgment see: Matthew Elliott, *Faithful Feelings: Rethinking Emotion in the New Testament* (Kregel, 2006), 54.

their motives (Ps 139:23–24), as well as habituation and reciprocity by imitating Christ's example as demonstrated in the next section (Luke 6:40, 43–45). For example, it requires faith to be motivated to act out of love to pray for enemies, but acting lovingly to pray for one's enemies through imitation (Luke 23:34) by habituation and reciprocity tends to cultivate love for one's enemies (Matt 5:43–48; Luke 6:27–36, 40). Self-love and pride are overcome, as Augustine interprets, by love of God and love of neighbor for God's sake as the root of humility (Matt 22:37–40; Phil 2:3–4).[51]

JESUS' EXAMPLE: IMITATION OF VIRTUE BY HABITUATION AND RECIPROCITY

Although they have traditionally been repudiated by the reformers and their heirs, two other aspects of virtue ethics having some consistency with the teaching of Jesus are habituation and reciprocity. While there are significant differences between the concepts of habituation and reciprocity and the teaching of Jesus, there are also similarities that perhaps are often overlooked. The traditional definitions of habituation and reciprocity must be modified in light of Jesus' teaching in order to be truly consistent with the Bible, but the modified definitions retain sufficient continuity with their original meanings so as to be considered the same concepts or at least part of the same family of ideas. Consequently, this book uses these two terms to describe Jesus' teaching because of the similarities and in order to emphasize consistency between virtue ethics and the Bible. Jesus' teaching that his virtuous example is to be imitated through a process that may be described as involving a type of habituation and reciprocity may have contacts or parallels with "Jewish [Rabbinic discipleship practices], Greco-Roman [virtue ethical tradition], or [a] somehow merged stream" of Jewish-Greco-Roman thought.[52] Although the following analysis is aimed at demonstrating the consistency of the virtue ethical tradition (particularly of Aristotle) with the teaching of Jesus, one should not lose sight of the Jewish contacts with Jesus' teaching. These Jewish contacts may themselves be influenced by the Greek virtue tradition in a "merged stream" of tradition.[53] Furthermore, while the argument makes use of source criticism, the intention is not to claim that Jesus as a man is dependent upon human sources, but rather that he as God may have drawn upon

---

51 Augustine, *Doctr. chr.* 2.7.10 (CCSL 32:37).
52 Carson and Moo, *Introduction*, 67.
53 Ibid., 67.

them in order to communicate his own message effectively to people through the culture and ideas with which they were familiar.

Imitating Christ's Example

Three selective evidences that Jesus' concept of and teaching on discipleship involves imitation of himself as a moral exemplar include: Matt 4:19, Luke 6:40; and John 13:34–35. In Matthew 4:19, Jesus' call to discipleship consists of the phrase "δεῦτε ὀπίσω μου," "come after me," which, according to Donald A. Hagner, is commonly understood as a technical expression from "the Jewish background of the rabbis and their disciples, where *imitation* of the master's *example*, and not only his teaching, is given great importance."[54] Consequently, Jesus' call to discipleship is itself a call to imitate his example.

In Luke 6:40 (cp. Matt 10:24–25; John 13:15–16; 15:20), Jesus claims that a disciple who is "fully trained ... will be like his teacher." By stating that a trained disciple "will be like his teacher," Jesus is expressing the idea that disciples were to emulate their teachers as examples.[55] Further confirmation that Jesus is implying that disciples should imitate their master's example in Luke 6:40 is found in John 13:15–16. In John 13:15–16, the first half of the saying in Luke 6:40, "a disciple is not greater than his teacher," appears in John 13:16 to make the point that the disciples will be like Jesus if they follow his example as he commanded them to do in John 13:15.[56] Accordingly, Jesus conceives of and teaches that discipleship involves imitation of the teacher's example.

In John 13:34–35, when Jesus is teaching specifically about the virtue of love (John 13:1), he gives the "new commandment." Most scholars agree that the newness of the "new commandment" is not its *content* "to love one another" that is found in the OT (Lev 19:18), but rather the *form* of the commandment, which is "just as I have loved you, so that you also may love one another" (John 13:34).[57] This phrase in John 13:34 is interpreted explicitly as meaning that Jesus is making himself a moral exemplar to be imitated as evidenced by Jesus' claim in John 13:15, "For I gave you an example, so that just as

---

54 Emphasis added. Donald A. Hagner, *Matthew 1–13*, WBC 33A (Word, 1998), 76. For a similar judgment see: Craig Blomberg, *Matthew*, NAC (B&H, 1992), 90; Leon Morris, *The Gospel According to Matthew*, PNTC (Eerdmans, 1992), 85; John Nolland, *The Gospel of Matthew: A Commentary on the Greek Text*, NIGTC (Eerdmans, 2005), 179.

55 Marshall, *Luke,* 269; Nolland, *Luke 1:1–9:20*, 307; Stein, *Luke*, 213.

56 Thomas Aquinas, ed., *Catena Aurea: Commentary on the Four Gospels, Collected Out of the Works of the Fathers, Volume 3: St. Luke*, trans. John Henry Newman (John Henry Parker, 1843) 224–225; Marshall, *Luke*, 269.

57 Carson, *John*, 484–485; Beasley-Murray, *John*, 247–248; Borchert, *John 12–21*, 99; Lincoln, *John*, 387–388.

I have done for you, also you may do." In the immediate context, the example the disciples are to follow is Jesus' example of love in the foot washing (John 13:1–17), which through John 13:3, 31–33, 36–38 and the parallel phrasing in John 15:12–17, ultimately points to his sacrificial death.[58] In John 13:35, this imitation of Jesus' example of love in the foot washing and his subsequent sacrificial death is the mark by which Jesus' followers would be known as his disciples. There has been much scholarly debate over the nature of imitation.[59] Much of this debate may be summarized by qualifying that it is not necessarily the actions of foot washing and death that are to be imitated or cognitively repeated (not mindlessly mimicked), but rather the virtue of self-sacrificial love exemplified by the actions.[60] There are numerous passages in the rest of the NT following Jesus' teaching that disciples should imitate their teachers.[61] Therefore, Jesus conceives of and teaches that the discipleship relationship involves imitation of his virtuous example by observation for the original disciples and through implication by reading about his example for contemporary disciples. In chapter 3, it was demonstrated that the virtue tradition taught that virtue is gained by observing and reading stories about moral exemplars, which is consistent with or at least similar to Jesus' teaching on this point.[62] Consequently, Jesus' teaching about imitating his moral example is considered a type of virtue ethic.

Imitation by Habituation

Although the Reformers rejected the concept of habituation as being inconsistent with *sola fide*, the idea has some similarities to Jesus' teaching that his virtuous example is to be imitated through the process of discipleship in Luke 6:40. Habituation was defined in chapter 3 as the process of repeated action which forms a habit or virtue.[63] In Luke 6:40, Jesus uses the word "κατηρτισμένος" or "fully trained" (NIV, NAS) to describe the process of imi-

---

58 Carson, *John*, 484; Lincoln, *John*, 387.
59 For a good overview of this research see: Jason G. Weaver, "Paul's Call to Imitation: The Rhetorical Function of the Theme of Imitation in Its Epistolary Context" (PhD. diss., The Catholic University of America, 2013), 10–45.
60 Jo-Ann Brant, "The Place of Mimēsis in Paul's Thought," *Studies in Religion/Sciences Religieuses* 22, no. 3 (1993): 287.
61 1 Cor 4:16; 11:1; Gal 4:12; Phil 3:17; 4:9; 1 Thess 1:6; 2:14; Heb 6:12, 13:7; 1 Pet 2:21; 1 John 2:6.
62 Observing: Aristotle, *An. post.* 1.33.89b5–11; 2.13.97b5–25 (*AO* 1:229, 250–251); Associating: idem, *Eth. nic.* 9.9.1170a.10–12; 9.12.1172a.1–15 (*AO* 9:190, 195); Reading: idem, *Pol.* 7.17.1336a.30–35; 8.3.1337a.20–23; 8.3.1337a.35–1337b.11; 8.3.1337b.24–28 (*AO* 10:216, 218–219); Imitating: "imitating the best," idem, *Mag. mor.* 1.19.1190a30–34 (*AO* 9:241–242).
63 Aristotle, *Eth. nic.* 2.1.1103a.18–b25; 2.2.1104a.34–b.3 (*AO* 9:23–26).

tation by which disciples are made to be like their teacher.⁶⁴ Contrary to L. John Topel, who finds it "amazing that all the commentators overlooked" the "obvious denotation" of the verb's "normal" usage of "the restoration or refurbishing of something that has lost its original good condition," there are several factors indicating that the word is being used contextually as an educational technical term that involves an athletic metaphor and connotes the idea of habituation.⁶⁵

First, as previously demonstrated, many scholars think that Jesus is teaching about virtues in the Beatitudes preceding Luke 6:40, which is part of the Sermon on the Mount/Plain. Moreover, Cyril of Alexandria interprets Jesus as teaching in v. 40 that disciples should gain a degree of virtue equal to their teachers by imitating them.⁶⁶ Consequently, according to the context and Cyril, v. 40 is concerned with Jesus' teaching on virtuous education.

Second and consistent with the NIV and NAS, Hans Dieter Betz claims that the term κατηρτισμένος had become common in Hellenistic Greek to refer to "developmental or correctional processes" in "the sphere of education" and particularly virtue based education based on parallel linguistic usages including references to Aristotle and Plutarch.⁶⁷ Similarly, Francois Bovon argues on the basis of the term's usage in several NT texts (1 Cor 1:10; 2 Cor 13:11; 1 Thess 3:10; Heb 13:21) that the word means "to educate" in Luke 6:40.⁶⁸ Accordingly, in addition to the context of virtue teaching in the Beatitudes preceding Luke 6:40, there is linguistic evidence that the term κατηρτισμένος is being used to refer to education and contextually virtue education.

Third, Debra Hawhee argues for a "connection between rhetorical and athletic training" in Hellenistic culture involving "forms of movement acquired through repetitive habituation—and their use in response to particular situations" so that "Pedagogically, they [athletic and rhetorical training] shared modes of knowledge production."⁶⁹ BDAG seems to support Hawhee's assertion by pointing to Epictetus's use of the word "κατηρτισμένος" as a tech-

---

64   Robertson claims that the biblical usage of the term implies a process. A.T. Robertson, *Word Pictures in the New Testament* (Broadman, 1933), s.v. "Luke 6:40."

65   L. John Topel, *Children of a Compassionate God: A Theological Exegesis of Luke 6:20–49* (Liturgical, 2001), 192.

66   Aquinas, *Catena Aurea*, 224.

67   Hans Dieter Betz, *The Sermon on the Mount: A Commentary on the Sermon on the Mount, Including the Sermon on the Plain*, ed. Adela Yarbro Collins, Hermeneia: A Critical and Historical Commentary on the Bible (Fortress Press, 1995), 624.

68   Francois Bovon, *Luke 1: A Commentary on the Gospel of Luke 1:1–9:50*, ed. Helmut Koester, trans. Christine M. Thomas, Hermeneia: A Critical & Historical Commentary on the Bible (Fortress, 2002), 249.

69   Debra Hawhee, *Bodily Arts: Rhetoric and Athletics in Ancient Greece* (University of Texas Press, 2004), 6, 147.

nical athletic term referring to "a trainer who adjusts parts of the body" in relation to the background meaning of the term in Luke 6:40.[70] In *Discourse* 3.20, Epictetus makes Hawhee's connection between moral education and athletics by arguing that an athlete's training, including the adjustment of a trainer, produces moral virtue in the athlete.[71] Consequently, in addition to the immediate context of teaching on virtue in Luke 6:40, there is further linguistic evidence attested by BDAG for taking the word κατηρτισμένος as an educational technical term which involves an athletic metaphor and points to the development of virtue by habituation.

Fourth, the *ISBE* claims that "during the Hellenistic period," the Jews drew on "ancient pedagogical methods" including "rote memory" as well as imitation, such that it "seems likely that Jesus himself taught and did so using the contemporary technique of repetition."[72] This repetition is consistent with habituation. In fact, there is evidence that Jesus did use repetition as a pedagogical method, which might be construed as habituation, such that he is referring to this method in Luke 6:40. For example, the three references to the feedings of the thousands (Matt 14:13–21; 15:29–39; 16:5–12; Mark 6:33–44; 8:1–21; Luke 9:10–17; John 6:1–14) indicate that Jesus was using habituation or repetitive exposure to particular situations in order to produce a response based on his example. In the case of the feedings, the response was the theological virtue of faith (Matt 16:8; Mark 8:17–19).

Finally, in the wider biblical context, two further evidences indicate that the term κατηρτισμένος may imply the idea of habituation. The idea that habituation is implied in the language of Luke 6:40 is further supported by the development of Jesus' teaching throughout the NT. In 1 Tim 4:7 and Heb 5:14; 12:11, the athletic metaphor is picked up from Jesus in Luke 6:40 by using the athletic term γυμνάζω, which is used "commonly in literature of gymnastic exercises in the nude: 'exercise naked, train'; but also fig. of mental and spiritual powers: *to train, undergo discipline*" to describe the discipleship process generally and the disciples' process of moral development explicitly.[73] Since the term γυμνάζω is from the language of the gymnasium and Hawhee points

---

70 BDAG, s.v. "καταρτίζω." For a similar judgment see: Richard B. Vinson, *Luke*, Smyth & Helwys Bible Commentary (Smyth & Helwys, 2008), 193.

71 Epictetus, *Disc.* 3.20 *The Discourses of Epictetus: With the Encheiridion and Fragments*, trans. George Long (A. L. Burt, 1900), 270.

72 B. Gerhardsson and J. T. Willis, "Tradition," *ISBE* 4:883, 885. Brant objects that imitation does not involve "rote repetition," but is rather a cognitive process. However, it seems that Brant is reading modern and/or post-modern pedagogical methods (that are opposed to rote memorization and favor free creativity in learning) back into classical methods in which "a cognitive process" was compatible with repetition. Brant, "Mimēsis," 287.

73 Emphasis original. BDAG, s.v. "γυμνάζω."

out that "the gymnasium combined the physical with the intellectual" and used the "repetition of movements while injecting the soul with forms of character," then the use of this gymnasium term γυμνάζω, following the use of a similar educational-athletic metaphor by Jesus, κατηρτισμένος, implies a process of moral habituation.[74]

Additionally, when other passages in the NT follow Jesus' pedagogy by using the word "imitation," the term itself may imply habituation. With respect to the use of imitation in the NT, C. J. Hemer notes that most "of the occurrences are in the present imperative ["imitate" Heb 13:7; 3 John 11; "be imitators" 1 Cor 11:1; 2 Cor 4:16; Eph 5:1], or an equivalent [1 Thess 1:6; 2:14; 2 Thess 3:7, 9; Heb 6:12], as exhortations to a habitual standard of conduct."[75] While the *ongoing process* of the Greek present imperative does not necessitate the idea of repetition or habituation to achieve the standard of conduct involved in the imitation, it allows for the idea of repetition and particularly "when an *action* is commanded, the force of the present imperative will usually be *iterative*" as seems to be the case in the command for imitation.[76] Thus, when other passages in the NT follow Jesus' pedagogy by using the word "imitation," the grammar involved in the term itself may imply habituation.

Therefore in Luke 6:40, by comparing the discipleship process to the repetition in athletic training by using a well-known athletic metaphor common in moral education at the time, Jesus implies that discipleship and sanctifying growth in virtue involves a process of imitation commensurate with habituation. The rest of the NT follows Jesus' pedagogy in implying the idea of imitation commensurate with habituation through the use of similar imagery and terminology. Similar to contemporary preachers, by drawing on a metaphor well known to his audience to make a theological point, Jesus does not necessarily endorse all for which the metaphor stands (all of the definition of habituation), and the following exegesis and argument shows that he uses it for his own purposes.

Imitation by Reciprocity

In considering the philosophical ideas being compared to the Bible, it is important to recognize that the concepts of habituation and reciprocity are logically related such that if habituation has some similarity to the teaching of Jesus as demonstrated in Luke 6:40, then one would also expect reciprocity

---

74 Hawhee, *Bodily Arts*, 110, 140.
75 C. J. Hemer, "Imitate," *ISBE* 2:806.
76 Emphasis original. Wallace, *Greek Grammar*, 722, 763.

to have some similarity to Jesus' teaching. Reciprocity was defined in chapter 3 as the concept that action leads to being, but being also leads to action.[77] Habituation and reciprocity are logically related not only because Aristotle discusses them together, but also because by definition the first half of reciprocity is habituation, "action leads to being" or the idea that repeated action leads to virtue. By definition, the reciprocity arises in connection to habituation through the converse that "being leads to action." Turning to consider the biblical consistency of reciprocity, in Luke 6:40, Jesus implied the first half of reciprocity through an idea of imitation commensurate with habituation or repetitive action which leads to being, and in the Sermon on the Mount/Plain, Jesus seems to explicitly state the second part of reciprocity that being leads to action.

The principle of reciprocity seems very similar to, but with some significant differences from, Jesus's teaching in the Sermon on the Mount/Plain (Matt 7:15–23; 12:33–35; Luke 6:43–45), where he gives a series of proverbs using an agricultural metaphor of trees and their fruit. In each of the passages, the trees are a metaphor for people (Matt 7:15; 12:35; Luke 6:45).[78] The metaphor of fruit has a slightly different emphasis in each passage with some verses in the context emphasizing that it symbolizes words (Matt 12:30–32, 34, 36–37; Luke 6:45), at least one v. highlighting words and deeds (Matt 7:21), and other verses focusing the symbolism on deeds (Matt 7:24–27; 12:35; Luke 6:46–49).[79] Perhaps the symbolism of the fruit in the passages may be harmonized by viewing the fruit overall as R. T. France's "predominantly an ethical metaphor" for one's deeds, with one's words as a type of deed.[80] Although the

---

77 Aristotle, *Eth. nic.* 2.1.1103a.18–b25; 2.2.1104a.34–b.3 (*AO* 9:23–26). For a similar judgment see: Cox and Kallenberg, "Character"; Stanley Hauerwas, *A Community of Character: Toward a Constructive Christian Social Ethic* (University of Notre Dame Press, 1981), 138–139; Kotva, *Case for Virtue*, 104–106.

78 Betz, *Sermon*, 629; Blomberg, *Matthew*, 205; Ulrich Luz, *Matthew 1–7*, ed. Helmut Koester, trans. James E. Crouch, Hermeneia: A Critical & Historical Commentary on the Bible (Fortress, 2007), 378; Morris, *Matthew*, 320–321, Stein, *Luke*, 215.

79 Morris seems to note a reference to deeds in Matthew 12:35, which Nolland denies, while Hagner points out the overall emphasis on words in the passage as a whole. BDAG, s.v. "καρπός;" Betz, *Sermon*, 634–635; Marshall, *Luke*, 272–273 Blomberg, *Matthew*, 132–133, 205; Bovon, *Luke 1*, 253; R. T. France, *The Gospel of Matthew*, NICNT (Eerdmans, 2007), 291, 484, 486; Hagner, *Matthew 1–13*, 181–184, 349–351; Arthur A. Just, Jr., ed. *Luke*, ACC (InterVarsity, 2003), 112–113; Craig S. Keener, *The Gospel of Matthew: A Socio-Rhetorical Commentary* (Eerdmans, 2009), 252; Luz, *Matthew 1–7*, 378; Morris, *Matthew*, 177, 322; Nolland, *Matthew*, 337–378, 506–507; Manlio Simonetti, ed. *Matthew 1–13*, ACC (InterVarsity, 2003), 155; David L. Turner, *Matthew*, BECNT (Baker Academic, 2008), 219–220; Vinson, *Luke*, 197.

80 France, *Matthew*, 291. For a similar judgment see: Keith Essex, "Sanctification: The Biblically Identifiable Fruit," *MSJ* 21, no. 2 (2010): 197–198.

contextual point and form of the proverbs are different in each passage, the basic meaning of the proverbs themselves remains essentially the same.[81]

The meaning of the proverbs in each context is to establish the relationship between a tree and its fruit or a person and their deeds. In Matt 7:15, the term ἔσωθεν, according to BDAG, refers to the *"inner nature"* of people in a number of verses (Matt 23:25–27; Mark 7:20–23; Luke 11:39–40) and Luke 6:45 mentions the heart.[82] Consequently, the meaning of the proverbs is such that in Matt 7:17–18; 12:33, 35; Luke 43, 45, the nature or heart of the tree/person determines and constrains the fruit or deeds/actions that can be produced, while in Matt 7:16, 20; 12:33; Luke 6:44, one's deeds make their inner nature or heart known or recognizable to the observer.[83] Earl Ellis has summarized the meaning of the verses as "character determines conduct and, on the other hand, what a man does reflects what he is."[84] Both the statement of the verses themselves and these interpretations indicate that the principle of reciprocity (action leads to being, but being also leads to action) is very similar to Jesus' teaching, but there are also differences.

There are at least three reasons for thinking that reciprocity is very similar to Jesus' teaching in these verses. First, Betz has argued that the phrase ὁ ἀγαθὸς ἄνθρωπος, "the good man" (Matt 12:35; Luke 6:45), is a technical term borrowed from Greek moral philosophy (particularly the virtue ethics of Aristotle) and common in Hellenistic Judaism, but generally rejected by the NT (Mark 10:17–18; Luke 18: 18–19) except in this proverb in which it is adapted by Jesus.[85] In Matt 12:35 and Luke 6:45, instead of one who works to make their soul good (actions lead to being) as in Greek moral philosophy, the good man is defined by Jesus as one whose heart is good so that good actions result (be-

---

81 For a similar judgment see: France, *Matthew*, 485; Nolland, *Matthew*, 506. On the difference of the contextual points, France elucidates that Matthew 7:15–20 deals with false prophecy/prophets and how to detect them, Matthew 12:33–35 is concerned with blasphemy against the Holy Spirit by "the current Jewish leadership" or Pharisees, and Luke 6:43–44 treats "hypocrisy on the part of any disciple." Hagner and Luz provide a good comparison of the different forms of the proverbs in the various passages. France, *Matthew*, 289–291, 484; Hagner, *Mathew 1–13*, 349; Luz, *Matthew 1–7*, 375–376; idem *Matthew 8–20*, 202.

82 Emphasis original. BDAG, s.v. "ἔσωθεν." See also: Morris, *Matthew*, 176; Nolland, *Matthew*, 336.

83 Betz, *Sermon*, 530–531; E. Earl Ellis, *The Gospel of Luke*, rev. ed., NCBC (Eerdmans; Marshall, Morgan, & Scott, 1974), 116; Craig A. Evans, *Matthew*, NCBC (Cambridge University Press, 2012), 176; France, *Matthew*, 290, 485; Joel B. Green, *The Gospel of Luke*, NICNT (Eerdmans; 1997), 279; Hagner, *Matthew 1–13*, 184, 349, 351; Ulrich Luz, *Matthew 8–20*, ed. Helmut Koester, trans. James E. Crouch, Hermeneia (Fortress, 2001), 177, 322.

84 Ellis, *Luke*, 116.

85 Betz, *Sermon*, 631–635.

ing leads to actions).⁸⁶ In Luke 6:46–49, the fruit or good actions of the good man are obeying the "words" or "teaching" of Jesus (similarly, Matt 7:21 does not include the good man but emphasizes doing the will of God), which in the context includes the virtues elaborated in the beatitudes or being a virtuous person.⁸⁷ Since Jesus may be using a technical term from Greek moral philosophy that would have been easily recognizable to his hearers as such, then it would not be surprising if he gave a principle commensurate with that milieu, reciprocity. However, the principle of reciprocity is adapted or reversed by Jesus' emphasis on the heart such that being leading to action is stressed rather than actions leading to being. Such an adaptation is not completely dissimilar from Aristotle, who while emphasizing the reverse (actions leading to being) also qualifies at the beginning of his ethics that students must start with some virtue or be virtuous to some degree to start in order for moral education to be effective.⁸⁸

Second, in Matt 7:16–18, 21, Jesus gives what were well-known proverbs and although there may be some parallels in the rabbinic literature (possibly indicating a mixed stream of tradition), the strongest parallels provided by Craig A. Evans and more widely attested by others seem to be found in the Greek moral philosophers and their heirs.⁸⁹ For example, Aesop (620–564 BC) taught that, "Clear proof will be the fruit produced of every tree growing, what nature it possesses." Aristotle (382–322 BC) claimed, "But this is the basic order of nature, for what is in potential, this the work reveals in the actuality." Seneca (4 BC–AD 65) held, "Therefore, good is not produced from evil, no more than figs from an olive tree. Things grow according to their seed, goods are not able to fall short of their standard."⁹⁰ The existence of this prov-

---

86 Several commentators ask the question about what makes the heart good in this passage and offer various answers. Betz, *Sermon*, 633–634; Marshall, *Luke*, 273; Stein, *Luke*, 215.

87 France and Nolland seem to place particular emphasis on recognizing that the wider context of the sermon and the book of Matthew define the fruit. France, *Matthew*, 291; Nolland, *Matthew*, 337.

88 Aristotle, *Eth. nic.* 1.4.1095b.5–14 (*AO* 9:4).

89 Evans, *Matthew*, 176, 259. Evans finds numerous parallels in the rabbinic literature to Matt 12:34, but this saying is absent from Matt 7:15–23 and Luke 6:43–45. Betz cites several Greek moral writers as having parallel sayings to Jesus' proverbs, but most notably, he mentions Aristotle, Aesop, and Diogenes. Nolland also cites Plutarch in his list, "Epict., *Diss.* 2.20.18–19; Plut., *Tranq. an.* 13; *Mor.* 472F; Seneca, *Ep.* 87.25," and sees some parallel to Sirach 27:6 and the Testament of Naphtali 2:6. When citing his parallels for Matthew 7, Luz claims that "There are no direct Jewish sources" and he describes Evan and Nolland's allusion to Sirach 27:6 as only "Somewhat similar." However, when citing parallels for Matthew 12, Luz sees some parallel to Sirach 27:6 (as does Turner) and the Testament of Naphtali 2:6. Betz, *Sermon*, 529, 536–537; Evans, *Matthew*, 176, 259; Nolland, *Matthew*, 337, 506; Luz, *Matthew 1–7*, 377–378; Luz, *Matthew 8–20*, 210; Turner, *Matthew*, 324.

90 "Δῆλος ἔλεγχος ὁ καρπὸς γενήσεται Παντὸς δένδρου <φυέντος> ἢν ἔχει φύσιν." Aesop, *Prov.* 51 Ben Edwin Perry, ed. *Aesopica: A Series of Texts Relating to Aesop or Ascribed to Him or Closely

erb tradition before the time of Christ in Aesop and Aristotle to the time of Christ in Seneca indicates that it was well known to Jesus and his hearers and suggests that like a good preacher, Jesus drew on the popular culture to make his own point in a way that his audience would understand. Consequently, Jesus' use of well-known proverbs and technical terms that would have been recognizable to the original hearers as overlapping with or possibly originating from Greek moral philosophy colors the immediate context as dealing with this milieu so that it would not be surprising to find Jesus presenting concepts commensurate with and possibly modified from virtue ethics such as reciprocity.

Third, the principle of reciprocity is very similar to the statements Jesus makes. In Luke 6:40, Jesus' use of the term κατηρτισμένος to describe the process by which disciples imitate their master implies habituation or that action leads to being, and in Luke 6:43, 45, Jesus' proverbs state that being leads to action.[91] Furthermore, in Matt 7:16, 20; 12:33 and Luke 6:44, Jesus' proverb that a tree is recognized by its fruit may imply the idea that action leads to being in a sense similar to but with significant differences from reciprocity.

These similarities and differences become apparent by examining the concepts of γινώσκω, "knowing or recognizing," and καρπός, "fruit," in Matt 7:16, 20; 12:33 and Luke 6:44. Interpreters (like Ellis) routinely infer that the way people's natures are known or recognized in these passages is that their fruit or actions "reveal" or "reflect" their inner nature.[92] In addition to the contextual explanations (Matt 7:17–18; 12:33, 35; Luke 6:43, 45), the term καρπός, "fruit," itself implies perhaps one way in which the inner nature is "recognized" or "reflected" to the observer. The term "fruit" is plural in Matt 7:16–18, 20 (καρπῶν, v. 16, 20; καρποὺς, v. 17–18, 20) and singular in Matt 7:19 (καρπὸν), Matt 12:33 (καρπὸν/καρποῦ), and Luke 6:43–44 (καρπὸν, v. 43; καρποῦ, v. 44). The plural in Matt 7 immediately lends itself to the idea that multiple human acts are in view, but the singular in Matt 7, 12 and Luke 6 does not necessarily limit the number of human deeds to a single occurrence because the singular indicates that the kind of fruit matches the type of tree rather than enumerating the amount of fruit or actions produced. If multiple actions are in view in the term fruit, then character may be in view, because biblically according

---

Connected with the Literary Tradition That Bears His Name (University of Illinois Press, 1952), 1:272. "τοῦτο δὲ φυσικόν· ὃ γάρ ἐστι δυνάμει, τοῦτο ἐνεργείᾳ τὸ ἔργον μηνύει." Aristotle, *Eth. nic.* 9.7.1168a.9 (AO 9:185); "*Non nascitur itaque ex malo bonum, non magis quam ficus ex olea. Ad semen nata respondent, bona degenerare non possunt.*" Seneca, *Ep.* 87.25 (Gummere, LCL 76).

91 For a similar judgment see: Cox and Kallenberg, "Character"; Kotva, *Case for Virtue*, 104–106; Hollinger, *Choosing the Good*, 87–90; Pink, *Sanctification*, 23, 41.

92 Ellis, *Luke*, 116; Evans, *Matthew*, 176; France, *Matthew*, 485; Luz, *Matthew 8–20*, 210; Nolland, *Matthew*, 507; Morris, *Matthew*, 322.

to BDAG, ἦθος or "character" (1 Cor 15:33) is "a pattern of behavior or practice that is habitual or characteristic of a group or an individual."[93] The Bible's view of character as an external "pattern of behavior" is different from the idea of character in contemporary ethics and popular culture, which is often or primarily thought of as "interior, private values."[94] On this interpretation of fruit, the idea in Matt 7:16, 20; 12:33; Luke 6:44 would be that people act and their actions form a pattern of behavior over time, which constitutes their character existentially or instantiates their inner nature.[95] Consequently, Jesus' proverb in these verses would be teaching that action leads to character. However, instead of actions habituating the soul ontologically as in Aristotle, actions form a pattern of behavior or character that existentially constitutes or instantiates one's inner nature.

As a further explanation of the difference between these ontological and existential changes, the Aristotelian ontological aspect is an internal change in the soul, while the biblical existential aspect is an external change in behavior. In Aristotelian reciprocity "action leads to being (habituation) and reciprocally being leads to action." For Aristotle, in habituation ("action leads to being") the "being" that is produced by the action is an internal ontological change in the soul or an actual change in "the nature" of the soul or a "molding of the hearer's soul by means of habit," repeated actions, or habituation.[96] Similarly and in terms of describing an internal change in the soul, Augustine speaks about the soul being "re-formed by ... God" and Aquinas speaks about infused grace "becoming accidental in the soul."[97] On the other hand, the existential change has to do with the reversed reciprocity in the teaching of Jesus, where "being leads to action and reciprocally action leads to being (habituation)." In this case, in the "being leading to action," the "being" is not

---

93 BDAG, s.v. "ἦθος." The term "δοκιμή" has a similar meaning in Rom 5:4. BDAG, s.v. "δοκιμή." This "external" definition of character is reflected in Morris's interpretation of the passage in which he insists that people speak (or act) out of the heart and not character. Morris, *Matthew*, 321.

94 Cox and Kallenberg point out that "character cannot be reduced to interior, private values." Cox and Kallenberg, "Character."

95 For a similar judgment see: Betz, *Sermon*, 536–537; Cox and Kallenberg, "Character." France allows that "fruit" may refer to character. France, *Matthew*, 291. Compare to Hauerwas' definition of character. Stanley Hauerwas, *Character and the Christian Life: A Study in Theological Ethics* (Trinity University Press, 1975), 117, 119, 221.

96 "τὴν φύσιν" of the soul or "προδιειργάσθαι τοῖς ἔθεσι τὴν τοῦ ἀκροατοῦ ψυχήν." Aristotle, *Eth. nic.* 2.3.1104b.19–21; 10.9.1179b.20–25 (*AO* 9:27, 214–215).

97 "*reformata per ... dei*" (Augustine) and "*accidentaliter fit in anima*" (Aquinas). Augustine, *Ver. rel.* 12.24 (CCSL 32:202); Aquinas, *STh.*, I–II q.110 a.2 ad 2 (*OOII* 7:313). For a similar judgment about the idea of the soul being described as "restructured" in salvation in the thought of Augustine see: Helene Tallon Russell, *Irigaray and Kierkegaard: On the Construction of the Self* (Mercer University Press, 2009), 46.

an internal change in the soul, but rather the presence of the Spirit and in the reciprocal "action leading to being," the "being" is an external existential change or the pattern of behavior resulting from the actions over time, not an internal change in the soul. Therefore, reciprocity is similar to Jesus' teaching in that in Matt 7:16, 20; 12:33; Luke 6:40, 44, Jesus teaches that actions lead to being and in Matt 7:17–18; 12:33, 35; Luke 6:43, 45, he teaches that being leads to action, although Jesus' emphasis is on the latter rather than the former as in Aristotle.

Objections (Sola fide) *and Responses*

Ulrich Luz points out that in the history of interpretation, understanding "the Matthean theology of fruit and judgment" (Matt 7:15–23; 12:33–35; Luke 6:43–45) in light of the doctrine of *sola fide* (salvation by grace through faith alone apart from works, Eph 2:8–19) has been problematic.[98] Following from Luz's observation, certainly the main objection to the presence of habituation and reciprocity in the teaching of Jesus is that these principles result in a works-based salvation. In responding to this important objection, at least two conditions must be met in sanctification in order to avoid a works-based salvation. First, there must not be an ontological change within people, because this would mean that people possess a righteousness of their own to justify them rather than Luther's alien righteousness (*"iusticia ... aliena"*) of Christ to justify them, so that Christ alone is their righteousness by faith alone (1 Cor 1:30; Phil 3:9).[99] Second, whatever behavioral or existential change occurs in sanctification, it must be a divine rather than a human work.[100] Consequently,

---

98 Luz, *Matthew 1–7*, 383.

99 Martin Luther, *Sermo de duplici iustitia* 1519 (WA 2:145).

100 Among many others, the following authors stress that sanctification is a divine rather than human work: G. C Berkouwer, *Faith and Sanctification*, Studies in Dogmatics (Eerdmans, 1952), 22; David G. Peterson, *Possessed by God: A New Testament Theology of Sanctification and Holiness*, NSBT 1 (InterVarsity, 1995), 23; Walter Marshall, *The Gospel-Mystery of Sanctification* (Southwick and Peluse, 1811), 30, 277; Pink, *Sanctification*, 40. More stringent Calvinists and perhaps Lutherans will likely require that the existential change in sanctification not only be initiated by God but wholly be a work of God (monergism). More moderate Calvinists, Pentecostals-Charismatics, Wesleyans, and others who tend to be more Arminian will likely require that the existential changes that occur in sanctification be initiated by God but also entail human participation or cooperation (synergism). Wilson has argued (presumably against more moderate Calvinists) that theologians should be consistent in their application of monergism and synergism in the *ordo salutis*. He claims that it is inconsistent to hold that justification is monergistic and that sanctification is synergistic. Wilson goes on to argue that both justification and sanctification be monergistic. Others such as Barrick, Snider, and Windward do not seem to have a problem mixing and matching these concepts in the *ordo salutis*. William D. Barrick, "Sanctification: The Work of the Holy Spirit and Scripture," *MSJ* 21, no. 2 (2010): 183, 87; Andrew V. Snider, "Sanctification and Justification: A Unity of Distinctions," *MSJ* 21, no. 2 (2010): 178;

if habituation and reciprocity can be explained in such a biblically consistent manner as to fulfill these two conditions, then they may be understood as not violating the important doctrine of *sola fide* (Eph 2:8–10).

Habituation and reciprocity may meet these two conditions as interpreted biblically through the following four explanations: (1) as mentioned earlier, Jesus' reciprocity is reversed by his emphasis on the heart so that "being leads to action" (Matt 7:17–18; 12:33, 35; Luke 43, 45) and "action leads to being" (habituation; Matt 7:16, 20; 12:33; Luke 6:40, 44) with the result that biblical reciprocity begins not with works, but rather with being, (2) Jesus teaches that the initial "being" that leads to action is a work of God in that God is the one who "makes the tree good" (Matt 12:33; cp. 1 Cor 1:2; 2 Thess 2:13; Titus 3:5),[101] (3) the "action" that leads to being (habituation) is a work of

---

Scott Sparling Wilson, "Trinity and Sanctification: A Proposal for Understanding the Doctrine of Sanctification According to a Triune Ordering" (PhD. diss., Southeastern Baptist Theological Seminary, 2009), 63; Stephen F. Winward, *Fruit of the Spirit* (Eerdmans, 1981), 21.

101 In Matthew 12:33, BDAG, Hagner, and Morris indicate that "make" likely means "suppose" and France explains that this is the case because the verb "make" is an imperative, but that v. 33 is the genre of a proverb so that "make" is not an actual command. With this meaning in mind, the expression "makes the tree good," is merely borrowed to use as a biblical allusion rather than as taken literally, and that Jesus is saying he makes the character of the trees, as Owen and Pink take the phrase. However, one must wonder whether the grammar and genre must be interpreted so strictly and if Jesus is making a veiled allusion to his divine power to create people with a particular nature (Rom 9:19–24). BDAG, s.v. "ποιέω;" France, *Matthew*, 484; Hagner, *Matthew 1–13*, 349–350; Morris, *Matthew*, 320; John Owen, *Πνευματολογια· or, a Discourse Concerning the Holy Spirit* (Works 3:469); Pink, *Sanctification*, 23, 41. The explicit biblical statement that the initial being in reciprocity is produced by God seems to remove all works-based salvation. However, how the nature of this being is understood determines whether there is an ontological change. If the traditional virtue ethics view of God's work in the believer's "being" is taken that an ontological change occurs through the infusion of virtues (Augustine and Aquinas) or the implantation, impartation, or infusion of a principle or disposition of holiness (Owen, Kuyper, Bavinck) then works-based salvation/sanctification may not be avoided. Aquinas, *STh.*, I q.43 a.6 s.c.; I q.43 a.6 ad.2 (*OOII* 4:451); idem, *STh.*, I–II q.110 a.3 resp. (*OOII* 7:313); Augustine, *Conf.* 8.12.29 (CSEL 33:195); idem, *Civ.* 4.20; 5.19 (CSEL 40/1:186–187, 252); idem, *C, du. ep. Pelag.* 1.8.13 (CSEL 60:435); Herman Bavinck, *Holy Spirit, Church, and New Creation*, vol. 4 of *Reformed Dogmatics*, ed. John Bolt, trans. John Vriend (Baker Academic, 2008), 70–72, 78, 94; Abraham Kuyper, *The Work of the Holy Spirit* (Funk & Wagnalls, 1900), 317, 456, 463, 485; Owen, *Holy Spirit* (Works 3:383–384, 405, 472, 530–531, 536, 553–554). Berkouwer defends Kuyper and Bavinck's use of infusion language by presenting convincing evidence that "Kuyper was as little interested as Bavinck in a substantialist view of grace." However, at best, their language is misleading and so objectionable despite their explicit qualifications and denials of a "heavenly substance" being introduced into "human nature." Bavinck, *Spirit, Chuch, and Creation*, 4:92–94; Berkouwer, *Sanctification*, 87–92.). Such an ontological change involves the possession of a quality (virtue) on the part of the believer that may be construed as an inherent righteousness which contributes to salvation by producing virtuous or good works that merit reward and so results in works-based salvation. Although believers' pre and post conversion works contribute nothing to their salvation so that their judgment for or placement in their eternal state depends solely on grace (Eph 2:8–10) or relationship to Christ (Rom 10:9–10), believers are judged for rewards on the basis of their post-salvation good works (Matt 16:27)

God in that reciprocity can be understood as "being leads to action leads to being," where the initial being is a work of God (Matt 12:33) and so the action is dependent upon that initial divine work,[102] and (4) the "being" resulting from the action leading to being may be understood as similar to S. Hauerwas' character or identical with the Bible's ἦθος, "character or pattern of behavior" (1 Cor 15:33). This character is not an ontological entity, but rather refers to the pattern of behavior that existentially instantiates or constitutes one's character or inner nature and that is the result of action produced by God.[103]

---

produced through them by the Trinity (Phil 2:13), who makes the works good because there is nothing good in a believer in and of themselves (Rom 7:18). As Augustine said, *"redditur quidem meritis tuis corona sua, sed dei dona sunt merita tua"* [indeed his crown is returned as merits to you, but your merits are God's gifts.] Augustine, *Gestis. Pelag.* 35 (CSEL 42:91). However, the change in "being" worked by God may be understood merely as the indwelling of Christ (Gal 2:20) by his Spirit (Rom 8:9, 11), who by his continual indwelling and an immediate operation "leads" (Rom 8:14; Gal 5:18) or "works in" (Phil 2:13) believers to think, act, and "be" virtuous (Gal 5:22–23) (On the indwelling of Christ see also: Rom 8:10; 2 Cor 13:5; Gal 4:19. On the Spirit's continual indwelling see also: John 14:23; Rom 8:9, 11; 1 Cor 3:16; 6:19; 2 Tim 1:14; 1 John 4:13.). By this interpretation of virtue, the believer is in possession of nothing and the only ontological change is the presence of Christ by his Spirit so that the believer contributes nothing to their salvation or sanctification ontologically and *sola fide* is preserved.

102 With respect to the second *sola fide* condition and the action in habituation, there are at least two senses in which habituation may be understood as a divine rather than as a human work. First and from a strong Calvinist view, the initial being or indwelling of the Spirit that causes the action which leads to being functions according to the popular Reformed dictum, "God acts and man responds." Thus, the repeated action that leads to being is initiated by the Spirit so that believers are being habituated by or to the Spirit and not by their own works and the second *sola fide* condition is met. However, because the strong Reformed position sees such a stringent cause and effect relationship between God's act and man's response, then an objection may be that there is no human role left for habituation to occur. In response, habituation (repetitive action that leads to being) may still be thought to occur in some way even if people are completely passive. Second and from a more moderate Calvinist or Arminianist view, the action in habituation is produced by a synergism of believers submitting their will to or yielding to the working or leading of the indwelling Spirit in the process of filling (Eph 5:18) (On the idea that the Spirit is transforming believers into the likeness of Christ by a process of submission in Ephesians 5:18 see the following sources: Lewis Sperry Chafer, *He That Is Spiritual: A Classic Study of the Biblical Doctrine of Spirituality* (Kessinger, 2010), ch. 3, 5, 6; Andrew T. Lincoln, *Ephesians*, WBC 42 (Word, 1990), 345; John F. MacArthur, Jr., *Ephesians*, Macarthur New Testament Commentary (Moody, 1986), 249–250; John F. Walvoord, *The Holy Spirit: A Comprehensive Study of the Person and Work of the Holy Spirit* (Zondervan, 2010), pt. 5, ch. 21.VII. On this view, believers' wills are habituated to the Spirit by the Spirit's prompting and empowerment and the second condition of *sola fide* is met.

103 Hauerwas, *Character*, 117, 119, 221. From a strict Reformed and monergistic perspective, in order to avoid a works-based sanctification, instead of God produced initial being leading to action leading to being leading to action leading to being etc. in an endless unbroken cycle as in Aristotle, biblically reciprocity may need to be understood as a finite repeating cycle of God produced being leading to action leading to being and repeat beginning with God produced being. However, Arminians may find the synergism involved in the endless unbroken cycle to be acceptable.

Someone might object that the "old man/new man" (Rom 6:6–7; Eph 2:15; 4:22–23; Col 3:9–10), "new creation" (Gal 6:15; Eph 4:24; 2 Cor 5:17), the NIV's "sinful nature" (Rom 7:5, 18, 25; 1 Cor 5:5; etc.), or other seemingly ontological language in the biblical text signals that some sort of ontological change takes place in sanctification. In response, while this language does *sound* ontological to a certain degree, there does not seem to be an infusion of grace/virtue or an implanted principle of holiness anywhere in Scripture. For example, in 1 John 3:9, the "seed" does not seem to be an "implanted principle of holiness" in the "new man" as in John Owen and others, because the implanted "seed" seems to be a metaphor for the Word or Gospel message (Matt 13:19; Mark 4:14; Luke 8:11; 1 Pet 1:23; cp. 1 John 2:14, 24; James 1:21) that believers "have" after they hear it.[104] The "new man" and other such ontological sounding language seems to be nothing more than metaphors which indicate the newness of life believers have when they are indwelt by the Spirit and if there is a "new principle," then it seems to be the Spirit himself (and perhaps the Word) and not something he infuses or implants in people.[105]

Therefore, from a Reformation perspective, if reciprocity and habituation are understood in any of these senses, they become important for explaining how sanctification can occur without ontological change, be a divine work rather than a human work, and yet in relation to justification not be a legal fiction as the Roman Catholics charge.

As another issue, those from the position-only view will likely object that imitation, habituation, and reciprocity and the passages cited in support do

---

104 The identification of the "seed" in 1 John 3:9 is highly controversial and while it is true that individual biblical authors may define terms differently according to their contexts, the canonical evidence seems overwhelming and decisive in this case and John himself even views the Word as living in the believer (1 John 2:14, 24). For a discussion of the different options and proponents, including those who hold to the view taken in this book (such as Augustine, B. F. Westcott, C. H. Dodd, W. Barclay, and R. C. H. Lenski), of the various identifications of the "seed" see the following sources: Daniel L. Akin, *1, 2, 3 John*, NAC (B&H, 2001), 148–149; Colin G. Kruse, *The Letters of John*, PNTC (Eerdmans, 2000), 124–125; J. du Perez, "'*Sperma Auto*' in 1 John 3:9," *Neotestamentica* 9 (1975): 105–110; Stephen S Smalley, *1, 2, 3 John*, WBC 51 (Word, 1989), 172–174.

105 For a discussion of ontology with respect to the "new nature" in sanctification see: Anthony A. Hoekema, "The Reformed Perspective," in *Five Views on Sanctification*, ed. Gundry, 78–82; John F. Walvoord, "The Augustinian-Dispensational Perspective," in *Five Views on Sanctification*, ed. Gundry, 199–209. Despite the fact that Niemelä's view is not convincing that the "new man" (Eph 2:15) is the church or the body of Christ in all instances, his claim demonstrates that some scholars are looking for a non-ontological interpretation of the "old man/new man" language. John H. Niemelä, "Where in the World Is the Old Man?: Old-Man and New-Man in Paul," (paper presented at the annual meeting of the Grace Evangelical Society, Fort Worth, TX, 24 April 2013), 1–6.

not have to do with or contain the term sanctification.[106] However, in chapter 2, it was demonstrated that growth in virtue is synonymous with sanctification (1 Thess 3:12, 2 Thess 1:3; 1 Pet 1:13–16; 2 Pet 1:5–9) and John 13:34–35 links growth in virtue to the idea of imitation, while habituation and reciprocity are linked to the idea of imitation through Luke 6:40. Moreover, since the Sermon on the Mount/Plain was addressed to Jesus' disciples or believers (Matt 5:1; Luke 6:17), then he is addressing concerns of sanctification rather than initial salvation when he introduces the teachings that are consistent with imitation, habituation, and reciprocity (Matt 7:15–23, 12:33; Luke 6:43–44).

Application: The Believer's Responsibility in Sanctification as a Process

In Luke 6:40, the description of imitation as κατηρτισμένος, "training," which implies habituation or a process of repeated action that produces virtue, has important implications for how progressive sanctification takes place. First, in chapter 2 the selective history of sanctification indicated that while the Lutheran, Reformed, Augustinian-Dispensational, and Contemplative views may be construed as viewing sanctification as a single stage continual process, the Wesleyan, Keswick, and Pentecostal views may be understood as involving an instantaneous crisis-event (entire sanctification, crisis experience, baptism of the Holy Spirit) which divides sanctification into an initial stage characterized by struggle with sin and relatively little spiritual growth and a second stage characterized by victory over sin and relatively vigorous spiritual growth. Although imitation, habituation, and reciprocity do not necessarily rule out a sudden advance in sanctification, these three concepts by definition stress the idea of a continual process as found in the Lutheran, Reformed, Augustinian-Dispensational, and Contemplative views over against an instantaneous sanctification. At the very least, these three concepts highlight the importance of the process, which the Wesleyan, Keswick, and Pentecostal views acknowledge does take place on either side of the instantaneous crisis-event.

Second, the idea of a process implies the concept of long term effort, which is contrary to the popular thinking of elements in both contemporary western Christianity and culture. It is likely that in the popular thinking of the Lutheran, Reformed, and Augustinian-Dispensational traditions, God's

---

106 Clarence Tucker Craig, "Paradox of Holiness," *Interpretation* 6 (Apr 1952): 149; William G. Coberly, "An Exegetical Argument for the Position-Only View of Sanctification" (M.T. thesis, The Master's Seminary, 2004), 36.

sovereignty is so emphasized that human responsibility is minimized in sanctification. Similarly, it is also likely that in the popular thinking of the Wesleyan, Keswick, and Pentecostal traditions, the miraculous and divinely caused instantaneous crisis-event takes such precedence over the idea of a process that human responsibility is also minimized in sanctification.[107] Moreover in the popular American culture of fast food, instantaneous electronic communication and information, and entertainment in thirty minute time slots, western Christians are culturally conditioned to expect spiritual growth to be fast and easy like their other cultural experiences. Consequently, perhaps many do not advance in spiritual maturity or progress in sanctification because: (1) they are not sufficiently aware of their responsibility in the process, (2) they have tried, but given up when success does not come as quickly or easily as the fast food culture falsely expects, or (3) they are either not willing or feel unable to put in the time and energy necessary to make progress due to hectic schedules and/or cultural distractions.

In contrast to this popular thinking, the concept of imitation by habituation and reciprocity implies that spiritual growth and sanctification involves human responsibility which entails great effort. For example, in 2 Pet 1:5, the command to believers to be sanctified by growing in virtue on the basis of God's work explicitly entails strenuous effort: "supply, making every effort with all diligence, by means of faith, virtue."[108] Also, facing circumstances in which Christians were not accepting sufficient responsibility for their spiritual growth, J. C. Ryle exhorted his readers, "The first thing I have to say is this: True Christianity is a fight ... In sanctification our own works are of vast importance, and God bids us fight, and watch, and pray, and strive, and take pains, and labour."[109] If believers want to grow spiritually and be sanctified as they are commanded, then all believers and particularly western Christians slumbering in their culturally conditioned complacency must renew their minds by the power of the Word (Rom 12:1) though the recognition that the Christian life entails not only great external suffering from trials (2 Tim 3:12)

---

107 Despite the fact that many Pentecostals and Charismatics likely teach that believers are to put in effort by seeking after or praying for the crisis-event (Luke 11:13; 1 Cor 12:31), the emphasis on the believer's involvement seems to end once the crisis-event is experienced.

108 For a similar judgment that 2 Peter 1:5 entails a command to believers involving human responsibility as well as divine sovereignty see: David A. Case and David W. Holdren, *1–2 Peter, 1–3 John, Jude: A Commentary for Bible Students* (Wesleyan, 2006), 160; Peter H. Davids, *The Letters of 2 Peter and Jude*, PNTC (Eerdmans, 2006), 179; J. N. D. Kelly, *The Epistles of Peter and of Jude*, BNTC (Continuum, 1969), 305; Thomas R. Schreiner, *1, 2 Peter, Jude*, NAC (B&H, 2003), 299.

109 J. C. Ryle, *Holiness: Its Nature, Hindrances, Difficulties and Roots* (William Hunt and Company, 1889), 45, 74.

but also great internal struggle with temptations to be progressively sanctified (2 Pet 1:5).

Jesus' Active Sanctification through the Word: Ephesians 5:25–33; Hebrews 4:12

This section deals with two related issues raised in chapter 2 that are involved with Jesus' teaching and example. First, chapter 2 noted that some question whether Jesus' teaching and example are really active, since as past events recorded in Scripture, they may merely be passive like the finished work of Christ on the cross. Responding to this objection involves the second issue of a more detailed discussion of sanctification in Eph 5:25–33 as well as a brief discussion of Heb 4:12.

Ephesians 5:25–33

While some scholars may be mistaken in *how* they interpret Eph 5:25–33 in order to find a present active role in progressive sanctification for Christ, they are correct that the passage does involve such an active role. In vv. 25–27, there are at least two if not three temporal aspects of sanctification as reflected by the three ἵνα-purpose clauses (translated as "that" in most English versions). In 5:25–26, the first purpose clause, the aorist verbs (ἠγάπησεν, παρέδωκεν, ἁγιάσῃ, and καθαρίσας; loved, gave, sanctified, having cleansed) along with the allusion to Christ's death on the cross ("gave himself") naturally lend themselves to the idea of a past-tense action, which theologically indicates that past positional sanctification is in view.[110] In the history of interpretation, some scholars incorrectly saw a present aspect of sanctification in these verses and while they seem mistaken about how they came to this conclusion, they were correct to recognize that there is a present aspect of sanctification in this passage as a whole.[111] Although they do not explicitly argue in the following manner, these scholars seem to be assuming (or at least the most plausible exegetical explanation for their interpretations seems to be) that the aorist verbs ἁγιάσῃ and καθαρίσας are gnomic aorists, which indicate "an action that in reality is iterative" so that a progressive idea is pres-

---

[110] Harold W. Hoehner, *Ephesians: An Exegetical Commentary* (Baker Academic, 2002), 757.
[111] Among others see: Calvin, *Inst.* 4.8.12 (CR 30:854); Thomas C. Oden, *Life in the Spirit*, vol. 3 of *Systematic Theology* (HarperSanFrancisco, 1992), 229; John R. W. Stott, *The Message of Ephesians*, BST (InterVarity, 1979), 228; Walvoord, *Holy Spirit*, ch. 22.3.

ent.¹¹² However, due to the connection to Christ's death (v. 25), these verbs are likely ingressive (inceptive or inchoative) aorists that "may be used to stress the beginning of an action or the entrance into a state" and thus they point to positional sanctification.¹¹³ Consequently, Christ is not actively, presently, and progressively sanctifying the church in v. 25–26.

In Eph 5:27a, the second purpose clause, the aorist (παραστήσῃ) does not grammatically necessitate a past tense and several factors indicate that the verb is a proleptic or futuristic aorist so that the clause is describing the future perfective aspect of sanctification (glorification).¹¹⁴ The phrase "not having any spot or wrinkle or any such things" seems to indicate a perfected spiritual state that is consistent with the future glorification of the believer.¹¹⁵ Further-

---

112 Wallace, *Greek Grammar*, 562. For example, Muddiman finds progressive sanctification in v. 26 by taking the phrase "by the word" with the participle "purifying" rather than with the phrase "by the washing" so that "if taken together, refer to the sanctifying effect of Christ's word, i.e. to the process of Christian nurture through preaching and teaching." But Muddiman's interpretation would seem to depend on "purifying" being a gnomic aorist, which the context will not support. John Muddiman, *The Epistle to the Ephesians*, BNTC (Continuum, 2001), 264–265. An alternate exegetical explanation for how some scholars (possibly including Muddiman) might be reading progressive sanctification into v. 25–26 is by assuming that the term "sanctification" itself refers to a process, but as was demonstrated in chapter 2, sanctification may refer to a past, present, or future aspect which is determined by context.

113 Wallace, *Greek Grammar*, 558. In the history of interpretation of the passage, many scholars have seen in the "washing with water by the word," a reference to baptism, where the "word" is the baptismal formula. However, the "word" likely refers to the Gospel message (John 15:3; 17:7; Eph 6:17; Rom 10:8, 17; Heb 6:5; 1 Pet 1:25) and the washing is probably a metaphor (possibly drawn from the prenuptial bridal bath of Ezek 16:8–14) for the Spirit's cleansing the believer from sin (1 John 1:9) rather than a reference to baptism. In either case, baptism or the initial cleansing of the Gospel would seem to indicate the beginning of the Christian life and so the entrance into a state or positional sanctification. Talbert takes the word as the Gospel, while Lincoln sides with the baptism view, but presents both interpretations. Muddiman seems to hold simultaneously that the word is the Gospel and the water is baptism, and Thielman argues that the water "is a metaphorical reference to the cleansing power of the gospel": Lincoln, *Ephesians*, 375–376; Muddiman, *Epheisans*, 264–266; Charles H. Talbert, *Ephesians and Colossians*, PCNT (Baker Academic, 2007), 141–142; Frank Thielman, *Ephesians*, BECNT (Baker Academic, 2010), 383–385.

114 Wallace, *Greek Grammar*, 563.

115 Markus Barth, *Ephesians: Translation and Commentary on Chapters 4–6*, AB 34A (Doubleday, 1974), 628; Hoehner, *Ephesians*, 761; Muddiman, *Ephesians*, 266. Lincoln dissents that "Impurity is what characterizes outsiders (cf. 4:19; 5:3); purity is the distinguishing mark of Christ's Church" so that "in line with this writer's more realized eschatology, glory and holiness are seen as present attributes of the Church and Christ's activity of endowing the Church with these qualities is a present and continuing one." Lincoln, *Ephesians*, 377. Schnackenburg objects to a future sense in v. 27 on the grounds that "because Baptism continually incorporates new people into the Church, this making splendid is also a present and continuing event— the metaphor of the Bride's bath as a unique event is shattered." Rudolf Schnackenburg, *Ephesians: A Commentary*, trans. Helen Heron (T&T Clark, 1991), 251. However, since the "word" likely refers to the Gospel and the metaphor of "washing with water" likely depicts the spiritual cleansing associated with belief in the Gospel (only drawing on the bridal bath as a metaphor), then

more, there are a number of parallel passages frequently cited (Rom 14:10; Acts 22:30; 27:34; 2 Cor 4:14; 11:2; Col 1:22, 28 [same term or cognate]; Luke 21:36; Jude 24 [same idea]) in which the verb παραστήσῃ, "to present," is used to refer to the final judgment or the *parousia*.[116] Consequently, Jesus is not actively, presently, and progressively sanctifying the church in v. 27a.

In Eph 5:27b, the third purpose clause may be taken in two senses where the first is more likely, but the second would indicate a present aspect of sanctification in the passage. It is most likely that the final purpose clause, "that she [the church] may be holy and blameless" is dependent and provides a further description of the perfective state in the first half of the verse. This dependent relationship is indicated in part by the use of the strong adversative ἀλλ', "but," which indicates that a positive description of the perfective state in the third clause ("holy and blameless") is being contrasted with a negative description of that same state in the second clause ("not having any spot or wrinkle or any such things").[117] The dependent relationship is also indicated by the fact that the phrase "holy and blameless" from the third purpose clause in v. 27b is used with the term "to present" from the second purpose clause in v. 27a to describe the perfective state in the parallel passage of Col 1:22, "to present you holy and blameless." If v. 27b is a further description of the church's state at the eschatological presentation, then Jesus is not actively, presently, and progressively sanctifying the church in v. 27b.

Although unlikely, there are several textual features which indicate that it is a possibility that the final purpose clause in Eph 5:27b is independent and describes a present aspect of sanctification. Structurally, the previous two ἵνα clauses each introduced a new purpose of Christ's death in v. 26–27a and so the introduction of a third ἵνα clause leads the reader to expect another new purpose.[118] In the third purpose clause, the verb ᾖ, "may be," is a main verb and

---

the idea of baptism upon which Schnackenburg's present tense depends does not occur in the passage.

116 Dunn, *Colossians and Philemon*, 110; Ralph P. Martin, *2 Corinthians*, WBC 40 (Word, 1998), 90; Douglas J. Moo, *The Letters to the Colossians and to Philemon*, PNTC (Eerdmans, 2008), 142; Garland and Dunn note that the word can be a technical term for standing or appear in court before a judge. James D. G. Dunn, *Romans 9–16*, WBC 38B (Word, 2002), 808–809; David E. Garland, *2 Corinthians*, NAC (B&H, 1999), 236.

117 For a similar judgment see: Barth, *Ephesians*, 626, 628; Gregory W. Dawes, *The Body in Question: Metaphor and Meaning in the Interpretation of Ephesians 5:21–33*, BibInt 30 (Brill, 1998), 95–96; Hoehner, *Ephesians*, 760; Albert L. Lukaszewski, Mark Dubis, and J. Ted Blakley, eds., *The Lexham Syntactic Greek New Testament*, SBL ed. (Logos Research Systems, 2011), s.v. "Eph. 5:25–27;" Thielman, *Ephesians*, 382.

118 Several scholars find the purpose clause in v. 27a to be subordinate to the purpose clause in v. 26. However, even if the purpose clauses in v. 27a and v. 27b are subordinate to the initial purpose in v. 26, they may still be separate but interrelated purposes. Barth, *Ephesians*,

so may indicate an independent clause (v. 27b), unlike the participle ἔχουσαν, "having," which is a dependent verb in the second purpose clause (v. 26). The fact that verb tense shifts from the aorist in v. 25–27a to the present tense in v. 27b indicates that the verb ᾖ, "may be," may point to a present aspect of sanctification. However, the participle ἔχουσαν, "having," in v. 27a is also present tense and weakens this suggestion. Finally, in the parallel passage of Col 1:22–23, the fact that the thought shifts from the future idea of the presentation using the aorist, "to present (παραστῆσαι) you holy and blameless," to the present tense idea of perseverance, "if indeed you remain (ἐπιμένετε) in the faith," indicates that there may be a similar transition in Eph 5:27 from future glorification to present progressive sanctification. Thus, if there is a present aspect of sanctification in v. 27b, then this verse depicts Christ as actively and presently sanctifying believers. However, even if v. 27b is part of the future sanctification (glorification) in v. 27a, v. 29 almost certainly depicts Christ as presently and actively sanctifying believers.

In Eph 5:29, there are at least three reasons why Christ has an active role in the present progressive sanctification of believers. First, the Christ-church/husband-wife analogy (5:22–33) indicates that Christ is progressively sanctifying the church. As Andrew Lincoln notes, "the use of comparative particles—ὡς (vv 23, 24), οὕτως (vv 24, 28), and καθώς (vv 25, 29)" running throughout and intricately woven into the passage indicates that the Christ-church relationship serves as an analogy or model for the husband-wife relationship to imitate."[119] Since in the model for husbands to imitate, sanctification by the Word is one of the concrete ways in which Jesus loves the church (v. 25–26), then "nurturing and caring for" (v. 29) may include sanctification by the Word.

Second, the transitional nature of v. 21 in the argument of Ephesians indicates that Christ is progressively sanctifying the church. Although there is much dispute whether v. 21 should be taken as the conclusion to v. 15–20 or as the introduction to 5:22–6:9, there seems to be agreement that v. 21 has a grammatical relationship to v. 15–20 and a thematic relationship to 5:22–6:9 that make it a transitional "hinge verse" or "link" between the two passages, and both of these relationships are important for interpreting v. 29.[120]

626, 628, Dawes, *Body in Question*, 95–96; Hoehner, *Ephesians*, 757; Lukaszewski, Dubis, Blakley, eds., *Lexham Syntactic Greek*, s.v. "Eph 5:25–27;" Thielman, *Ephesians*, 382.

119 Lincoln, *Ephesians*, 352–353, 378.

120 Whether one emphasizes the grammatical relationship as a conclusion or the thematic relationship as an introduction and whether one holds to the presupposition of egalitarianism or complimentarianism in the debate over women's issues determines whether v. 21 is taken with 5:15–20 or 5:22–6:9. Dawes, *Body in Question*, 18–21; Hoehner *Ephesians*, 716–717, 719–720; Lincoln, *Ephesians*, 352; Muddiman, *Ephesians*, 257; Schnackenburg, *Ephesians*, 244; Talbert, *Ephesians*, 130–132; Theilman, *Ephesians*, 372.

For the grammatical relationship, the participle ὑποτασσόμενοι, "submitting" (v. 21), is the last of a string of five participles (λαλοῦντες, ᾄδοντες, ψάλλοντες, εὐχαριστοῦντες, and ὑποτασσόμενοι, v. 19–21) that describe the results of being filled with the Spirit (v. 18). For the thematic relationship, the motif of submission in v. 21 runs throughout the household code (5:22, 24, 33; 6:1–2, 5). Taking both of these relationships into account indicates that in the structure of the argument of Eph, 5:22–6:9 are an elaboration on the theme of submission as a result of being filled with the Spirit in 5:18. As mentioned previously, L. S. Chafer and John F. Walvoord understand the filling of the Spirit (5:18), which for them involves yielding to the Spirit, to be an aspect of progressive sanctification.[121] Since the filling of the Spirit in 5:18–20 is a discussion of sanctification, 5:26–27 continue the theme of sanctification, and the hinge v. of 5:21 indicates that 5:22–6:9 are generally a discussion of submission as an aspect of sanctification, then it is reasonable to assume that the "nurturing and caring for" (v. 29) have something to do with sanctification.

Third, the phrase "nurtures and cares for" (v. 29) indicates that Christ is actively and progressively sanctifying the church. The two verbs ἐκτρέφει καὶ θάλπει, "nurtures and cares for," are in the present tense and through this tense and as determined by the context, these verbs refer to what Christ himself is doing at the present time and refer to the progressive action involved as part of the ongoing Christ-church and husband-wife relationships.[122] In 6:4, the verb "nurture" occurs again and the phrase "in the training and instruction of the Lord" seems to imply that nurturing involves a religious based education entailing in part instruction in the Word. If nurturing in 6:4 entails instruction in the Word, then it may involve the same in 5:29. Since the present progressive nurturing by instruction in the Word by husbands in 5:29 needs to correspond to something that Christ is doing through the analogy, "just as Christ also [does for] the church," and Jesus' instruction in the Word in 5:26 entails past positional sanctification, then the corresponding act of Christ in 5:29 would be nurture and care by instruction through the Word that presently and progressively sanctifies.[123] Therefore, through the Christ-church/husband-wife analogy, Eph 5:21–33 indicates that Jesus is actively, presently, and progressively sanctifying the church.

There are at least two important objections to this interpretation. First, G. W. Dawes objects that the analogy is limited and he restricts the extent of the analogy to the attitude of love (vv. 25, 28) rather than the actions which de-

---

121 Chafer, *He That Is Spiritual*, ch. 3, 4; Walvoord, *Holy Spirit*, ch. 23.
122 Wallace, *Greek Grammar*, 501.
123 For a similar judgment see: Hoehner, *Ephesians*, 761, 768; Lincoln, *Ephesians*, 379–380.

fine Christ's love, explicitly excluding sanctification (vv. 26–27).[124] In response, while it is true that the analogy is limited, it is not so limited as to exclude all of Christ's actions which define his love and particularly sanctification. For example, husbands both figuratively and literally are able to give their lives up for their wives (v. 25). In fact, John 15:13 and 1 John 3:16 explicitly state that believers are to imitate Christ's action of self-sacrifice as a means of following his attitude of love. Furthermore, since the positional sanctification is done through the instrument of the Word in v. 26 and not by divine fiat, then analogously, husbands (and the church) can use the Word as an instrument by which the Trinity is the underlying means or cause that provides progressive sanctification and similarly the Trinity and particularly Christ can be understood as presently using the written Word as an instrument.

Second, someone may object that the term "nurture" does not have the same meaning in the husband-wife relationship (5:29) that it has in the father-child relationship (6:4). However, in a society in which women generally did not receive either secular or religious formal education and in which the entire household was expected to follow the religion of the household head or husband/father, a wife's religious training was the husband's responsibility and so he would be expected to instruct her in the Word (1 Cor 14:33–35; 1 Tim 2:11–12).[125] Moreover, in Eph 5:22–33, the spiritual and metaphorical nature of the context indicates that Paul has in mind not merely physical "feeding and care," through his use of the typical marriage terminology of the time, "nurture and care," (v. 29) but also spiritual religious instruction.[126]

Hebrews 4:12

In Heb 4:12, which is a summary conclusion for Heb 3:7–4:11, the phrase "living and active" not only indicates the power of the written Word of God to "judge the reflections and thoughts of the heart," but also through the quote of Ps 95:7–11 in Heb 3:7, the phrase involves the dynamic power of the written Word to speak in the present ("today") through the Spirit.[127] This present

---

124 Dawes, *Body in Question*, 94.

125 Keener, *IVPBBCNT*, s.v. "1 Tim. 2:11"; Thomas D. Lea and Hayne P. Griffin, *1, 2 Timothy, Titus*, NAC (B&H, 1992), 97; Lincoln, *Ephesians*, 358; William D. Mounce, *Pastoral Epistles*, WBC 46 (Word, 2000), 119.

126 For a similar judgment see: Hoehner, *Ephesians*, 767–768; Thielman, *Ephesians*, 388. For an opposing judgment see: Muddiman, *Ephesians*, 267–268; Schnackenburg, *Ephesians*, 253–254.

127 Gareth Lee Cockerill, *The Epistle to the Hebrews*, NICNT (Eerdmans, 2012), 214–215; Paul Ellingworth, *The Epistle to the Hebrews: A Commentary on the Greek Text*, NIGTC (Eerdmans, 1993), 260–261; William L. Lane, *Hebrews 1–8*, WBC 47A (Word, 2002), 102–103; Thomas

day speaking is not a Barthian existential encounter in which the Bible, "can become the Word of God," but rather is best understood in terms of Calvin and Zwingli's Word-Spirit correlation (the inseparable working of the Word and Spirit by which they mutually confirm each other), by which the Spirit illuminates (Eph 1:17–19) the Word (1 Thess 2:13) to the reader.[128]

In this process by which the reader encounters (Heb 4:12) Jesus' teaching and example and the historical account of Christ's death, the nature of these two aspects of the biblical text and the reader's interaction with them is different. For instance, the death of Christ may be replayed in the mind of readers as they read the text, but there is no sense in which the death of Christ is actually repeated in the act of reading or else it loses its "once for all" (Rom 6:10; Heb 7:27; 9:12, 26) and final nature as it does in the theology of the Roman Catholic mass, which sees the mass as an actual repetition of Christ's sacrifice. In the case of Christ's death, the Spirit applies the benefits of the past event of Christ's death to new believers by uniting them to Christ, who is passive, as they read the text (Eph 1:13–14).

In the case of Jesus' teaching, of which his example is one aspect, there is a sense in which Jesus is actively teaching as the Spirit illuminates the reader's mind. The case of John Vernon McGee (1904–1988) illustrates this active sense. McGee, pastor of the historic Church of the Open Door in downtown Los Angeles (1949–1970) and professor at Biola University in La Mirada, CA (1943–1953), had a radio ministry from 1941–1988, with his most famous broadcast being his *Thru the Bible* program, which continues to be aired internationally as of the time of writing.[129] Currently, McGee's voice, teaching content, and personality are communicated to at least thousands if not millions

---

D. Lea, *Hebrews, James*, HNTC 10 (B&H, 1999), 71–72; James W. Thompson, *Hebrews*, PCNT (Baker Academic, 2008), 96–97. Allen makes a thoughtful and persuasive but ultimately unconvincing argument that "the word of God" is Jesus based on four points. Ellingworth's discussion and the BDAG effectively counter Allen's first three points. Allen's fourth point is that "A final argument in favor of taking the 'word' in 4:12 to refer to Jesus is the connection of these verses with the prologue, Heb 1:1–2 to form an *inclusio*." Since the two halves of an *inclusio* are typically connected by the repetition of words (catchwords or linking words) and phrases (cp. Prov 10:6, 11; Matt 7:16, 20; John 15:12, 17; for a canonical *inclusio* cf. Deut 4:2 and Rev 22:18–19) and Heb 1:1–2; 4:12 are connected by merely weak conceptual similarity, then it is difficult to see how these verses form an *inclusio*. David L Allen, *Hebrews*, NAC (B&H, 2010), 284–286; BDAG, s.v. "μάχαιρα;" Ellingworth, *Hebrews*, 260–261.

128 Karl Barth, *CD* 1.1:xiii, 111, 138, 383; Calvin, *Inst.* 1.9.3 (CR 30:71–72); Ulrich Zwingli, *Von Klarheit und Gewißheit des Wortes Gottes* 47–53 (CR 88:379–384). Some argue that Zwingli had a Spirit-Word correlation and while the different emphasis due to the word order is important, the idea of correlation is basically the same in this case. In existentialism, existence precedes essence, but in the Bible, essence precedes existence (Lev. 19:2) so that existentialism and the Barthian conception of revelation that is based on existentialism are biblically inconsistent.

129 Gertrude L. Cutler, ed. *The Whole Word for the Whole World: The Life and Ministry of J. Vernon Mcgee* (Thru the Bible Radio Network, 1991), 51–52, 58–59, 79, 93.

of people even though McGee is no longer alive. Someone may object that it is the electromagnetic recording of McGee that is teaching and not McGee himself who is active. However, there is something in and communicated by the recording that is McGee, for the recording would not exist without McGee and it is McGee's voice, content, and personality that are communicated. In a similar way, as believers read the biblical text and encounter the words of Jesus, there is a sense in which his voice, his content, and his personality are actively communicated or taught to the reader. Jesus does not continue to die as the account of his death is read, but he does continue to teach and through his teaching set an example as the Spirit illuminates the biblical text as it is read. And as argued from Eph 5:25–33, this active teaching of Jesus has a sanctifying function. Therefore, Jesus' role as a teacher and example of virtue is an active sanctifying role (Eph 5:25–33; Heb 4:12) along with the other persons of the Trinity.

STATEMENT OF VIRTUE ETHICAL TRINITARIAN SANCTIFICATION ORDERED BY THE TRIUNE PREMISE

This section draws together some of the observations made and conclusions reached so far in order to formulate two statements of virtue ethical Trinitarian sanctification ordered by the Triune premise through a theological synthesis. These statements demonstrate that virtue ethics is key to understanding Trinitarian progressive sanctification by indicating how the Trinity progressively sanctifies believers on the basis of Jesus' active roles as a teacher and example of virtue.

In his role as a teacher of virtue, Jesus' instruction on moral motivation functions in relation to the Father and the Spirit to sanctify the believer. In chapter three, the exegetical argument for moral realism based on value demonstrated that the Father is the source of the value that exists in the creation order and which reflects his character and is the basis of his moral commands (Gen 1:1, 25, 31; Lev 19:2; Ps 19:1; Acts 14:17; Rom 1:19–20). The sections on moral motivation, demonstrated that through his teaching, Jesus reveals the commands or value of the Father (John 8:38; 14:15, 21, 23–24) and he taught that the emotion-virtues provide motivation to obey these commands (Luke 8:1–15; 18:1–8; John 14:15, 23–24). Based on the value argument in chapter three, these moral motivation sections also demonstrated that emotion-virtues motivate moral action by producing emotions which detect or recognize the value of the creation order (Rom 2:14–15) and Jesus' teaching and person (Rom 12:2, 9). However, due to the noetic effects of sin (Mic 3:2; Rom 1:18;

7:18–20), the empowerment of the Spirit (Eph 1:17–19; 1 Cor 2:14) is required in order for believers' emotion-virtues to function properly in recognizing and providing motivation from the value that the emotion-virtues detect. Therefore, as ordered by the Triune premise, Jesus' active role as a teacher of virtue functions to sanctify believers along with the Father and the Spirit such that the value (moral facts/commands) having its source *from* the Father (Gen 1:1, 25, 31; Lev 19:2; Ps 19:1; Acts 14:17; Rom 1:19–20), is revealed *through* the Son to motivate believers (Luke 8:1–15; 18:1–8; John 14:15, 21, 23–24), who are empowered to be motivated/obey *by* the Spirit (Eph 1:17–19; 1 Cor 2:14).

Similarly, in his role as a moral example of virtue, Jesus' example functions in relation to the Father and the Spirit to sanctify the believer. In John 8:38; 14:9–10, Jesus teaches that the Father is the source of the character or virtues that he is revealing through his life and example. The sections dealing with imitation, habituation, and reciprocity, demonstrated that Jesus intended his example to be imitated by a kind of habituation and reciprocity in order for believers to be made like their teacher (Luke 6:40) or conformed to his image (Rom 8:29). The section dealing with objections to imitation by habituation and reciprocity demonstrated that due to sin (Mic 3:2; Rom 1:18; 7:18–20), the continual indwelling and immediate operation of the Spirit is needed to "lead" (Rom 8:14; Gal 5:18) and "work in" (Phil 2:13) believers in order for them to imitate Christ's example to think, act, and "be" virtuous (Gal 5:22–23). Therefore, as ordered by the Triune principle, Jesus' active role as an example of virtue functions to sanctify believers along with the Father and the Spirit such that the character that is *from* the Father (John 8:38; 14:9–10) is revealed *through* the Son's example (John 14:9–10) that is to be imitated by the believer through habituation and reciprocity (Luke 6:40, 6:43–45), *by* the Spirit's "leading" (Rom 8:14; Gal 5:18) and "working" (Phil 2:13).

Conclusion

Therefore, a number of arguments have supported the main claim of this chapter that virtue ethics is key to understanding Trinitarian progressive sanctification because Jesus' active roles as a teacher and example of virtue are crucial to understanding how the Trinity progressively sanctifies believers. As groundwork for understanding Jesus' active roles as a teacher and example of virtue, it was demonstrated that the theological virtues Jesus taught were not the traditional theological virtues (faith, hope, and love; 1 Cor 13:13), but rather faith, love, and endurance (Matt 24:10–13). The reason for the difference between the theological virtue lists of Jesus and the later NT authors may be that endurance was more important than hope before the resurrection as part of progressive revelation.

Having established the existence and content of the theological virtues in the teaching of Jesus, it was demonstrated that Jesus taught that the theological virtues provide moral motivation (Luke 8:1–15; 18:1–8; John 14:15, 23–24). In John 14:15, 21, 23–24, motivational weak internalism is consistent with Jesus' teaching, which implies that motivational strong internalism and externalism are not biblically consistent. Moreover, the emotion-virtues and namely the theological virtues provide moral motivation by generating the necessary emotions which motivate moral action.

It was also demonstrated that an adapted form of habituation and reciprocity is consistent with Jesus' teaching on how his moral example is to be imitated (Matt 7:15–23; 12:33–35; Luke 6:40, 43–45). In Jesus' teaching, reciprocity is reversed through his emphasis on the heart so that the stress is on being leading to action rather than habituation. Furthermore, several theological understandings of reciprocity and habituation were offered which allow these concepts to be consistent with *sola fide* and to explain from a Reformation perspective how sanctification can occur without ontological change, be a divine work rather than a human work, and yet in relation to justification not be a legal fiction as the Roman Catholics charge.

Finally, a theological synthesis of the conclusions reached so far and ordered by the Triune premise demonstrated how the Trinity progressively sanctifies believers on the basis of Jesus' active roles as a teacher and example of virtue: (1) the value having its source *from* the Father, is revealed *through* the teaching of the Son to motivate believers, who are empowered to be motivated *by* the Spirit and (2) the character that is *from* the Father is revealed *through* the Son's example that is to be imitated by the believer through habituation and reciprocity, *by* the Spirit's "leading" and "working."

CHAPTER 4

JESUS' ROLE AS PRIEST

The main claim of this chapter is that virtue ethics is key to understanding Trinitarian progressive sanctification because Jesus' present and active priestly role of heavenly intercession aimed at manifesting virtue in believers is crucial to understanding how the Trinity progressively sanctifies believers. This claim is defended through an in-depth exegesis of select verses in Rom 8 in conjunction with biblical-theological synthesis of other select intercession passages. A Trinitarian statement structured according to the Triune premise and based on the exegesis of this chapter explains the roles of the Father, Son, and Spirit in virtue ethical Trinitarian sanctification. The chapter closes with a final application to the church from Rom 8 that the prayers of believers are directed *primarily* to the Father rather than to all three persons of the Trinity.

AN INTRODUCTION TO THE DOCTRINE OF CHRIST'S HEAVENLY INTERCESSION

Before proceeding to the main chapter claim, it is important to recognize that the background of Jesus' present and active heavenly intercession is an aspect of his exalted state in his session in heaven involving his role as priest and which has four historic interpretations. Understanding the basic concept of the intercession and its historic interpretations is important because some of the interpretations tend to make Jesus' intercession passive and appropriate the sanctifying aspect of the intercession to the Spirit. The term ἐντυγχάνω, "to intercede" (Rom 8:34; Heb 7:25), means "to make an earnest request through contact with the pers. approached ... *approach* or *appeal to someone* ... *plead for someone* ... *appeal to someone against a third* person ... Since petitions are also directed toward God, ἐ. can be rendered *pray*."¹ Traditionally, there are two states of Christ: his state of humiliation during the incarnation (Phil 2:6–8) and his state of exaltation in heaven after the ascension (Eph 1:20; Phil 2:9–11; Heb 8:1).² Christ's heavenly intercession is part of his state of exaltation. The term "session" refers to Christ's sitting at the right hand of God (Ps 110; Heb 1:3, 13) to conduct the business of his traditional threefold office of prophet (John 14:16; 15:26; Acts 2:33), priest (Heb 8:1–2) and king (Eph 1:19–23)."³ While there is some overlap between the offices, the intercession is typically thought of as that aspect of the session that belongs to the priestly

---

1 Emphasis original. BDAG, s.v. "ἐντυγχάνω."
2 The doctrine of the "states of Christ" is present in the church fathers and reformers, but was more fully developed by the Lutherans and adapted by the Reformed in the period of Protestant Scholasticism (1648–1700). However, according to Berkhof, some also prefer a third state of Christ as his "pre-existent state of eternal divine being" prior to the incarnation (John 1:1). Berkhof, *Theology*, 331–332; Wayne A. Grudem, *Systematic Theology: An Introduction to Biblical Doctrine* (Zondervan, 2004), 1241, 1244; Veli-Matti Kärkkäinen, *Christology: A Global Introduction* (Baker Academic, 2003), 20, 54–55.
3 Gary Brady, *What Jesus Is Doing Now* (EP Books, 2012), 34, 58. David M. Hay, *Glory at the Right Hand: Psalm 110 in Early Christianity*, ed. Robert A. Kraft and Leander Keck, SBLMS (Abingdon, 1973), 130; Arthur J. Tait, *The Heavenly Session of Our Lord: An Introduction to the History of the Doctrine* (Robert Scott, 1912), 3, 8. Although Christ is pictured as standing in Acts 7:55–56 and Revelation 5:6, others follow Tait, who seems to be elaborating on Calvin by arguing that the difference between "standing" and "sitting" is not problematic since both are metaphorical descriptions of the session and merely describe different aspects of it. Brady, *Jesus Now*, 61–63; John Calvin, *Inst.* 2.16.15 (CR 30:383); Hay, *Right Hand*, 160; Tait, *Heavenly Session*, 23–24. Among others, Bavinck sees Christ's fulfillment of his promise to send the Spirit as part of his prophetic role carried out during the session. Herman Bavinck, *Sin and Salvation in Christ*, vol. 3 of *Reformed Dogmatics*, ed. John Bolt, trans., John Vriend (Baker Academic, 2006), 475. Since the Socinians errantly resolved the intercession into the kingly office in order to make the intercession figurative like their view of the atonement, then in response, later authors stressed that the heavenly intercession is a priestly activity, but Murray aptly notes that while the intercession is properly priestly, there is an overlap or "inter-permeation of the various offices." John Murray, "The Heavenly, Priestly Activity of Christ," in *The Claims of Truth*, vol. 1 of *Collected Writings of John Murray: Professor of Systematic Theology, Westminster Theological Seminary, Philadelphia, Pennsylvania, 1937–1966* (Banner of Truth Trust, 1976), 47. Faustus Socinus (1539–1604) and his followers denied the divinity of Christ and the Trinity and argued for the moral example theory of the atonement or the idea, as Enns states, that "Christ's death was an example of obedience that should inspire others" rather than a penal substitutionary bearing of sin that made God gracious or favorably disposed toward people. Paul P. Enns, *The Moody Handbook of Theology* (Moody, 1989), 450; John Miley, *Systematic Theology* (Hunt & Eaton, 1893), 2:54–55. On the overlap of offices see: Brady, *Jesus Now*, 35; John Mauchline, "Jesus Christ as Intercessor," *Expository Times* 64, no. 12 (1953): 356. On the Socinian interpretation of the intercession see: Franz Pieper, *Christliche Dogmatik* (Evangelisch-Lutherischen Synode von Missouri und Anderen Staaten, 1946), 422; William Symington, *The Atonement and Intercession of Jesus Christ*, rep. ed. (Reformation Heritage Books, 2006), 257; Francis Turretin, *Inst.* 14.15.6 (2:424). On the later emphasis on the priestly office see: Brady, *Jesus Now*, 139; Stephen Charnock, *Christ's Intercession* (Works 5:95, 100); Thomas Houston, *The Intercession of Christ* (James Gemmell, 1882), 51, 151.

office. Thus, Christ's heavenly intercession is an aspect of his session in heaven involving his office or role of priest.

Four Historic Interpretations of the Intercession

Jesus' heavenly intercession has four historic interpretations, which impact the active or passive nature of the intercession and determine whether the sanctifying aspect of the intercession should be appropriated to the Spirit. In *The Heavenly Session of Our Lord: An Introduction to the History of the Doctrine*, Arthur J. Tait has written what seems to be the definitive Protestant history of the doctrine of the heavenly intercession of Christ.[4]

Table A4 in Appendix 4 summarizes Tait's history and indicates that the church has historically held to four interpretations of the intercession.[5] These interpretations or views of the intercession may be classified in the following manner: (1) the "metaphor or anthropomorphic" view of Chrysostom (347–407) claims that the intercession is a symbol of God's love, (2) the "passive presence" view of Gregory of Nazianzus (330–389) that is generally followed by the Reformed is the idea that Christ's intercession is real, but involves his passive presence in heaven rather than literal prayer, (3) the "continual propitiation/sacrifice" view of Leo the Great (440–461) and the Roman Catholic Church is that Christ actually continues to make propitiation in heaven, and (4) the "*vocalis et realis*" view of Melanchthon that is generally followed by the Lutherans holds that Christ not only presents his sacrifice by his presence, but also actually prays for people.[6]

---

4 Arthur J. Tait, *The Heavenly Session of Our Lord: An Introduction to the History of the Doctrine* (Robert Scott, 1912). In comparison, Peterson treats only the post-Reformation history in a single but helpful footnote. David G Peterson, *Hebrews and Perfection: An Examination of the Concept of Perfection in the "Epistle to the Hebrews,"* ed. R. McL. Wilson, SNTSMS 47 (Cambridge University Press, 1982), 248. Owen claims that the Roman Catholics have extensive histories. John Owen, *An Exposition of the Epistle to the Hebrews* (Works 22:537).

5 Table A4 in Appendix 4 demonstrates that Tait's history has significant gaps. Some of the gaps have been partially filled primarily by citing more recent proponents of these views. However, Tait's overall history is sufficient to demonstrate the point that there have been numerous proponents of the four views of the intercession over time and particularly the passive presence and *vocalis et realis* views.

6 Tait, *Heavenly Session*, 150, 152, 157–159, 163; Peterson, *Hebrews and Perfection*, 248. One of the later adherents of something close to the metaphor view may be Alexander Nairne, *The Epistle of Priesthood, Studies in the Epistle to the Hebrews* (T&T Clarke, 1913), 183–184, 198–202. Gregory of Nazianzus wrote "οὐχ ὡς ὑπὲρ ἡμῶν προκαλινδούμενον τοῦ Πατρός, καὶ προσπίπτοντα δουλικῶς. ... ἀλλ' οἷς πέπονθεν, ὡς ἄνθρωπος, πείθει καρτερεῖν, ὡς Λόγος καὶ παραινέτης. Τοῦτο νοεῖταί μοι ἡ παράκλησις" [as on behalf of us not prostrating to the Father, and falling as a slave, ... but by what he suffered, as man, continues to persuade, as the Word and Advocate. This is the meaning of the Advocacy to me]. Gregory Nazianzus, *Or.* 30.14 (SC 250:256). In his comments on Rom 8:34 and in *Institutes* 3:20.20, Calvin uses similar language to Gregory to qualify

Several important qualifications and explanations are needed in regard to these four historic views of the intercession. First, in practice there is some overlap or mixing and matching between the views among the actual statements of the various proponents. Second, the Roman Catholic view of continual propitiation is correctly and summarily dismissed by Protestants as violating the "once for all" statements in Scripture which indicate that the propitiation is completed on earth and not repeated in heaven (Rom 6:10; Heb 7:27; 9:26; 10:10; 1 Pet 3:18; see also Heb 9:25).[7] Third, despite the recognition of passive presence proponents that Christ is still actively working in his session and efforts to qualify their view to that effect, their view by definition (that the intercession consists primarily, if not exclusively in some cases, of the presence of Christ) tends to make Christ passive and inactive in their interpretations.[8] Fourth, Tait seems to conflate the metaphor and passive pres-

---

that the intercession is not actual prayer and so unequivocally demonstrates that he is following in the passive presence position as Tait and Peterson claim and as consistent with his comments in *Institutes* 2.15.6; 3.20.18. Calvin claims concerning Rom 8:34, "*Non enim cogitandus est supplex, flexis genibus, manibus expansis, patrem deprecari: sed quia apparet ipse assidue cum morte et resurrectione sua, quae vice sunt aeternae intercessionis, et vivae orationis efficaciam habent, ut patrem nobis concilient, atque exorabilem reddant, merito dicitur intercedere.*" [Not indeed should we think he is supplicating, *bowing on knees, hands spread out, praying to the Father*: but because he appears continually with his death and resurrection, *which are* in turn eternal *intercession*, and have the efficacy of living prayer, in order to render the Father favorably disposed to us, and also capable of being moved by entreaty to restore, rightly he is said to intercede.] Empahsis added. John Calvin, *Commentarius in Epistolam Pauli ad Romanos* 8:34 (CR 77:165); Peterson, *Hebrews and Perfection*, 248; Tait, *Heavenly Session*, 163–164. Others in the passive presence tradition follow or affirm this language from Gregory and Calvin: Brady, *Jesus Now*, 141; Henry Barclay Swete, *The Ascended Christ: A Study in the Earliest Christian Teaching* (Macmillan and Co., 1910), 95–96; Turretin, *Inst.* 14.15.7, 11, 13 (2:425). MacLeod argues that interpretations like Tait's are a common Protestant "misrepresentation" of Roman Catholic theology because "Catholic theologians reject this interpretation and argue that the Mass is not a 'repetition' but a 'realization' of the sacrifice of Christ in the present." However, Leo's language seems to support the idea of a continuing or repeated propitiation or sacrifice. David J MacLeod, "Christ, the Believer's High Priest: An Exposition of Hebrews 7:26–28," *BSac* 162, no. 647 (Jl–S 2005): 340. Also in the West, Tait claims that "Gregory the Great [540–604] seems to have been the first to treat specifically the question as to whether Christ's Intercession is to be regarded as *vocalis et realis* [vocal and real], or as the intercession of His presence in our nature with the Father" and Gregory argued against the *vocalis et realis* position. Tait, *Heavenly Session*, 159–60.

7 Brady, *Jesus Now*, 129; Bavinck, *Sin and Salvation*, 478–479; Charnock, *Intercession*, Works 5:100–101; Pieper, *Dogmatik*, 422; Symington, *Atonement and Intercession*, 260; Swete, *Ascended Christ*, 43.

8 For a similar judgment see: Mauchline, "Intercessor," 358. For example of the passive tendency see: Brady, *Jesus Now*, 67, 143; Charnock, *Intercession*, Works 5:99, 102, 104; Houston, *Intercession*, 50; Symington, *Atonement and Intercession*, 260; Tait, *Heavenly Session*, 12, 19; Turretin, *Inst.* 14.15.7, 11, 13 (2:425). In fact, in their qualifications, Murray and Tait seem to acknowledge that the presence view they hold tends to be misunderstood as representing Christ as passive. Murray, "Priestly Activity," 47; Tait, *Heavenly Session*, 19.

ence views.⁹ While it is true that there is an affinity between these views, they are historically distinct and there seems to be some appropriation of the idea of metaphor by the *vocalis et realis* view.¹⁰

Fifth, both the passive presence and the *vocalis et realis* views acknowledge a salvific-forensic (focusing on application of the accomplished atonement to forgive daily sins) and a sanctifying-supplicatory or non-forensic component (including intercessory supplication for issues other than forgiveness of sin such as perseverance, purification of believers, manifestation of virtue in believers, etc.) to Christ's intercession.¹¹ However, they differ in emphasis and in explanation of how Christ actually applies the sanctifying aspect. The passive presence view tends to emphasize the salvific-forensic and minimize the sanctifying-supplicatory aspect, while the *vocalis et realis* view tends toward more of a balanced approach. Furthermore, the *vocalis et realis* view described by J. T. Mueller depicts Christ as actively sanctifying and by John Bunyan and Franz Pieper as actively supporting the perseverance of believers through his actual prayer, while the passive presence view may argue as William Symington does that the symbol of Christ's presence "intimates" or implies requests or along the lines of Francis Turretin and Gary Brady that Christ's intercession merely has the "substance" but not the form of prayer and is something like "effective speaking."¹² However, both views

---

9 Tait, *Heavenly Session*, 150, 163–164.
10 John Theodore Mueller, *Christian Dogmatics* (Concordia Publishing House, 1999), 313–314.
11 Berkhof, *Theology*, 402; Brady, *Jesus Now*, 51, 95–97, 124–125, 165–166, 168; Charnock, *Intercession*, Works 5:95–96, 105, 122, 129–130, 131–133, 136, 143; Millard J. Erickson, *Christian Theology*, 3rd ed. (Baker Academic, 2013), 703. Houston, *Intercession*, 51, 83, 87–88, 92–93, 97–98, 205, 210–213; Mueller, *Dogmatics*, 313–314; Murray, "Priestly Activity," 48, 51; Symington, *Atonement and Intercession*, 256–258, 272–273, 278–279, 282.
12 Brady, *Jesus Now*, 141; John Bunyan, *Christ a Complete Saviour or the Intercession of Christ and Who Are Privileged in It* (Works 1:203, 207, 215, 228); Mueller, *Dogmatics*, 313–314; Pieper, *Dogmatik*, 422; Symington, *Atonement and Intercession*, 263–267; Turretin, *Inst.* 14.15.7, 11, 13 (2:425). Symington and Charnock argue that Christ's presence in heaven communicates as a silent symbol like the rainbow of the flood or the blood of the passover lamb. Additionally, Symington offers the helpful extra-biblical illustration of Amintas to explain the passive presence position: "Amintas had performed meritorious services in behalf of the commonwealth, in course of which he had lost a hand. When his brother Aechylus is about to be condemned to death for some offence of which he has been guilty, Amintas rushes into the court; without uttering a syllable he holds up the mutilated limb; the judges are moved; and Aechylus is set free. Thus the sacrifice of our Redeemer," symbolized by his presence, functions the same way in heaven. Cody has the metaphor of Christ's blood "speaking" (Heb 9:12; 12:24). Charnock, *Intercession* (Works 5:113, 141); Aelred Cody, *Heavenly Sanctuary and Liturgy in the Epistle to the Hebrews: The Achievement of Salvation in the Epistle's Perspective* (Grail Publications, 1960), 193, 195, 197–198; Owen, *Hebrews* (Works 22:540–541). See also Heppe who approvingly cites Beza and Turretin: Heinrich Heppe, *Die Dogmatik der evangelisch-reformierte Kirche: Dargestellt und aus den Quellen belegt*, 2nd ed. (Neukirchener Verlag, Kreis Moers, 1958), 382–383.

have the potential to downplay the active role of Christ by appropriating the application of salvation to the Spirit.[13]

In defending the main claim of this chapter, this book is only concerned with demonstrating that Jesus' intercession is active and sanctifying in a manner that involves the Trinity and virtue.[14] However, defense of this claim necessarily involves the debate between three of the four historic views of the nature of the intercession, because the passive presence view tends to make Jesus' intercession passive and salvific-forensic while at the same time all three views may at times appropriate the sanctifying-non-forensic aspect of the intercession to the Spirit. While the position taken in this book, *agilis et realis*, "active and real," may most closely fit with a mediating view between the passive presence and *vocalis et realis* views, the intention is not to defend an existing or develop a new view of the nature of the intercession, but rather to demonstrate that the biblical evidence supports the main claim which entails an active and sanctifying priestly role for Christ in the intercession.[15]

---

13 For example see: Houston, *Intercession*, 81, 86; Mueller, *Dogmatics*, 313–314.

14 There are many other controversial issues that are debated in relation to the session generally that bear on the intercession and others specifically regarding the intercession, but these are out of the scope of this argument. For example, Tait lists a number of controversies surrounding the session in the Patristic period such as: (1) the issue of whether Christ's exalted glory was a return to the pre-incarnate glory or a new economic glory, (2) the debate surrounding whether or not the hypostatic union of the incarnation continued into eternity, and (3) the controversy of whether the "right hand" position indicates equality or subordination. Tait, *Heavenly Session*, 53–54. In addition to these issues, a number of authors debate the extent of the intercession (for all people or only the elect) typically by linking their view of its extent to the atonement. Brady, *Jesus Now*, 219–222; Charles Hodge, *Systematic Theology* (Logos Research Systems, 1997), 2:594; Houston, *Intercession*, 79; 153–154; Mueller, *Dogmatics*, 313; Murray, "Priestly Activity," 55–57; Pieper, *Dogmatik*, 421; Swete, *Ascended Christ*, 98–99; Augustus Hopkins Strong, *Systematic Theology* (American Baptist Publication Society, 1907), 2:774; Symington, *Atonement and Intercession*, 268–269.

15 Brady and Strong's views might be interpreted as such a mediating view. Brady, *Jesus Now*, 138–143; Strong, *Theology*, 2:774. In keeping with the method of the unity of all doctrine, interpretation of the intercession has been impacted by other doctrines. The passive presence view was developed through two stages of polemics against perceived heresies. In the Patristic era, the passive presence view was given in response to Arianism's rejection of Jesus' deity and it was used by Protestants in the Reformation to counter the Roman Catholic doctrine of a continuing propitiation. Furthermore, while emphasis on heaven as a place prior to the nineteenth century did not result in the literal *vocalis et realis* view, the reversal of highlighting heaven as a state after the nineteenth century does seem to reinforce the idea of a symbolic passive presence. Tait, *Heavenly Session*, 25–28, 58, 36–38, 127, 212–217, 231–232. Since the historic theological concerns in the development of the passive presence view were to guard Jesus' divinity by cautiously presenting his exalted humanity and to counter the Roman Catholic idea of a continuing active heavenly sacrifice, then perhaps the true interpretation of the intercession lies somewhere in between the passive presence and *vocalis et realis* views. In Kurianal's view, the passive presence and *vocalis et realis* views split respectively along Protestant and Roman Catholic lines. However, following a careful exegesis of the text, Kurianal's own position is something in between and seems closer to the passive presence view. Kurianal's anal-

LINGUISTIC AND THEMATIC CONNECTION OF INTERCESSION PASSAGES

Turning to the biblical evidence, there are several main (standard) passages commonly addressed by discussions of the intercession which demonstrate that Jesus' present and active priestly role of heavenly intercession produces virtue in believers through a process of Trinitarian progressive sanctification. Since not all of these standard passages (Luke 22:31–32; John 17:6–26; Rom 8:34; Heb 2:14–18; 4:14–16; 7:23–28; 9:23–28; 1 John 2:1–2) are equally relevant for the issue of virtue ethical Trinitarian sanctification, they are treated selectively in this chapter's argument. While the other passages are touched upon briefly, the focus of this book is on the standard passages of John 17:6–26, Rom 8:34, and Heb 2:14–18; 4:14–16, with the addition of Zech 3:1–2 as mentioned by Symington, because they demonstrate the sanctifying-supplicatory aspect of the intercession.[16] Hebrews 7:23–28; 9:23–28, the main passages supporting the passive presence view, are passed over because it is not disputed that these passages emphasize a salvific-forensic aspect of the intercession.[17] Authors discussing the intercession commonly assume that these passages are interrelated, but do not always explicitly explain why they are all intercession passages.[18] Table A5 in Appendix 5 indicates that there are at least eight common key words and/or themes which link these standard intercession passages: high priest, suffer, help, temptation, weakness, sacrifice, intercede, and exaltation (right hand, etc.). Since the passages are all interconnected and only present different aspects of the intercession, then it is necessary to

---

ysis may demonstrate that when scholars are not engaged in polemics, they may more closely approach the meaning of the text. James Kurianal, *Jesus Our High Priest: Ps 110,4 as the Substructure of Heb 5,1–7,28*, European University Studies, Series 23 (Peter Lang, 2000), 135–136, 217–219. Whatever view is taken, both Jesus' divinity and exalted humanity need to be respected in the description of the intercession and accomplishing this dual task is difficult.

16 Symington, *Atonement and Intercession*, 276–277.

17 For some passive presence interpretations of these passages see: Charnock, *Intercession* (Works 5:99, 101–102, 109); Houston, *Intercession*, 45–48, 100; Owen, *Hebrews* (Works 22:541); Swete, *Ascended Christ*, 43; Symington, *Atonement and Intercession*, 263–265; Turretin, *Inst.* 14.15.7, 11, 13 (2:425). On the idea of the salvific-forensic emphasis of the context see: David L. Allen, *Hebrews*, NAC (B&H, 2010), 488; William L. Lane, *Hebrews 9–13*, WBC (Word, 2002), 206, 248, 251 252.

18 Brady, *Jesus Now*, 134; Charnock, *Intercession* (Works 5:93–94, 101–102, 105, 107, 109, 125, 129–130); Cody, *Heavenly Sanctuary*, 193; David Michael Crump, *Jesus the Intercessor: Prayer and Christology in Luke-Acts*, WUNT 2.49 (J. B. C. Mohr, 1992), 14–19; Hay, *Right Hand*, 130–134, 152; Houston, *Intercession*, 45, 47–48, 52, 89, 97; Murray, "Priestly Activity," 45–46, 51, 55–56; Allen James McNicole, "The Relationship of the Image of the Highest Angel to the High Priest Concept in Hebrews" (PhD. diss., Vanderbilt University, 1974), 187; Swete, *Ascended Christ*, 94–95; Symington, *Atonement and Intercession*, 258–259, 262–264, 266; Tait, *Heavenly Session*, 23–24; Turretin, *Inst.* 14.15 (2:424–426).

treat them together in order to gain a more complete picture of the intercession and how it involves an active, sanctifying, and priestly role for Christ.[19]

VIRTUE ETHICAL TRINITARIAN SANCTIFICATION IN ROMANS 8:14–16, 26–28, 34

In Rom 8:34, the nature of Christ's intercession is shown to be active and sanctifying by comparing the immediate, the wider, and the canonical contexts. The immediate context emphasizes a salvific-forensic but active aspect of the intercession. The wider context of Rom 8:26–34 connects the intercession of the Son to the work of the Spirit and the Father, making this possibly the only intercession passage where all three persons of the Trinity explicitly interact with each other and also possibly the only passage in which the entire Trinity interacts with the believer in prayer. For this reason, Rom 8:26–34 is treated as the main intercession passage with the other passages serving to interpret the intercession involved in the Trinitarian action in Rom 8. Furthermore, the wider context emphasizes the active and sanctifying aspects of the Son's intercession. Similarly, the canonical context of Heb 2:14–18; 4:14–16; John 17:6–26, and Zech 3:1–2 highlight that the Son's intercession is not only salvific-forensic, but also active and sanctifying-supplicatory.

Romans 8:34: The Son's Intercession

In Rom 8:34, the explicit emphasis of the immediate context is on the salvific-forensic aspect of the intercession.[20] In the immediate context and taking vv. 33–34 as a unit, the forensic language "charges," "justifies," and "condemns," places a strong but not exclusive emphasis on the intercession as salvific-forensic.[21] The present active verb, ἐντυγχάνει, "intercedes" (8:34), implies that

---

19 For a similar judgment that the intercession passages should be taken together in order to get a better picture of the intercession as a whole see: Gordon Rupp, "The Finished Work of Christ in Word and Sacrament," in *The Finality of Christ*, ed. Dow Kirkpatrick (Abingdon, 1966), 189.

20 For a similar judgment see: Aquinas, *Super Epistolam B. Pauli ad Romanos lectura* C.8 L.7.719–20, ed. J. Mortensen and E. Alarcón, trans. F. R. Larcher, Under the title *Commentary on the Letter of Saint Paul to the Romans*, Latin/English ed., Biblical Commentaries 37 (The Aquinas Institute, 2012), 239–240; Calvin, *Rom* 8.34 (CR.77:147, 165); Martin Luther, *Der Breief an die Römer* (WA 56:78); Abraham Kuyper, *The Work of the Holy Spirit*, trans. Henri de Vries (Funk and Wagnalls, 1900), 462, 456, 637–638.

21 For a similar judgment see: Hodge, *Theology*, 2:593; William R. G Loader, *Sohn und Hoherpriester: eine traditionsgeschichtliche Untersuchung zur Christologie des Hebräerbriefes*, WMANT 53 (Neukirchener Verlag, 1981), 154–155; Mauchline, "Intercessor," 359. For the dispute over the relationship of the questions in v. 33–34 see: Douglas J. Moo, *The Epistle to the Romans*,

Jesus' intercession is active. The contrast between Christ's intercession (8:34) and the forensic language (8:33–34), along with the idea that nothing will separate believers from the love of God (8:35–39), seems to imply that like in the biblical scenes in which Satan attacks believers before God through accusations (Job 1:6–12; 2:1–7; Zech 3:1–2), Jesus defends them through his intercession against daily and other sins (Zech 3:1–2; Luke 22:31–32; 1 John 2:1–2) on the basis of his death (Rom 8:34).[22] Therefore, in Rom 8:34 the immediate context emphasizes a salvific-forensic but active aspect of the intercession.

Romans 8:14–16, 26–27: The Spirit's Intercession

While the immediate context shows the Son's intercession (Rom 8:34) as primarily salvific-forensic, in the wider context, the Spirit's salvific-forensic (Rom 8:14–16) and sanctifying-supplicatory (Rom 8:26–27) intercession implies that the Son's intercession also has a sanctifying-supplicatory dimension. Scholars have long recognized that there is some relationship between the intercession of the Son and the Spirit and have primarily described this relationship in geographic terms such that the Son intercedes in heaven and the Spirit on earth and also have sometimes divided the intercessions such that the Son's intercession is salvific-forensic and the Spirit's intercession is sanctifying-supplicatory.[23] However, some scholars have suggested that the close syntactical parallel between Christ's work in v. 34, ἐντυγχάνει ὑπὲρ ἡμῶν, "intercedes on our behalf," and the Spirit's work in v. 27, ἐντυγχάνει ὑπὲρ ἁγίων, "intercedes on behalf of the saints," implies that the intercessions are not just related, but that they are somehow similar in content or character.[24] For example Ulrich Wilckens claims, "the earthly [Spirit's intercession] *reflects* the

---

NICNT (Eerdmans, 1996), 541; John Murray, *The Epistle to the Romans*, NICNT (Eerdmans, 1968), 1:326–327.

22 For a similar judgment see: Brady, *Jesus Now*, 96–97, 142, 145; Bunyan, *Intercession* (Works 1:238); Charnock, *Intercession* (Works 5:129); Houston, *Intercession*, 83–84, 87–88; Murray, "Priestly Activity," 54–55; Symington, *Atonement and Intercession*, 276–277; Turretin, *Inst.* 14.15.8, 14 (2:424, 426).

23 Basil, *Spir.* 19.50, (SC 17:422); Brady, *Jesus Now*, 124–125, 165–166; Gregory Nazianzus, *Or.* 30.14, (SC 250:256); Houston, *Intercession*, 52, 147–158; Kuyper, *Holy Spirit*, 637–638; Moo, *Romans*, 527; Leon Morris, *The Epistle to the Romans*, PNTC (Eerdmans, 1988), 327; Murray, *Romans*, 1:311; Peter T. O'Brien, "Romans 8:26, 27: A Revolutionary Approach to Prayer?," *RTR* 46 (1987): 72; Hermann Olshausen, *The Epistle of St Paul to the Romans*, Biblical Commentary on the New Testament: Adapted Especially for Preachers and Students, trans. n. t. (T&T Clark, 1849), 297; Augustus Strong, *Theology*, 2:774; Symington, *Atonement and Intercession*, 292–293.

24 Murray, "Priestly Activity," 51; E. A. Obeng, "The Origins of the Spirit Intercession Motif in Romans 8:26," *New Testament Studies* 32, no. 4 (1986): 623; James E. Rosscup, "The Spirit's Intercession," *MSJ* 10, no. 1 (1999): 151; Ulrich Wilckens, *Der Brief an die Römer*, EKKNT 6 (Neukirchener Verlag, 1978), 161.

heavenly [intercession of Christ]."[25] Therefore, the exegesis in this chapter demonstrates that since the Spirit's work has both a salvific-forensic (legal adoption, Rom 8:14–16) and an active sanctifying-supplicatory aspect (Rom 8:26–27), then the linguistic parallel (Rom 8:27, 34) may imply that Christ's intercession has these features as well. Moreover, the study of the canonical context in this chapter reinforces the similarity of the intercessions implied in Rom 8 by demonstrating that Christ's intercession does have an active sanctifying-supplicatory aspect (Zech 3:1–2; John 17:17, 19; Heb 2:14–18; 4:14–16).

Just as scholars have seen a connection between the intercessions of the Son and the Spirit (Rom 8:26, 34) such that the intercession of the Spirit helps define the intercession of the Son, so also some scholars have seen a close connection between the relation of the *testimonium Spiritus sancti internum*, "inner testimony of the Holy Spirit" (Rom 8:14–16), to the Spirit's intercession (Rom 8:26–27) and others have even conflated them, such that the *testimonium* helps to define the Spirit's intercession.[26]

In Rom 8:14–16, the *testimonium internum* has both a past salvific-forensic and a present sanctifying-supplicatory aspect.[27] In v. 15, the "for" indicates that the Spirit's work is an example of the Spirit's "leading" in v. 14.[28] In the history of interpretation of the passage, whether the Spirit leads by working "on" or working "with/for" the believer has been a source of contention.[29] Up to the Reformation, the *testimonium internum* and the Spirit's intercession were viewed as a "working on" the believer, but in the modern period, these were

---

25 "*irdische Spiegelung dessen ... was der himmlische.*" Emphasis added. Wilckens, *Römer*, 161.

26 F. F. Bruce, *Romans*, rev. ed., TNTC 6 (Eerdmans, 1993), 158; Calvin, *Rom.* 8.26 (CR 77:157); James D. G. Dunn, *Romans 1–8*, WBC 38A (Word, 2002), 454; Luther, *In epistolam S. Pauli ad Galatas Commentarius ex praeclectione* [1531.] 1535 (WA 40:579, 581); Moo, *Romans*, 501–503; Geoffrey Smith, "The Function of 'Likewise' (Osautos) in Romans 8:26," *TynBul* 49, no. 1 (1998): 33–34.

27 For a similar judgment see: Aquinas, *Rom.* C.8 L.5.680, 226; Calvin, *Rom.* 8.14, 28 (CR 77:147, 158–159).

28 Moo, *Romans*, 498–499.

29 Adherents of the "working on" view include: Basil, *Spir.* 28.70, (SC 17:496, 498); Aquinas, *Rom* C.8 L.3.645; C8 L.5.693, 217, 229; Calvin, *Rom* 8.15, 26 (CR 77: 150, 157); Olshausen, *Romans*, 297. Adherents of the "working with/for" view include: Herman Bavinck, *Holy Spirit, Church, and New Creation*, vol. 4 of *Reformed Dogmatics*, ed. John Bolt, trans. John Vriend (Baker Academic, 2008), 219, 251; Donald G. Bloesch, *The Christian Life and Salvation* (Eerdmans, 1967), 247, 302; Bruce, *Romans*, 165; Dunn, *Romans 1–8*, 454, 476–478; Gregory Nazianzus *Or.* 31.12, (SC 250:296, 298, 300); Kuyper, *Holy Spirit*, 639; Rosscup, "Intercession," 149–153; Wilckens, *Römer*, 161; John A. Witmer, *Romans*, in *BKC*, ed. John F. Walvoord and Roy B. Zuck (Victor Books, 1985), 2:473. Some argue that the *testimonium* is "working on," but the intercession is "working with:" Moo, *Romans*, 504, 524; Morris, *Romans*, 317, 328; Murray, *Romans*, 1:297.

understood as a "working with/for" the believer.[30] The textual evidence best seems to support Luther's transitional interpretation that "the Spirit gives testimony first to our spirit within us, then also publicly to the world, so that we say."[31] Luther seems to be claiming that the Spirit "works on" the believer by testifying to them with the result that the Spirit "works with" the believer as the Spirit testifies with the believer to God and to the world.[32]

The following evidence seems to support Luther's interpretation. In Rom 8:15a, the aorist ἐλάβετε, "have received," seems to refer to the initial sending of the crying Spirit into the heart of the believer (Gal 4:6) as part of their adoption (Rom 8:15). In Rom 8:15b, the phrase ἐν ᾧ κράζομεν, "by whom we cry out," best seems to be taken as dative of agency describing the Spirit's present personal influence to cause the believer to cry out rather than the Spirit's use as an impersonal instrument, which the believer uses to cry out.[33] In Rom 8:16, while grammatically the "συν-" prefix on the present tense, συμμαρτυρεῖ, "testifying," allows for either an intensive ("really testifying") or a cooperative ("testifying with") sense, the use of eight other "συν-" terms in the immediate context (Rom 8:17, 22, 26, 28, 29) indicates that the prefix is functioning as "with" rather than as an intensifier.[34] From these observations, the picture in Rom 8:14–16 shows that the Spirit is "received" (Rom 8:15a) or sent into the believer's heart crying "Abba Father" (Gal 4:6), which causes the believer to "cry 'Abba Father'" (Rom 8:15b) along "with" the Spirit (Rom 8:16). Consequently, in Rom 8:15, the Spirit's past initial working on the believer is a salvific-forensic act as part of the believer's adoption.

Not only does the Spirit have a past salvific-forensic function (v. 15), but he also has a present sanctifying-non-forensic function (v. 16). In v. 16, since

---

30 Kuyper claims that "expositors of an earlier period judged with Calvin that the intercession of the Holy Spirit signified a working upon us." Kuyper, *Holy Spirit*, 636.

31 "*Spiritus testimonium reddit primum spiritui nostro intra nos, deinde etiam coram mundo, ut loquamur.*" Luther, *Borlesung über den 1. Brief des Johannes*. 1527 (WA 20:723).

32 *Ut* plus the subjunctive, *loquamur*, indicates a result clause or cause and effect. John F, Collins, *A Primer of Ecclesiastical Latin* (The Catholic University Press, 1985), 196–197.

33 Moo argues for the instrumental, but Murry argues for agency. It seems decisive that theologically the Spirit is a personal agent rather than an impersonal instrument and that in the immediate context even Moo recognizes that the Spirit is acting as an agent in "making alive," (v. 11), "helping," and "interceding," (v. 26). Moo, *Romans*, 502–503; Murray, *Romans*, 1:296.

34 Dunn, *Romans*, 454, 477; Morris, *Romans*, 317. There are at least nine "συν-" terms in the immediate context: συμμαρτυρεῖ, "to bear witness with" (v. 16), συγκληρονόμοι, "co-inheritor," συμπάσχομεν, "to suffer with," and συνδοξασθῶμεν, "to be glorified together" (v. 17), συστενάζει, "to groan together," and συνωδίνει, "to suffer together" (v. 22), συναντιλαμβάνεται, "to help" (v. 26), συνεργεῖ, "to work together" (v. 28), and συμμόρφους, "be conformed to" (v. 29). In all the instances except v. 22, the "συν-" terms indicate solidarity between people and God and in v. 22 the solidarity is between people and the creation, but the idea of solidarity is still highlighted. The idea of the solidarity is to give assurance to believers so that they may endure the suffering in the passage through the virtue of hope.

the Spirit is testifying with the believer through the cry or prayer, "Abba Father," then the content of the cry seems to indicate that the prayer is directed toward the Father.[35] However, the repetition of the word "children" serves to link v. 16 to v. 17 and the following argument in the passage (vv. 17–25), which indicates that the prayer is also intended to have a sanctifying impact on the believer praying it. The general thrust of the argument in vv. 17–25 is that in the face of the "the sufferings of the present time" (v. 18), believers are to manifest the virtue of endurance (Rom 8:25) and the traditional theological virtue of hope (Rom 8:20, 24–25). The implication of the key word link between the prayer that one is a child of God (v. 16) and the virtues that God's children are to manifest in the face of suffering (vv. 17–25) seems to be that the Spirit-empowered prayer provides an assurance that one is a child of God so that believers may endure and hope. This promotion of virtue on the part of the Spirit is a sanctifying-non-forensic work (1 Thess 3:12, 2 Thess 1:3; 1 Pet 1:13–16; 2 Pet 1:5–9).

Just as the prayer involved in the *testimonium internum* (Rom 8:14–16) involves the Spirit's leading and a sanctifying-non-forensic work, through the parallel indicted in the text, the Spirit's intercession also has these features (Rom 8:26–27). In Rom 8:26, Luther and Geoffrey Smith have argued that the word "likewise" connects the intercession to the *testimonium* so that the two actions have parallel characteristics.[36] The parallel established by the term "likewise" implies that just as the Spirit's "leading" (v. 14) prompts the believer's "cry" (v. 15), likewise the Spirit's "help" prompts the believer's prayer (v. 26) and just as the Spirit leads the believer by "testifying with" them (v. 16), likewise the Spirit "helps" the believer to pray by praying with them or interceding (vv. 26–27). Since the Spirit is helping believers (implied by "our" or inclusion of Paul in being helped) through his intercession in their prayers to deal with their "weakness" (v. 26), to know what to pray (v. 26), and to pray

---

35 Moo, *Romans*, 503–504.

36 Luther, *Gal* (WA 40:579, 581); Smith, "Likewise," 33–34. Luther conflates the two acts. Luther, *Gal* (WA 40:579, 581). Smith argues that (1) grammatically, "BDAG seems to treat [ὁμοίως] as a virtual synonym for ὡσαύτως" and "ὁμοίως functions to connect 1 Peter 3:1 to 2:18 in a comparative fashion [to Rom 8:16, 26], bridging a lengthy section of material in the process," (2) structurally, "Romans 8:16 and 8:26 share an obvious common syntactical structure: the same subject operates in relation to a compound verb, a dative substantive, and a first person plural possessive pronoun," and (3) conceptually, ὡσαύτως is "connecting two similar actions [carrying/testifying (v. 15–16) and intercession/groaning (v. 26)] to a single subject [the believer]." Smith, "Likewise," 33–34. Rosscup has objected primarily to Smith's grammatical and conceptual arguments but his objections are not persuasive; Rosscup, "Intercession," 141. Dunn argues for other linguistic links between the *testimonium* and intercession. Dunn, *Romans 1–8*, 454.

"according to the will of God" (v. 27), then the content of the help or aim of the intercession is a sanctifying-non-forensic act.[37]

Therefore, since the work of the Spirit has both a salvific-forensic and a present sanctifying-supplicatory/non-forensic aspect involving prayer in Rom (8:14–16, 26–27), then the parallel between Christ's work in v. 34, ἐντυγχάνει ὑπὲρ ἡμῶν, "intercedes on our behalf," and the Spirit's work in v. 27, ἐντυγχάνει ὑπὲρ ἁγίων, "intercedes on behalf of the saints," implies that Christ's work has not only a salvific-forensic aspect, but also a present sanctifying-supplicatory/non-forensic aspect (Rom 8:34). The study of the canonical context will confirm this implication. This parallel also implies that the Son and Spirit cooperate and this implication is treated in the section on virtue ethical Trinitarian sanctification.

Romans 8:27–28, 33: The Father and the Intercession

In Rom 8:27–28, 33, like the Son and the Spirit, the Father is also involved in a salvific-forensic work and a sanctifying-supplicatory work. In v. 33, the Father's salvific-forensic work is that of justifying the believer. In v. 27, based on a number of passages (1 Chr 28:9; 29:17; Ps 7:9; 139:1, 23; Jer 17:10) it is the Father and not the Son or the Spirit that is "the one searching the hearts."[38] On this reading of the phrase, the idea in v. 27 is that since the Father knows the believer's prayer, then believers have the assurance that their prayers will be answered. Furthermore, James E. Rosscup has claimed that the parallel between κατὰ θεόν, "according to God" (v. 27), and κατὰ πρόθεσιν, "according to his purpose" (v. 28), indicates that the Father and not the Spirit is the subject of v. 28 and is the one "working all things for good" as the response to the

---

37 Although Morris indicates that some might wish to take the "weakness" to be the sin nature from v. 3, with the implication that the intercession only deals with sin, others take the weakness to be the suffering of vv. 17–18 (Smith, Wilckens) or the specific inability to pray from v. 26 (Basil and Kuyper). However, the majority seem to take the weakness to include all of these suggestions and more by taking the weakness to be a reference to the general condition of humanity under sin in the present age (Aquinas, Harrison, Moo, Morris, Murray, Rosscup, Witmar). The implication of this broad and general reference is that the intercession has a wide range of application, including sanctification. Aquinas, *Rom* C.8 L.5.687–688, 227–228; Basil, *Spir.* 19.50 (SC 17:422); Everett F. Harrison, *Romans*, Vol. 10 of *EBC*, ed. Frank E. Gaebelein and J. D. Douglas (Zondervan, 1981), 95; Kuyper, *Holy Spirit*, 638; Moo, *Romans*, 523; Morris, *Romans*, 326; Murray, *Romans*, 1:311; Rosscup, "Intercession," 143–144; Smith, "Likewise," 37; Wilckens, *Römer*, 175; Witmar, *Romans*, 2:471–473.

38 Calvin, Dunn, Morris, and Rosscup also take the one searching to be the Father. Calvin, *Rom* 8.14, 28 (CR 77:147, 158–159); Dunn, *Romans 1–8*, 479; Morris, *Romans*, 329; Rosscup, "Intercession," 157–159. MacRae takes the one searching to be the Spirit. George MacRae, "A Note on Romans 8:26–27," *HTR* 73 (1980): 228–229.

believer's prayer which is according to God's will or purpose.[39] In this way, the Father is involved in a sanctifying-supplicatory work in vv. 27–28 by responding to the believer's prayer. In Rom 8:14–16, 26–28, 34, since the Father, Son, and Spirit are all involved in both a salvific-forensic work and a sanctifying-supplicatory work, then this implies that they are working together. This cooperative idea is further explored in the section dealing with virtue ethical Trinitarian sanctification after the canonical context is used to further define the Son's intercession.

The Canonical Context: Brief Consideration of Supplementary Intercession Passages

While the immediate context of Rom 8:34 emphasizes the salvific-forensic nature of Christ's intercession, like the wider context of Rom 8:14–16, 26–27, 28–33, the canonical context of Heb 2:14–18; 4:14–16; John 17:6–26, and Zech 3:1–2 highlights the Son's intercession as not only salvific-forensic, but also active and sanctifying-supplicatory. The following subsections examine the description of Christ's intercession in these other passages, and the next main section on "Jesus' Active Intercessory Sanctification" analyzes and summarizes the examination of these other passages.

Hebrews 2:14–18; 4:14–16

Whereas Heb 7:23–28; 9:23–28 focus on the salvific-forensic aspect of Jesus' heavenly intercession, the parallel passages of Heb 2:14–18; 4:14–16 imply a present, active, and sanctifying-supplicatory/non-forensic aspect to the intercession that is more explicit in John 17:17, 19. There is disagreement whether the explicit statement that Jesus sanctifies (Heb 2:11) is a reference to salvation generally (including progressive sanctification) or refers to positional sanctification only.[40] In Heb 2:14, both the "therefore" and the catchword link through the repetition of the phrase "the children" (vv. 13, 14) indicates that 2:14–18 is closely linked to and draws a conclusion from the preceding argu-

---

39 Rosscup, "Intercession," 149.

40 Peterson and Lane argue for positional sanctification, while Allen, Ellingworth, and Hughes argue for a general reference to the whole of salvation, which includes a progressive idea. Allen, *Hebrews*, 216; Paul Ellingworth, *The Epistle to the Hebrews: A Commentary on the Greek Text*, NIGTC (Eerdmans, 1993), 163–164; Philip Edgcumbe Hughes, *A Commentary on the Epistle to the Hebrews*, rep. ed. (Eerdmans, 1977), 103; William L. Lane, *Hebrews 1–8*, WBC (Word, 2002), 58; David G. Peterson, *Possessed by God: A New Testament Theology of Sanctification and Holiness*, NSBT 1 (InterVarsity, 1995), 35.

ment, which provides content for the type of sanctification in 2:11.[41] Since some later passages in Hebrews refer to positional sanctification (Heb 10:10, 14; 13:12) and, as is being argued, Heb 2:14–18; 4:14–16 refer to progressive sanctification, then sanctification in 2:11 encompasses all of salvation, including both positional and progressive sanctification.

In Heb 2:18; 4:15–16, the idea of Jesus' currently helping in his high priestly role those who are presently being tempted, presumably to resist temptation, indicates a sanctification issue of separating from sin and vice unto virtue (the implied incipient theological virtue of endurance) rather than a salvific-forensic issue of forgiving sin.[42] Despite the reference to the atonement (propitiation) in Heb 2:17, Heb 2:18b refers to sanctification rather than forgiveness of sin (atonement) for at least three reasons. First, Heb 2:15 indicates that not all the purposes of Jesus' death listed in the context are salvific-forensic. The constructions "ἵνα ... καὶ" [so that ... and] (2:14–15), the "ὅθεν ... ἵνα ... καὶ" [therefore ... so that ... and] (v. 17), γάρ, "for" (v. 18), indicate five purposes for or consequences of Jesus' incarnation and death.[43] Since the purpose or result of being released from the fear of death (2:15) has to do with the sanctification idea of having hope after death and since the sanctifying idea of 2:15 stands alongside the salvific purpose of making propitiation or atoning for sins in 2:17, then despite the close connection of 2:17–18, 2:18 may contain a sanctifying-non-forensic idea like 2:15 does.

Second, the temptation of believers in 2:18b is paralleled with the temptation of Christ in 2:18a and since Christ resisted temptation rather than giving into it (as in the parallel passage in Heb 4:15), then this suggests that Christ's help in 2:18b is for believers to resist temptation rather than merely to forgive them when giving into it.[44] Furthermore, in Heb 12:4, as consistent with the rest of the teaching of Scripture with regard to temptation (James 4:7–8), the challenge for the readers to struggle and resist sin rather than merely to be forgiven for giving into it suggests that Jesus is providing aid in this struggle in Heb 2:18; 4:16.

Third, in the parallel passage in Heb 4:14–16, the trial or temptation for which help is being provided (2:18; 4:16) seems to be "holding onto the confession [of faith]" (4:14) or resisting apostasy (denying the faith).[45] If the apos-

---

41 Allen, *Hebrews*, 218; Ellingworth, *Hebrews*, 170–171; Lane, *Hebrews 1–8*, 60.

42 For a similar judgment see: Symington, *Atonement and Intercession*, 277–278.

43 Allen, *Hebrews*, 219, 223; F. F. Bruce, *The Epistle to the Hebrews*, rev. ed., NICNT (Eerdmans, 1990); 85, 88; Ellingworth, *Hebrews*, 170, 174, 190; Lane, *Hebrews 1–8*, 60–61, 64–65.

44 O'Brien, *Hebrews*, 123.

45 Allen claims, "Historically, the most common purpose advocated [for the writing of Heb] suggests the author is attempting to dissuade his Jewish Christian readers from a relapse into Judaism brought on by increasing persecution and a desire for the stability of the old

tasy became permanent as the passages seem to imply is the danger (whether hypothetical or real is debated), then this would be an unforgivable sin and so Christ's help would be toward avoiding this situation. The help that Christ provides in "holding onto the confession [of faith]" (4:14), in resisting apostasy or persevering is presumably the empowerment to manifest or an arrangement of the circumstances to facilitate the practice of the incipient theological virtue of endurance.[46] The manipulation of circumstances or spiritual empowerment is in view as indicated by the word βοηθῆσαι, "help" (Heb 2:18; 4:16). The word βοηθῆσαι, "help," in the Septuagint (Greek translation of the OT) refers to the provision of external aid and the external sense of the help conjures the image of the circumstantial "way out" of temptation provided by God in 1 Cor 10:13.[47] However, the help may refer metaphorically to internal spiritual empowering provided by the Spirit (Phil 2:13). For example, in Luke 22:31–32, Jesus prays for a need that Peter does not even know he has, that his faith may not fail.[48] Regardless of the nature of the help Jesus' provides through his intercession, the term συμπαθῆσαι, "sympathize," as noted by Lane, "extends beyond the sharing of feelings (i.e., compassion). It always includes the element of *active* help."[49] If Jesus' active intercessory help to manifest the incipient theological virtue of endurance is in view in Heb 2:14–18; 4:14–16, then this is similar to the emphasis in Rom 8:12–32 of manifesting endurance (Rom 8:25) and the traditional theological virtue of hope (Rom 8:20, 24–25).

In light of the point concerning endurance, someone might object that it is perseverance rather than sanctification that is involved in Heb 2:17–18 and 4:14–16. In response, not only is "holding on to the confession [of faith]" (Heb 4:14) or perseverance in view in the context, but so is resisting temptation generally (2:18), which is an issue of sanctification. Much like in Rom 8:26, there is some scholarly agreement that the plural ἀσθενείαις, "weaknesses" (Heb 4:15), refers to the whole range of human frailties (physical, moral, social, etc.) with which people need help and not just the inability to save

---

faith." Allen, *Hebrews*, 79; Bruce, *Hebrews*, 89, 115. On the discussion whether πεπειρασμένον should be translated or understood as "trial," "temptation," or both, see: Allen, *Hebrews*, 308.

46 For a similar judgment see: Bruce, *Hebrews*, 115; Lane, *Hebrews 1–8*, 189.
47 Allen, *Hebrews*, 226; Ellingworth, *Hebrews*, 191–192.
48 For a similar judgment see: Berkhof, *Theology*, 403.
49 Lane, *Hebrews 1–8*, 114. Emphasis added. Songer argues that against the socio-religious background of the first century and the context of Heb 2, 4 that "help" should be understood in a broad and comprehensive sense of "any act of a king which revealed his favor." Harold S. Songer, "A Superior Priesthood: Hebrews 4:14–7:27," *RevExp* 82, no. 3 (1985): 345–347. Allen, *Hebrews*, 304; Ellingworth, *Hebrews*, 268.

themselves.⁵⁰ On this interpretation of "weaknesses," the help that Jesus' intercession provides is widened beyond the present dilemma of the need to persevere in the face of the temptation to apostatize, but also includes all sorts of physical and moral failings with which one may need help to resist. Consequently, Jesus' intercession is depicted as being for non-forensic sanctification and not only perseverance and forensic salvation.

Furthermore, there is a close if not a reciprocal relationship between perseverance and sanctification in general and particularly in these two parallel passages.⁵¹ Even if the general idea of temptation (Heb 2:18) is restricted to falling away from the faith (Heb 4:14), then sanctification is still in view because by definition if one endures in "holding on to the confession [of faith]" (Heb 4:14) in the face of trials or temptations, then one has been sanctified by manifesting the virtue of endurance (Rom 5:3–5; James 1:2–4; 1 Pet 1:13–16; 2 Pet 1:5–8). Therefore, the parallel passages of Heb 2:14–18; 4:14–16 imply a present, active, and sanctifying aspect to the intercession that is more explicit in John 17:17, 19.

John 17:17, 19

John 17:6–26 indicates that Jesus is presently and actively sanctifying believers. John 17:6–26 is an intercession passage because by definition the term ἐντυγχάνω, "to intercede" (Rom 8:34; Heb 7:25), means to *"plead for someone ... can be rendered pray"* and since in John 17:9, 20 Jesus prays to the Father on behalf of his disciples and all believers, then by definition Jesus is interceding for them.⁵² Despite the fact that John 17:6–26 is describing Jesus' earthly intercession, most writers on the heavenly intercession accept as a hermeneutic principle the idea that there is some continuity between the earthly and heavenly intercessions.⁵³ The difference between the passive presence and *vocalis et realis* views is that the passive presence sees more discontinuity such that the heavenly intercession only has the substance but not the form of the earthly prayer, while the *vocalis et realis* view sees the two intercessions as having such a high degree of continuity that they are nearly the same, except that the manner of the heavenly prayer is more dignified as fitting Jesus' ex-

---

50 Alen, *Hebrews*, 304; Ellingworth, *Hebrews*, 268.
51 For a similar judgment see: Symington, *Atonement and Intercession*, 278–283.
52 Emphasis original. BDAG, s.v. "ἐντυγχάνω."
53 Berkhof, *Theology*, 403; Brady, *Jesus Now*, 142, 145; Charnock, *Intercession*, Works 5:92, 98, 107–109, 119, 122, 130, 134, 140; Crump, *Intercessor*, 14; Houston, *Intercession*, 51, 79, 196; Murray, "Priestly Activity," 49, 53–54; Swete, *Ascended Christ*, 95–97; Symington, *Atonement and Intercession*, 261–262.

alted state. If as Symington argues, Jesus' heavenly intercession only consists of the symbol of Christ's presence "intimating" or implying requests, then Jesus' heavenly intercession is passive, but if it is *vocalis et realis* as described by Mueller or Brady's "effective speaking" or John Owen's communication without words, then Jesus' heavenly intercession is active.[54]

In John 17:17, 19, Jesus explicitly prays for the sanctification of his disciples and all believers. W. Coberly and D. G. Peterson have convincingly argued that the sanctification for which Jesus prays in John 17:17, 19 is positional rather than progressive sanctification.[55] Their strongest argument is the one supported by the commentary tradition that since the sanctification of Jesus is the same as that of the disciples in v. 19 and since Jesus as the holy God cannot be progressively sanctified in v. 19, then the sanctification of both Jesus and the disciples (vv. 17, 19) is the positional dedication or consecration for the mission of preaching the gospel in v. 18.[56] However, both Coberly and Peterson heavily base their argument on the highly controversial claim that the expressions ἐν (τῇ) ἀληθείᾳ (vv. 17, 19) should be taken as locatives, "in the truth" (sanctification into the sphere of a status), rather than as instrumentals "by the truth" (sanctification by means of the Word as truth).[57] Although reliable sources take both sides in the debate over the meaning of the preposition ἐν in John 17:17, 19, it seems decisive in favor of the instrumental meaning that a parallel idea occurs through the preposition, "διά," in John 17:20 and Rom 10:17, both of which indicate that the Word is "the immediate means

---

54 Brady, *Jesus Now*, 141; Mueller, *Dogmatics*, 313–314; Owen, *Hebrews*, Works 22:540–541; Symington, *Atonement and Intercession*, 266–267. Owen claims, "It must be granted that there is no need of the *use of words* in the immediate presence of God." Empahsis original.

55 William G. Coberly, "An Exegetical Argument for the Position-Only View of Sanctification" (M.T. thesis, The Master's Seminary, 2004), 41–44; Peterson, *Possessed by God*, 30–32.

56 George R. Beasley-Murray, *John*, 2nd ed., WBC (Word, 2002), 301; Gerald L. Borchert, *John 1–11*, NAC (B&H, 1996), 203; D. A. Carson, *The Gospel According to John*, PNTC (Eerdmans, 1991), 567; Coberly, "Position-Only," 44; Andrew T. Lincoln, *The Gospel According to Saint John*, BNTC (Continuum, 2005), 438; Peterson, *Possessed by God*, 30; Rodney A. Whitacre, *John*, IVPNTC (InterVarsity, 1999), 414.

57 Coberly, "Position-Only," 41–42; Peterson, *Possessed by God*, 31. That the exegetical decision is controversial, but weighted in favor of the instrumental, is indicated by the fact that Beasley-Murray, Schnackenburg , and Whitacre argue for the locative, Luther, Calvin, Carson, Gangel, and Harris argue for the instrumental, and Borchert argues for both. Beasley-Murray, *John*, 300; Borchert, *John 1–11*, 197; John Calvin, *Commentary on the Gospel According to John*, trans. William Pringle, CC 2 (Logos Bible Software, 2010), 179; Carson, *John*, 566; Kenneth O. Gangel, *John*, HNTC 4 (B&H, 2000), 324; Murray Harris, *Prepositions and Theology in the Greek New Testament: An Essential Reference Resource for Exegesis* (Zondervan, 2012), 133–134; Martin Luther, *Word and Sacrament II* (*LW* 36:245); Rudolf Schnackenburg, *The Gospel According to St. John*, NTSR 3 (Crossroad, 1982), 185; Whitacre, *John*, 414.

[instrument] or cause of justification or salvation."⁵⁸ If Jesus prays for the positional sanctification of believers by the instrument of the Word (Gospel) in John 17:17, 19, then by the hermeneutic principle of the continuity between the earthly and heavenly intercession, Jesus' active progressive sanctification of believers by means of the Word in Eph 5:29 (as argued in chapter 4) would refer to Jesus' heavenly intercession. If ἐν in John 17:17, 19 is instrumental then this strengthens the parallel between John 17:17, 19 and Eph 5:29, but if it is not, then Eph 5:29 still indicates present, active, and progressive sanctification by the instrument of the Word and may be understood as the heavenly parallel to the earthly intercession in John 17:17, 19. Furthermore, even if Eph 5:29 does not refer to progressive sanctification, then the fact that Jesus explicitly prays for positional sanctification in John 17:17, 19 still implies that he prays for progressive sanctification in heaven.⁵⁹ Therefore, John 17:6–26 indicates that Jesus is presently and actively sanctifying believers.

Zechariah 3:1–2

In Zech 3:1–2, there is evidence that Jesus' intercession may be *vocalis et realis* or at least involve actual active communication beyond silent intimations or implications resulting from the symbol of his passive presence. Symington, who seems to prefer the passive presence position, cites Zech 3:1 as a parallel passage to 1 John 2:1 (also parallel to Rom 8:34), which he uses as evidence of the advocacy function of the intercession as defending against the accusations of Satan against daily sins.⁶⁰ In Zech 3:1–2, the high priest Joshua stands before the angel of the Lord while Satan accuses him (v. 1) and the Lord or the angel defends Joshua (v. 2). If "the angel of the Lord" in v. 1 is a Christophany (pre-incarnate appearance of Christ) and is identified as the speaker, "The Lord," in v. 2, then these verses represent a pre-incarnate Christ verbally de-

---

58 Henry Alford, *Alford's Greek Testament: An Exegetical and Critical Commentary* (Logos Bible Software, 2010), 2:422; Harris, *Prepositions Greek*, 112–113; R. C. H. Lenski, *The Interpretation of St. Paul's Epistle to the Romans* (Lutheran Book Concern, 1936), 667; Robert A. Mounce, *Romans*, NAC (B&H, 1995), 212. Although Rom 10:17 has ῥῆμα, "word," instead of λόγος, "word" (John 17:17, 19, 20), the difference seems insignificant in this case as both refer to the Gospel message.
59 For a similar judgment see: Gustaf Aulén, *Eucharist and Sacrifice* (Muhlenberg, 1958), 153–154; Brady, *Jesus Now*, 96–97, 168; Charnock, *Intercession* (Works 5:122, 131–133, 136, 143); Houston, *Intercession*, 51, 83, 92–93, 97–98, 205, 210–213; Symington, *Atonement and Intercession*, 272–273, 277–280, 282.
60 Symington, *Atonement and Intercession*, 276–277. Symington has a long qualification stating that he is not endorsing any position, but he seems to prefer the passive presence view.

fending his people against Satan before the throne of God.[61] The implication would be that if Christ defended his people verbally before the incarnation, then it is likely that he does the same thing afterward through the intercession during his exaltation. Even if the angel of the Lord in v. 1 is not a Christophany, then the implication would still seem to hold. For if the angel of the Lord defends God's people verbally before God, then Christ would seem to do no less in his intercession. If the angel of the Lord in v. 1 is not identified as the speaker in v. 2, then the verses would still seem to imply that like God, Christ defends his people in heaven. Therefore, Zech 3:1–2 indicates that Jesus' intercession may be *vocalis et realis* or at least involve some type of actual active communication beyond silent intimations or implications resulting from the symbol of his passive presence.

JESUS' ACTIVE INTERCESSORY SANCTIFICATION

The standard intercession passages taken as a whole indicate that Jesus' priestly intercession is not only his passive salvific-forensic presence, but also his active supplication, which is aimed at manifesting virtue in believers through a process of Trinitarian progressive sanctification. On the one hand, Rom 8:34, Heb 7:23–28; 9:23–28, and 1 John 2:1–2 offer the best support for the passive salvific-forensic presence view that Jesus' presence in heaven is a symbol or memorial of his propitiation, which serves as his intercession to forgive daily and other sins and to defend against Satan's accusations. On the other hand, Zech 3:1–2; Luke 22:31–32, John 17:6–26, Rom 8:14–16, 26–27, 34, and Heb 2:14–18; 4:14–16 offer the best support for the *vocalis et realis* view that Jesus' intercession consists of his actively offering supplications, which are aimed not only at perseverance and resisting temptation, but also manifesting virtue (faith, endurance, hope) in believers through a process of Trin-

---

61 Calvin and Lindsey interpret the verse in this manner, concurring Chambers says that most commentators give this interpretation, and Klein merely notes that this is the traditional interpretation of most of the angel of the Lord passages. Going beyond these, Clark and Hatton provide the rationale that since Joshua and Satan are standing before the angel (vv. 1, 3) and the angel is named explicitly as the one who speaks throughout the passage, then the angel must be speaking in v. 2. Representing the dissenting position of critical interpretation, Smith takes the speaker in v. 2 to be God rather than the angel, although he allows that the angel may be identical to God in other passages. John Calvin, *Commentaries on the Twelve Minor Prophets*, trans., John Owen, Calvin's Commentaries (Logos Bible Software, 2010), 5:83; Talbot W. Chambers, *The Book of Zechariah*, ed. John Peter Lange, trans., Philip Schaff, A Commentary on the Holy Scriptures (Logos Bible Software, 2008), 36; David J. Clark and Howard A. Hatton, *A Handbook on Zechariah*, UBS Handbook Series (United Bible Societies, 2002), 119–120; George L. Klein, *Zechariah*, NAC (B&H, 2008), 99–100; F. Duane Lindsey, *Zechariah*, in *BKC*, ed. John F. Walvoord and Roy B. Zuck (Victor Books, 1985), 1:1554; Ralph L. Smith, *Micah-Malachi*, WBC (Word, 1998), 189, 198, 275, 328.

itarian progressive sanctification. Even if the supplication in these *vocalis et realis* passages is taken metaphorically so that it refers not to actual speech but merely some sort of active communication, then both views would agree that Jesus' intercession is active and sanctifying as is claimed by this book. The Trinitarian nature of the intercession is most apparent in Rom 8.

Of the many actual and possible objections to Jesus' intercession as active supplication, which includes sanctification, two seem the most important.[62] First, the phrase "sitting at the right hand" to describe the session might be taken by some as implying inactivity or passivity. However, the standard response to this objection seems to be that "sitting" is a metaphor, which points to Christ's exalted position of honor and authority rather than indicating inactivity.[63] Second, the passive presence view objects that if the supplication of the ascended Christ is active (verbal) prayer as in the incarnation, then this mode of intercession is inconsistent with Jesus' exalted status in the session.[64] In response, the mediating view presented in this book that Jesus' supplication is *agilis et realis*, "active and real," communication and not necessarily *vocalis*, is an application of the metaphor view to the *vocalis et realis* view. This results in a description that respects both Jesus' exalted divine and human natures in that he still actively asks through actual communication as a man and that his asking is not necessarily with words as God, but neither is it merely the implication of a passive symbol.[65] Moreover, if Jesus' intercession is depicted as *agilis et realis*, then this description avoids the misunderstanding of the presence view that Jesus is passive, which proponents of that view acknowledge and wish to avoid. Therefore, Jesus' priestly intercession is not only his passive salvific-forensic presence, but also his active supplication aimed at manifesting virtue in believers through a process of Trinitarian progressive sanctification.

---

62 Among others who field objections to Christ's intercession, Mauchline deals with some intriguing and important issues. Mauchline, "Intercessor," 359–360.

63 Brady, *Jesus Now*, 61–63, 66 67, 70–71; John Calvin, *Inst.* 2.16.15 (CR 30:383); Hay, *Right Hand*, 160; Tait, *Heavenly Session*, 4–8; 23–24.

64 Calvin, *Rom* 8:34 (CR 77:165); Gregory Nazianzus *Or.* 30.14, (SC 250:256); Murray, "Priestly Activity," 51–52; Swete, *Ascended Christ*, 95–96; Tait, *Heavenly Session*, 163–164; Turretin, *Inst.* 14.15.13 (2:425).

65 If the Son's intercession in Scripture is taken as figurative supplication rather than literal vocal words, then the Bible does not seem to give a description of how the intercession actually takes place or its mode, but it does affirm through the metaphor of prayer that actual active communication is occurring.

Statement of Virtue Ethical Trinitarian Sanctification Ordered by the Triune Premise

As possibly the only intercession passage where all three persons of the Trinity explicitly interact with each other, Rom 8:14–34 connects the intercession of the Son to the work of the Spirit and the Father. In this section, a theological synthesis is drawn, based on the previous historical investigation of the intercession and exegetical analysis of the wider and canonical contexts of Rom 8:14–34, which indicates that the Son works in Trinitarian cooperation according to the Triune premise with the works of the Spirit and the Father in both salvific-forensic and sanctifying-supplicatory acts.

In the salvific-forensic act, the Son's work is to intercede by providing the basis for justification through his death (Rom 8:34), the Father's work is to send the Son (Rom 8:32) in order to justify on the basis of the Son's work (Rom 8:33), and the Spirit's work is to testify to the Father and Son's work (Rom 8:15–16). According to the Triune premise, the salvific-forensic aspect of the intercession works such that justification from sin is *from* the Father's sending the Son (Rom 8:32–33), *through* the Son's work on the cross which is presented by his intercessory presence in heaven (Rom 8:34; Heb 7:23–28; 9:23–28; 1 John 2:1–2), and *by* the Spirit's testifying of the Son's work to believers (Rom 8:14–16).

In the sanctifying-supplicatory act, the Spirit's work is to initiate and lead the submitting believer's prayer into the revealed will of God in the Word by the example of his own intercessory prayer with the believer (Rom 8:7, 14–16, 26–27; John 15:26; 16:13), the Son's work is to complement the Spirit's leading with omniscient intercessory prayer, not to make the believer's prayer pleasing to God (John 16:26–27) but to meet needs that believers are not aware of in their finite creaturely condition (Rom 8:34; Luke 22:31–32), and the Father's work is to answer the prayer (Rom 8:27–28).[66] The sanctifying-supplicatory act works according to the reversed Triune premise (Eph 2:18) such that believers are led *by* the Spirit's intercession into prayer (Rom 8:14–16, 26–27), to be helped *through* the Son's intercession (Rom 8:34), in order to receive an answer *from* the Father (Rom 8:27–28).[67]

---

66 Historically, John 16:26–27 has been seen as problematic for the idea of the Son's intercession or even as a potential contradiction in Scripture that threatens inerrancy. A harmonization which seeks to solve the problem and defend inerrancy is included in Appendix 6. Brady, *Jesus Now*, 141, 213–214; Charnock, *Intercession* (Works 5:125); Hay, *Right Hand*, 131; Murray, "Priestly Activity," 51–53, 57.

67 For a similar judgment see: Houston, *Intercession*, 144–146, 152; Robert Letham, *The Holy Trinity: In Scripture, History, Theology, and Worship* (P&R, 2004), 68; Swete, *Ascended Christ*, 100; Symington, *Atonement and Intercession*, 274; James B. Torrance, *Worship, Communi-*

In the context of Rom 8 and other intercession passages, the purpose of each work of the Trinitarian salvific-forensic and sanctifying-supplicatory acts is to provide assurance of salvation in the face of present suffering (Rom 8:18; Heb 2:14–18; 4:14–16) in order to sanctify believers progressively by conforming them generally to the image of Christ's character (Rom 8:29) and specifically by manifesting the Son's virtue of "hope through patient-enduring" (Rom 8:20, 24–25).[68]

APPLICATION: THE BELIEVER'S EXPERIENCE OF PRAYER ("FATHER PRIMARILY" PRAYER)

In Rom 8, where the believer's prayer is directed to the Father with the help of the Son and the Spirit, the application of the Trinity's sanctifying work through prayer to the believer's experience of prayer is complicated by a debate over which Trinitarian person is the proper object of prayer, the Father alone (the "Father only" view) or all three persons of the Trinity ("all three" view).[69] Much of this debate might be summarized by noting that while there are some special cases where prayer is offered to the Son (Acts 7:59–60; 1 Cor 16:22; 2 Cor 12:8–9; Rev 22:20)[70] and it is biblically consistent to pray to the

---

ty, and the Triune God of Grace (InterVarsity, 1996), 32; Scott Sparling Wilson, "Trinity and Sanctification: A Proposal for Understanding the Doctrine of Sanctification According to a Triune Ordering" (PhD. diss., Southeastern Baptist Theological Seminary, 2009), 46–47, 214.

68 For a similar judgment see: Lane, *Hebrews 1–8*, 189; Moo, *Romans*, 523; Morris, *Romans*, 326; Murray, "Priestly Activity," 55; Murray, *Romans*, 1:310–311, 329; Owen, *Hebrews*, Works 22:538–539; Tait, *Heavenly Session*, 12, 230–231, 234.

69 The division of the debate into two positions with the terms "Father only" view and "all three" view are taken from: Millard J. Erickson, *Making Sense of the Trinity: Three Crucial Questions* (Baker Academic, 2000), ch. 3. No one seems to argue for prayer to the Trinity or the Godhead as a whole or a synthesized unitary collective, as this position seems tantamount to making the Godhead a fourth hypostasis and results in the error of a "quatrinity/quadtrinity." On the general danger of creating a fourth hypostasis in one's interpretation of the Trinity see: Karl Barth, *CD* 1.1:365; Friedrich Schleiermacher, *The Christian Faith*, ed. H. R. Mackintosh; and J. S. Stewart, 1st Paperback ed. (T&T Clark, 1999), 744. On the use of the term "Quad-Trinity" in this regard see: John W. Wright, ed. *Postliberal Theology and the Church Catholic: Conversations with George Lindbeck, David Burrell, and Stanley Hauerwas* (Baker Academic, 2012), 59. Although Erickson speaks of prayer "directed to the Trinity as a whole," he seems to mean by this all three persons simultaneously rather than a collective or the Godhead. Erickson, *Trinity*, 838, cf. 843.

70 Erickson, *Trinity*, 846–853; J. I. Packer, *Keep in Step with the Spirit* (F. H. Revell, 1984), 261. Cole, who mentions some of these passages, may represent a mediating view, but he does emphasize prayer to the Father in his conclusion. Graham A. Cole, *Engaging with the Holy Spirit: Real Questions, Practical Answers* (Crossway, 2007), ch. 3. Although Torrance does not seem to cite the relevant passages, he explicitly argues for the all three position. Torrance, *Triune God*, 36. While not dealing with the details of the debate, Wilson seems to speak favorably of Erickson's view and so may support the all three view. Wilson, "Trinity and Sanctification," 3.

Spirit (some appeal to 1 Cor 6:19–20; Phil 3:3) since he is God (Acts 5:3–4),[71] the emphasis of Scripture is on directing prayer to the Father (Matt 6:6, 9; 26:39; Mark 14:35; Luke 11:2, 5–13; John 17:1; James 1:17; Rom 8:26–34; Eph 2:18; 3:14–19).[72]

Someone may object to both the Father only and all three views that believers may pray without having any of the persons of the Trinity in view by generically praying to "God." In response, while it may be acceptable for believers to pray generically to an undifferentiated "God," and since contemporary believers also live in a pluralistic culture and maintain allegiance to a specific God (a Trinitarian God), then it may be appropriate and beneficial for them to follow the example of the OT believers and explicitly identify the God to whom they are praying in a Christian, biblical, and implicitly Trinitarian manner as Father.[73]

---

71 Charles W. Lowry, *The Trinity and Christian Devotion* (Eyre and Spottiswoode, 1946), 122–123; Erickson, *Trinity*, 857–883.

72 Fred Sanders, *The Deep Things of God: How the Trinity Changes Everything* (Crossway, 2010), 211–214, 224–225; Bruce A. Ware, *Father, Son, and Holy Spirit: Relationships, Roles, and Relevance* (Crossway, 2005), ch. 1, 3, 5, 6; Arthur William Wainwright, *The Trinity in the New Testament* (S.P.C.K., 1962), 97; Geoffrey Wainwright, *Doxology: The Praise of God in Worship, Doctrine, and Life: A Systematic Theology* (Oxford University Press, 1980), 62, 94. Both the Father only and all three views seem to agree that Ephesians 2:18 contains a reversed ordering of the Triune premise by which prayer is "through him [the Son] ... to the Father by one Spirit" or *by* the Spirit, *through* the Son *to* the Father. However, as was argued in chapter 2 of this book and as the biblical evidence for prayer to the Son indicates, the Triune premise cannot and should not be rigidly applied so as to exclude prayer to all three persons of the Trinity. While not specifically addressing Ephesians 2:18, Erickson seems to acknowledge the validity of the Triune premise but disputes its rigid application. Erickson, *Trinity*, 884–886. Cessario, who does not appear to be taking a position on the object of prayer, notes that this reverse understanding of the Triune premise with respect to prayer is "commonplace" in contemporary thought. Romanus Cessario, "The Trinitarian Imprint on the Moral Life," in *The Oxford Handbook of the Trinity*, ed. Gilles Emery and Matthew Levering (Oxford University Press, 2011), 489. Bradshaw argues that the use of the Triune premise in worship was not as widespread so early in church history as many claim and that its ubiquitous use as a liturgial structuring principle was much later. However, the argument in Eph 2:18 is not regarding the church's actual historical practice, but rather what should be normative for the church's practice. Paul Bradshaw, "God, Christ, and the Holy Spirit in Early Christian Praying," in *The Place of Christ in Liturgical Prayer: Trinity, Christology, and Liturgical Theology* ed. Bryan D. Spinks (Liturgical Press, 2008), 51, 61–62. Therefore, Father only proponents are correct that the Triune premise does indicate the "standard" form, "pattern," or "paradigm" of Christian prayer, but the all three view is correct that the premise does not exclude prayer to the Son and Spirit. Erickson, *Trinity*, 884–886; Leonard Hodgson, *The Doctrine of the Trinity: Croall Lectures, 1942–1943* (C. Scribner's Sons, 1944), 232; Sanders, *Deep Things*, 224; Ware, *Father, Son, and Holy Spirit*, ch. 6.8–9. For a potentially mediating view see: Houston, *Intercession*, 281–284.

73 In the syncretistic culture of the OT, it seems that believers prayed by using some specific name of God such as his covenant names or names which identified him as the God of Israel (Gen 24:12; 32:9; Judg 13:8; 16:28; 1 Kgs 8:28; 18:36; 2 Kgs 6:17; 19:15; Ezra 9:6; Ps 69:13; Dan 9:4; Jonah 4:2). Cole argues that when Christians pray with the generic address, "God," then

Therefore, since the emphasis of Scripture is on directing prayer to the Father (Matt 6:6, 9; 26:39; Mark 14:35; Luke 11:2, 5–13; John 17:1; James 1:17; Rom 8:26–34; Eph 2:18; 3:14–19), then this emphasis means that the majority of the believer's experience of prayer will be prayer directed to the Father.[74]

There are at least three benefits to Trinitarian oriented, Father-primarily directed prayer. First, in Rom 8, believers may be assured, be encouraged, and have faith to pray because of the intercessory activity of both the Son (Rom 8:34) and the Spirit (Rom 8:26), and that the Trinity is working not only so their prayers will be answered, but that they will be effective by being in conformity with the Father's will (Rom 8:27; 1 John 5:14–15).[75] If believers pray to their intercessors, then no one is left to mediate for them, but if they have faith that the Father is favorably disposed to them because of the Son's death (Eph 2:16–18) and that both the Son and the Spirit are helping their prayers be effective, then believers may "approach with confidence the throne of grace" in prayer (Heb 4:16; 10:19–22). Second, Fred Sanders points out that the Spirit's leading means that "the Trinitarian dynamic of Christian prayer ...takes the pressure off us to make prayer happen" so that believers do not need to work "up the right response in prayer or worship" to the Father.[76] Believers striving to be sensitive to the Spirit will pray when and as the Spirit leads. If believers are busy praying to the Spirit rather than the Father, then they may be less aware of the Spirit's leading in and into prayer. Third, Sanders also argues that praying to the Father implies the Father-son relationship involved in the adoption of believers (Eph 1:5), which is "a reminder of our privilege and our need at the same time."[77] Building on Sanders' insight, when believers address the Father in prayer, that address points them to all that the Father-child relationship of adoption entails such as: intimacy, the security felt by children seeking to have their needs met by a caring parent, an attitude of submission and a corresponding expectation on the part of the children of potential discipline and correction from the parent as well as aid, etc.[78] Certainly there

---

they not only lose the uniqueness of Christianity in a pluralistic culture, but they also become functional Unitarians. Cole, *Holy Spirit*, ch. 3.

74 For a similar judgment see: Cole, *Holy Spirit*, ch. 3; Houston, *Intercession*, 284; Packer, *Keep in Step*, 261; Sanders, *Deep Things*, 224–225. There may be some special circumstances in which it is appropriate to direct prayers to the Son (such as praying for his return, 1 Cor 16:22; Rev 22:20) or the Spirit (such as asking for help in prayer, Rom 8:26), but this is not the norm.

75 For a similar judgment see: Brady, *Jesus Now*, 160, 195–196; Bunyan, *Intercession* (Works 1:239); Houston, *Intercession*, 261–262, 270.

76 Sanders, *Deep Things*, 215.

77 Ibid., 216–220.

78 In the contemporary culture of broken homes, abuse, and other family tragedies, many may not be able to relate positively to the healthy relationship between a parent and child and particularly between a father and child. However, many may have a positive father or parental

may be benefits to Trinitarian oriented prayer that primarily addresses the Father other than those listed in this section.

Conclusion

Therefore, virtue ethics is key to understanding Trinitarian progressive sanctification because Jesus' present and active priestly role of heavenly intercession aimed at manifesting virtue in believers is crucial to understanding how the Trinity progressively sanctifies believers. Although the intercession is not the whole of Jesus' heavenly session nor is the intercession all about sanctification, neither is it wholly about the forgiveness of sins as the passive presence view may tend to imply. Furthermore, the full witness of Scripture concerning the intercession, in conjunction with Rom 8, indicates that the priestly intercession of Christ in heaven is not only active, but it is also part of a Trinitarian work of sanctification aimed at manifesting virtue in believers and particularly the virtues of faith, hope, and endurance. It is invaluable for believers' motivation to pray to recognize that the entire Trinity is working with them for their sanctification in their prayers so that their faith may be assured and so that they may be able to endure patiently with hope in the face of the present sufferings of this life. In this light, prayer is not just for getting an answer, but it is also about building character. Finally, while prayer to the Son and/or the Spirit may not be theologically incorrect, prayer directed to the Father is the norm of Scripture and the Christian life.

---

figure with whom they can identify and to whom they may relate this kind of prayer relationship. For those who do not have such a parental figure, if they are able to find one, then their prayer life may be enriched.

Conclusion

The thesis of this book is that virtue ethics is key to understanding Trinitarian progressive sanctification. The book argues that while some have overemphasized the role of the Spirit and others have depicted Christ as having a primarily passive role in progressive sanctification, the emphasis on the active role of Christ in conjunction with a recovery of virtue ethics demonstrates how a virtue ethical view of Trinitarian sanctification functions.

This book sought to recover the pre-Reformation virtue ethical emphasis of the tradition's biblical interpretation of sanctification in a way compatible with Reformation and post-Reformation evangelical sensibilities concerning salvation by grace though faith alone apart from works (Eph 2:8–10), while at the same time employing an emphasis on the Trinity similar to that of the contemporary Trinitarian proponents. The primary concern of this book is not merely to retrieve virtue ethics, but rather to argue that progressive sanctification functions biblically in a virtue ethical and Trinitarian manner actively involving Christ and not only the Spirit.

Four reasons support the thesis as to why virtue ethics is key to understanding Trinitarian progressive sanctification which include: (1) the Trinity, virtue ethics, and sanctification are historically and conceptually interconnected in the tradition of interpretation and Scripture, (2) virtue ethics based on metaphysical realism is the most biblically consistent ethical framework for Trinitarian progressive sanctification, (3) Jesus' active roles as a teacher and example of virtue play an important part in understanding how the Trinity progressively sanctifies believers, and (4) Jesus' present and active priestly role of heavenly intercession aimed at manifesting virtue in believers is crucial to understanding how the Trinity progressively sanctifies believers.

Summary of Conclusions

Defense of the thesis through these four reasons results in several conclusions which involve terms and concepts that are programmatic for the argument. In investigating the doctrinal interconnections in the history of interpretation, it is concluded that the three histories of virtue ethics, sanctification, and the Trinity are intricately connected in that the eclipse and resurgence of virtue ethics has radically changed how the nature of the doctrine of sanctification is perceived by theologians, and the Trinitarian description of sanctification has been impacted by the contemporary Trinitarian proponents and perhaps by the eclipse of virtue. It is demonstrated that virtue ethics was part of the church's doctrine of Trinitarian sanctification until the Reformation, after which sanctification was described in increasingly deontological terms and at times the role of the Spirit in sanctification was emphasized to the neglect of Christ, the Father, and the mutual cooperation of all three persons of the Trinity. Moreover, the biblical doctrine of the finished work of Christ had the unfortunate historical tendency to depict Christ's work in sanctification as passive, but while Christ's work is finished in accomplishing redemption, he is not finished working in actively applying redemption in sanctification. Additionally, the position-only view of sanctification popularized by David G. Peterson is rejected in favor of the traditional three aspect view of sanctification as positional, progressive, and perfective.[1]

With respect to the investigation of the nature and function of virtue ethics, it is concluded that the popular distinction between teleological and deontological ethics based on ends is inadequate, because it fails to account for the different meaning of the term "ends" in virtue ethics (final cause) and utilitarianism or consequentialism (consequence of an action). By using the historic definition of the terms in which teleology is based on metaphysical realism and deontology is based on a conception of duty, obligation, and utility that is consistent with metaphysical nominalism, a more helpful distinction is drawn between these two broad classifications of ethical theories. This metaphysical distinction is used in conjunction with arguments based on history, theology, and exegesis to conclude that realism and hence teleology is consistent with the Bible, and nominalism and hence deontology is not biblically consistent. Consequently, teleological virtue ethics rather than any deontological type of ethics, including the agent based and linguistic virtue

---

[1] David G. Peterson, *Possessed by God: A New Testament Theology of Sanctification and Holiness*, NSBT 1 (InterVarsity, 1995), 13–14, 115–116, 136–137.

ethics of the resurgence of virtue ethics, is the type of ethics most consistent with the Bible and its Trinitarian progressive sanctification. Furthermore, one function of virtue ethics in sanctification is that progress in exemplifying the virtues is a key aspect of sanctification (1 Thess 3:12; 2 Thess 1:3; 1 Pet 1:13–16; 2 Pet 1:5–9).

In regard to Jesus' active roles as a teacher and example of virtue, it is concluded that while Jesus taught that the theological virtues provide moral motivation (Luke 8:1–15; 18:1–8; John 14:15, 23–24) in a manner consistent with motivational weak internalism, he did not teach on the traditional theological virtues (faith, hope, and love), but rather he taught on the incipient or transitional theological virtues of faith, love, and endurance (Matt 24:10–13). It is also concluded that the concepts of habituation and reciprocity are similar to Jesus' teaching on how his moral example was to be imitated (Matt 7:15–23; 12:33–35; Luke 6:40, 43–45) and the manner in which Jesus teaches these concepts is consistent with *sola fide* in which the Spirit initiates and empowers the imitation. Finally, a theological synthesis ordered by the Triune premise concludes that the Trinity progressively sanctifies believers on the basis of Jesus' active roles as a teacher and example of virtue such that: (1) the value of all things having its source *from* the Father is revealed *through* the teaching of the Son to motivate believers, who are empowered to be motivated *by* the Spirit and (2) the character that is *from* the Father is revealed *through* the Son's example, that is to be imitated by the believer through habituation and reciprocity, *by* the Spirit's "leading" and "working."

With respect to Jesus' role as a priest, it is concluded that the description of Jesus' heavenly intercession in Scripture is best interpreted as being *agilis et realis*, "active and real." Jesus' *agilis et realis* role as priest works with the other persons of the Trinity to sanctify believers progressively according to the reversed Triune premise (Eph 2:18) such that believers are led *by* the Spirit's intercession into prayer (Rom 8:14 16, 26–27), to be helped *through* the Son's intercession (Rom 8:34), in order to receive an answer *from* the Father (Rom 8:27–28), and all of which is aimed at conforming believers generally to the image of Christ's character (Rom 8:29) and specifically by manifesting the Son's virtue of "hope through patient-enduring" (Rom 8:20, 24–25).

Contribution

This book seeks to make several contributions to the fields of theology and ethics. First, this book does not seek to correct the tradition, but rather as part of J. Webster's "theology of retrieval," it seeks to add to the insights of the past.[2] For example, rather than rejecting an aspect of the tradition, pre-Reformation virtue ethics, the Reformation doctrine of *sola fide*, and the contemporary Trinitarian resurgence's emphasis on Trinitarian sanctification have been synthesized. Second, this book offers an interdisciplinary approach by attempting to add new insights and depth of understanding to the doctrine of sanctification by reuniting theology with ethics, namely virtue ethics, and clarifying through virtue ethics how progressive sanctification takes place. For instance, it has been demonstrated how the virtues function as moral motivation for sanctification and how imitation by habituation and reciprocity is part of the biblical manner of manifesting the virtues in progressive sanctification. Third, while others have presented Trinitarian views of sanctification, this book focuses on the Trinitarian work from a Christological perspective. This contribution is accomplished by focusing on Jesus' roles as teacher, example, and priest and then framing these roles as part of Trinitarian statements that are ordered by the Triune premise. Fourth, by shifting the methodological paradigm from building the doctrine of sanctification based on theological constructions, such as the so-called Triune premise, to textual exegesis, this book demonstrates that Christ has an active role in applying his finished work in cooperation with the Spirit and Father. This active aspect of Jesus' participation in sanctification is emphasized through his roles as teacher, example, and priest. Fifth, by interpreting reciprocity and habituation as Spirit initiated and led actions, these concepts help provide an important explanation for how sanctification can occur without ontological change, be a divine work rather than a human work, and yet in relation to justification not be a legal fiction as the Roman Catholics charge. Sixth, while not the main concern, this book also offers the mediating view of Jesus' heavenly intercession as *agilis et realis*, which seems to affirm both the best of the passive presence, vocalis et realis, and metaphor views while avoiding their weaknesses and to describe the biblical evidence most accurately. Finally, this book suggests how a virtue ethical view of Trinitarian sanctification applies to the current debate about sanctification in relation to the believer's practical spiritual experience. In this regard, virtue ethics implies that sanctification is a process rather than an instantaneous event and the norm, but not the iron clad rule, of the believer's prayer life is that prayer is addressed primarily to the Father.

---

2 John Webster, "Theologies of Retrieval," in *OHST*, eds. Kathryn Tanner, John Webster, and Iain Torrance (Oxford University Press, 2007), 584.

Continued Research

In this book, there are many omissions due to the normal space and time constraints accompanying any written project as well as content limitations due to confining the material to the scope of the argument rather than tangents, prior questions, or background considerations. Certainly there may also be some issues overlooked due to human finiteness. All of these considerations and possibly more contribute to a body of material that may be pursued for further research.

Some of the omitted issues are more important for further consideration. Since the history of sanctification included in this book is necessarily highly selective, then future work might concentrate on providing a more detailed history of sanctification that covers the traditional views, but it should *not* make any one controversy the focus or lens for interpreting the history as, for example, R. A. Muller's history does in tracing the idea of perfection and Timothy P. Jenney's history does in focusing on the development of Pentecostalism.[3] Such a history would need to take into account not only the traditional debate issues, justification, and regeneration, but also the systematic perspective as well as the individual historical figures. The goal of the history would be to establish a more standardized and complete history of sanctification.

Another area for further consideration is that of the other aspects of metaethics not covered by this book. Although this book discusses the metaethical issue of moral motivation in relation to Trinitarian progressive sanctification, there are other important metaethical issues such as moral epistemology or how morality is known. For example, since this book argues that virtue ethics is key to Trinitarian progressive sanctification and Smith has argued aptly that moral epistemology is crucial for virtue ethics, then these joint claims, if true, mean that moral epistemology is crucial for Trinitarian progressive sanctification.[4] A future work might explore this connection between moral epistemology and sanctification.

A final selection of future research topics may include: (1) one might continue S. S. Wilson's project by considering Trinitarian sanctification from the

---

[3] Timothy P. Jenney, "The Holy Spirit and Sanctification," in *Systematic Theology: A Pentecostal Perspective*, ed. Stanley M. Horton (Gospel Publishing House, 2012), ch. 12; R. A. Muller, "Sanctification," *ISBE* 4:321–331.

[4] R. Scott Smith, *Virtue Ethics and Moral Knowledge: Philosophy of Language after Macintyre and Hauerwas*, Ashgate New Critical Thinking in Philosophy (Ashgate, 2003), 213–214, 216–217.

perspective of the Father and the Spirit respectively, (2) the issue of how union with Christ impacts one's description of sanctification and particularly the active or passive nature of Christ's role might be investigated, (3) a more detailed analysis of the progress of the theological virtues from Jesus to Paul may be provided, (4) one might interact more with the significant amount of literature on imitation and other specialized topics only touched on by this book's argument, (5) Aristotle's use of the term *padia* (teaching) in his virtue ethics may be explored in order to determine whether it is consistent with the use of the term in the NT, (6) one might go beyond what J. Kotva did in establishing the biblical consistency of the idea of *telos*, (7) a consideration might be made of whether or not there are other better ways of explaining the biblical consistency of reciprocity and habituation, (8) a more detailed history of the interpretation of Christ's heavenly intercession might be provided, (9) other ways that Christ has an active role in progressive sanctification may be considered, and (10) one might expand the application sections into a practical work which explores in greater depth how to live out Christian virtue ethics as an aspect of sanctification.[5]

A Final Exhortation to the Church

Therefore, since virtue ethics is key to Trinitarian progressive sanctification, the following words adapted from J. C. Ryle are still applicable in the present generation. "Such is the working of a virtue ethical view of Trinitarian sanctification. Let the reader along with the author examine themselves for, strive after, and pray by the Spirit through the Son to the Father to manifest the virtues that make and mark a sanctified life."[6]

---

5 Joseph J. Kotva, Jr., *The Christian Case for Virtue Ethics* (Georgetown University Press, 1996), 76–78, 106–108, 147–148, 154; Scott Sparling Wilson, "Trinity and Sanctification: A Proposal for Understanding the Doctrine of Sanctification According to a Triune Ordering" (Ph.D. diss., Southeastern Baptist Theological Seminary, 2009), 253.

6 Adapted from: J. C. Ryle, *Holiness: Its Nature, Hindrances, Difficulties and Roots* (William Hunt and Company, 1889), 57.

APPENDIX 1 TABLE A1: OVERVIEW OF THE HISTORY OF SANCTIFICATION

Classical & Patristic	Medieval (590–1527)	Reformation (1517–1648) to Protestant Scholasticism (1700)	Revival (1700) to Modernity (1914) Enlightenment (1650/1700-1790/1800)	Late Modernity (1914–1950) to Post-Modernity (1950–)
Aristotle (384–322 BC)	Bernard of Clairvaux (1090–1153): Contemplative view	Luther (1483–1546) rejects justification as infused grace	John Wesley (1703–1791): forerunner of Pentecostalism and Keswick views	Lewis Sperry Chafer (1871–1952): Dispensational view
Clement of Rome (AD 30–100)	Aquinas (1225–1274): a progress of infused virtue	Ignatius of Loyola (1491–1556): Contemplative view	Jonathan Edwards (1703–1758)	Louis Berkhof (1873–1957): Reformed view
Barnabas (100)	Ockham (1280–1349): prepared for distinction of sanctification and justification by separating God's will from his nature	Melanchthon (1497–1560) distinguished justification from sanctification/regeneration	F. D. E. Schleiermacher (1768–1834)	John Theodore Mueller (1885–1967): Lutheran view
Clement of Alexandria (155–220)		Calvin (1509-1564)	G. W. F. Hegel (1770–1831)	Karl Barth (1886–1968)
Tertullian (160–225): tied sanctification to virtue		John of the Cross (1542–1591): Contemplative view	Charles Finney (1792–1875): forerunner of Pentecostalism	John Murray (1898–1975)
Origen (185–254)		Council of Trent (1545–1563)	Charles Hodge (1797–1878) distinguished regeneration and sanctification	G. C. Berkouwer (1903–1996)
Gregory of Nyssa (330–395): Trinitarian sanctification		William Ames (1576–1633)	Asa Mahan (1799–1889)	John Walvoord (1910–2002): Dispensational view
Augustine (354–430)		Johannes Maccovius (1588–1644)	William Shedd (1820–1894)	Thomas Merton (1915–1968): Contemplative view

	Francis Turretin (1623–1687): conflated regeneration and sanctification	Abraham Kuyper (1837–1920)
		Hermann Bavinck (1854–1921): Reformed view
		Franz Pieper (1852–1931): Lutheran view

Sources: Aquinas, *STh.*, I q.43 a.6 s.c.; I q.43 a.6 ad 2; I–II q.113 a.6 resp.; I–II q.112 a.2 ad.1; I q.112 a.3; Augustine, *Mor. eccl.* 13.22; 13.23; 19.36; 25.46 (PL 32:1320–1321, 1326–1327, 1330–1331); idem, *Bapt.* 4.24.32 (PL 43:173); idem, *spir. et litt.* 26.45; 33.66 (PL 44:228, 245); Frederick S. Carney, "The Structure of Augustine's Ethic," in *The Ethics of St. Augustine*, ed. William S. Babcock, JRSER 3 (Scholars Press, 1991), 11, 15, 33; (Gregory's *De Sancta Trinitate* was incorrectly attributed to Basil when Migne's work was compiled). Basil, *Ep.* 189 (PG 32:693); Barnabas, *Barn.* 5 (PG 2:733–734); Clement of Alexandria, *Paed.* 1.6 (PG 8: 260); Clement of Rome, *1 Cor.* 30 (PG 1: 269, 272); Gregory of Nyssa, *Cont. Eun. duo.* 2.2 (PG 45:472); Origen, *Princ.* 1.4.2 (PG 11:156); Tertullian, *Bapt.* 7.10.27–31 (CSEL 20:209); idem, *Res.* 44.3–6 (CSEL 47:91); idem, *Prax.* 2.11–14 (CSEL 47:229); John Calvin, *Inst.* 2.2.1–2.2.4; 2.2.8; 2.2.9; 2.7.12; 3.2.8; 3.6.1; 3.16.1 (CR 30:175–178, 183–184, 261, 266–309, 404, 501–502, 586); Martin Luther, *Dictata super Psalterium: Psalmus* 119:88 (WA 4:350); idem, *In Epistolam S. Pauli ad Galatas Commentarius ex praelectione* (WA 40.1:228–229); idem, *Vorrede zum ersten Bande der Gesamtausgaben seiner lateinischen Schriften, Wittenberg 1545* (WA 54:186); idem, *Der Brief an Die Römer* (WA 56:201; Philip Melanchthon, *Loci Communes Theologici* (MW 2.1:68; 239–240; 281; idem, *Loci Communes Theologici* (MW 2.2:359, 431–433, 783, 800; idem, *Confessio Augustana* (CR 26: 299–300); idem, *Apologia Confessionis Ex Editione Principe A. 1531 4th Edita* (CR 27: 429, 447–448, 526, 543, 587, 619); Bernard of Clairvaux, *On Loving God* (Wyatt North, 2012), ch. 2.1, 5; Steven Barabas, *So Great Salvation: The History and Message of the Keswick Convention* (Marshall, Morgan, & Scott, 1952), 17–27, 39–155; Lewis Sperry Chafer, *Systematic Theology* (Kregel, 1947), 148, 234–237, 303, 347; 2.5, 74, 163, 202; Lewis Sperry Chafer, *He That Is Spiritual: A Classic Study of the Biblical Doctrine of Spirituality* (Kessinger, 2010), ch. 3, 5, 6; Lawrence S. Cunningham, s.v. "Lecture XVIII.4; XXIII.1.2, II.2, V.2; ch. 13.IV.3; idem, *Systematic Theology*, Original, Unabridged 1851 ed. (Holiness, 2011), s.v. "Lecture 3.3; 4.III.4; 5.III.29, 39; 5.IV.2; E. Glenn Hinson, "The Contemplative View," in *Christian Spirituality: Five Views of Sanctification*, ed. Donald Alexander (InterVarsity, 1988), 174; Stanley M. Horton, "The Pentecostal Perspective," in *Five Views on Sanctification*, ed. Stanley N. Gundry of Zondervan Counterpoints Collection (Zondervan, 1987), 103–135; Ignatius Loyola, *The Spiritual Exercises of St. Ignatius Loyola: Spanish and English with a Continuous Commentary*, ed. and trans. Joseph Rickaby (Burns & Oates, 1915), 75, 98, 124, 127, 175; Timothy P. Jenney, "The Holy Spirit and Sanctification," in *Systematic Theology: A Pentecostal Perspective*, ed. Stanley M. Horton (Gospel Publishing House, 2012), ch. 12; John of the Cross, *Dark Night of the Soul* (Neeland Media, 2010), 15–32, 40–42, 47–48, 67–68, 96, 110–113; Asa Mahan, *Out of Darkness into Light* (Amazon Digital Services, 2010), pt. 1, ch. 3; pt. 2, ch. 1; idem, *Christian Perfection* (Amazon Digital Services, 2012), s.v. "Discourse 1.2; 3.I.7; 5: 8; J. Robertson McQuilkin, "The Keswick Perspective," in *Five Views on Sanctification*, ed. Gundry, 149–183; Russell P. Spittler, "The Pentecostal-Dispensational Perspective," in *Christian Spirituality: Five Views of Sanctification*, ed. Donald Alexander (InterVarsity, 1988), 133–170; John F. Walvoord, "The Augustinian-Dispensational Perspective," in *Five Views on Sanctification*, ed. Gundry, 197–226; idem, *The Holy Spirit: A Comprehensive Study of the Person and Work of the Holy Spirit* (Zondervan, 2010). pt. 5, ch. 21, 23.

Appendix 2 Table A2:
Theological and Associated Virtues in the Epistles

Virtues	Virtues [BDAG]	Reference	Relationship Between Virtues
πίστις, ἐλπίς, ἀγάπη	Faith, hope, love	1 Cor 13:13; Col 1:4–5; Gal 5:5–6; Eph 1:15–18; Heb 10:22–24; 1 Pet 1:3–8, 21–22	
πίστις, ἐλπίς, ἀγάπη, ὑπομονή	Faith, hope, love, endurance	1 Thess 1:3; Rom 5:1–5	1 Thess 1:3 "ὑπομονῆς τῆς ἐλπίδος" possibly an ablative of source so that endurance comes from hope. Rom 5:3–4 endurance ultimately leads to or κατεργάζεται, "produces," hope.
πίστις, ἀγάπη, ὑπομονή	Faith, love, endurance	1 Tim 6:11; Titus 2:2; 2 Pet 1:5–7; Rev 2:19	1 Tim 6:11; Titus 2:2; Rev 2:19 have lists. 2 Pet 1:5 endurance is something that is indirectly ἐπιχορηγήσατε, "supplied," to faith as part of a chain of virtues.
πίστις, ἀγάπη, ὑπομονή, μακροθυμία	Faith, love, endurance, patience	2 Tim 3:10	2 Tim 3:10 has a list.
πίστις, ἐλπίς, ἀγάπη, μακροθυμία	Faith, hope, love, patience	Heb 6:10–12	
πίστις, ἐλπίς, ἀγάπη, νήφω	Faith, hope, love, sober	1 Thess 5:8	
πίστις, ὑπομονή	Faith, endurance	James 1:3; Rev 13:10; 14:12	James 1:3 τῆς πίστεως κατεργάζεται ὑπομονήν, "faith produces endurance" and endurance produces sanctification, "mature, perfect complete not lacking anything." Rev 13:10; 14:12 listed together.

Appendix 2 Table A2

Virtues	Virtues [BDAG]	Reference	Relationship Between Virtues
ἐλπίς, ὑπομονή	Hope, endurance	Rom 8:25; 15:4	Rom 8:25 a list. Rom 15:4 endurance leads to hope.
ἀγάπη, ὑπομονή	Love, endurance	2 Cor 6:4–6; 2 Thess 3:5; Rev 2:3–4	2 Cor 6:4–6; 2 Thess 3:5 have lists. Rev 2:3–4 has endurance existing without love.

---

1 Hunter claims that since faith, hope, and love occur in the *same sequences* in some passages (1 Pet 1:21–22; Heb 10:22–24; Gal 5:5–6; 1 Cor 13:13) that this "suggests that the triad in Paul is not his own creation, but something common and apostolic, perhaps a sort of compendium of the Christian life current in the early apostolic church." Archibald M. Hunter, *Paul and His Predecessors*, rev. ed. (The Westminster Press, 1961), 34. The chart demonstrates that endurance has a reciprocal relationship with both faith and hope and that endurance can exist without love.

APPENDIX 3 TABLE A3:
THEOLOGICAL AND ASSOCIATED VIRTUES
IN THE GOSPELS

Virtue(s)	Virtue(s) [BDAG]	Reference	Location Description	Significance
πίστις [σκανδαλίζω], ἀγάπη, ὑπομένω	Faith (implied by "being caused to stumble [in or from their faith]" as in the NIV), endurance, love	Matt 24:10–13	Signs of the End of the Age	This is the only possible occurrence where faith (implied), endurance, and love may occur together in the Gospels. Jesus relates all three to salvation.
πίστις, ἀγαπάω	Faith and love	Luke 7:42, 47, 50	Jesus Anointed by a Sinful Woman	Jesus relates faith and love to forgiveness and salvation.
πιστεύω, ἀγαπάω	Faith and love	John 12:42–43	The Jews Continue in Their Unbelief	Jesus is rebuking the Jews for lack of these virtues. Serves as a negative example for the disciples of those lacking faith and love.
πίστις	Faith	Matt 17:20; Luke 17:5–6	Saying Concerning the Mustard Seed	Jesus relates faith to power to accomplish spiritual things.
		Matt 21:21–22; Mark 11:22	Saying Concerning the Tree Thrown into the Sea	Jesus relates faith to power in prayer and to accomplish spiritual things.
		Mark 4:40; Luke 8:25	Calming of the Storm	Jesus rebukes the disciples for having little faith.
		Luke 18:8	The Parable of the Persistent Widow	Jesus teaches that faith motivates prayer.
		Luke 22:31–32	The Last Supper	Faith not fail when Satan sift like wheat.

Appendix 3 Table A3

Virtue(s)	Virtue(s) [BDAG]	Reference	Location Description	Significance
πίστις	Faith	Matt 23:23	Seven Woes	Jesus rebukes the Pharisees for neglecting faithfulness and love as a more important matters of the law.
		Matt 8:10; Luke 7:9	The Faith of the Centurion	Jesus upholds the faith of the Centurion as a positive example to the disciples.
		Matt 9:29; Mark 10:52; Luke 18:42; Matt 15:28; Luke 9:2; Mark 5:34; Matt 9:22; Luke 8:48; Mark 2:5; Luke 5:20; Luke 17:19	Healing of two blind men and/or Bartimaeus The Syrophoenician Woman Jesus Heals a Paralytic A Dead Girl and a Sick Woman Jesus Heals a Paralytic Ten Healed of Leprosy	Numerous passages where people are healed in response to faith that do not involved a direct teaching of the disciples by Jesus but indirectly teach them by the example of those healed.
ἐλπίζω	Hope (to hope)	Matt 12:21 (Is 42:1–4) Luke 24:21	God's Chosen Servant On the Road to Emmaus	The proper response to Jesus' coming is Messianic hope.
ὑπομονή	Endurance	Luke 8:15	The Parable of the Sower	Jesus teaches that endurance is needed to "bear fruit," possibly good works.
		Luke 21:19	Signs of the End of the Age	Jesus teaches that endurance is related to salvation.
ἀγάπη	Love	John 13:34–35	The New Commandment	Jesus commands love.
		John 15:9–13	The Vine and the Branches	Jesus teaches that love motivates obedience
		John 5:42	Testimonies About Jesus	Jesus rebukes the Jews for lack of love. They are a negative example of lack of love.

Virtue(s)	Virtue(s) [BDAG]	Reference	Location Description	Significance
ἀγάπη	Love	John 17:26	Jesus Prays for All Believers	Jesus exalts love as a virtue to be possessed.
		Luke 11:42	Seven Woes	Jesus rebukes the Pharisees for neglecting faithfulness and love as more important matters of the law.
ἀπιστίαν	Lack of Love (A related vice)	Matt 13:58; Mark 6:6	A Prophet Without Honor	Jesus' rebuke of his home town for not having faith serves as a negative example for the disciples.
		Mark 16:14	Post-Resurrection Appearance	Jesus rebukes the disciples for lack of faith.
ὀλιγόπιστοι	Little Faith (A related vice)	Matt 6:20; Matt 8:26; Matt 14:31; Matt 16:8; Matt 12:28	Sermon on the Mount, Do Not Worry Calming of the Storm Jesus Walks on Water The Yeast of the Pharisees and Sadducees Sermon on the Mount, Do Not Worry	Jesus rebukes the disciples for having little faith.
πιστός	Faithfulness	Matt 25:45; Luke 12:42	The Day and Hour Unknown	Jesus teaches that faithfulness is the proper virtue with respect to the nature of service done while waiting for the second coming.
		Matt 25:21–23	The Parable of the Talents	Jesus teaches that those who are good stewards are faithful.

Appendix 3 Table A3

Virtue(s)	Virtue(s) [BDAG]	Reference	Location Description	Significance
πιστεύω	Faith (to put or place faith in)	John 2:11; John 7:31; John 8:30; John 11:45; John 12:11; John 14:12	Wedding at Cana, Water Turned into Wine, Is Jesus the Christ? The Validity of Jesus' Testimony, The Plot to Kill Jesus, Jesus Anointed at Bethany, Jesus the Way to the Father	Passages where the disciples and others put their faith in Jesus, mostly as a result of his miracles. The placing of faith in Christ depicted as a positive narrative example.
ὑπομένω	Endurance (to endure)	Matt 10:22	Jesus Sends Out the Twelve	Jesus relates endurance to salvation.
		Mark 13:13; Matt 24:13	Signs of the End of the Age	Jesus relates endurance to salvation.
ἀγαπάω	Love (to love)	Matt 5:34; Luke 6:27–36	Sermon on the Mount, Love for Enemies	Jesus commands love and that love motivates or is acted out by praying for enemies.
		Matt 19:19	The Rich Young Ruler	Jesus quotes Lev 19:18 to command love.
		Matt 22:37–40; Mark 12:29–31	The Greatest Commandment	Jesus quotes Deut 6:5; Deut 19:18 to command love.
		John 13:34–35	New Commandment	Jesus commands love based on the example of his sacrifice on the cross.
		Matt 6:24; Luke 16:13–14	Sermon on the Mount, Saying on Loving God or Money	Jesus teaches that love needs to have the right object, God.
		John 8:42	The Children of the Devil	Jesus rebukes the Jews for lacking love. Love connected with salvation.

Virtue(s)	Virtue(s) [BDAG]	Reference	Location Description	Significance
ἀγαπάω	Love (to love)	John 14:15, 21, 23–24, 28	First Paraclete Passage in the Upper Room Discourse	Jesus teaches that love motivates obedience.
		John 14:31	First Paraclete Passage in the Upper Room Discourse	Jesus teaches that the world must know that Jesus' obedience is motivated by love for the Father.
		John 15:9–13, 17	The Vine and the Branches	Jesus commands the disciples to love as he has loved by laying down one's life for one's friends.
		John 16:27	The Disciple's Grief will Turn to Joy	Jesus relates love to salvation.
		John 17:23	Jesus Prays for all Believers	Jesus teaches that unity is motivated by love.
		John 17:26	Jesus Prays for all Believers	Jesus relates love to salvation.
φιλέω	Love	John 12:25	Jesus Predicts His Death	Jesus teaches that eternal goods are the proper object of love.
ἀγαπάω and φιλέω	Love	John 21:15–17	Reinstatement of Peter	Jesus teaches that God is the proper object of love and that love motivates service.

2

---

2 Source: Some location descriptions taken from the NIV and NAS section' headings. Note: Table A2 is not an exhaustive list of all occurrences.

Appendix 4 Table A4: Four Views of the Intercession of Christ

Time Period	Metaphor (Anthropomorphism)	Passive Presence	*Vocalis et Realis*	Perpetual Offering (Roman Catholic)
Patristic	Chrysostom (347–407), Theodoret (393–458), Gennadius of Marseilles (496 d.)	Gregory of Nazianzus (330–389), Ambrose (339–397), Primasius of Hadrumetum (560 d.)		Jerome (345–419), Ambrose (339–397), Leo the Great (440–461)
Medieval (590–1527)	John of Damascus (675–749) Oecumenius (900s)	Gregory the Great (540–604), Walafridus Strabo (808–849), Bruno of Chartreuse (the Carthusian) (1030–1101), Radulphus Ardens (1200 d., Herveus of Bordeaux (1080–1150), Abelard (1079–1142), The Abott	Thomas Aquinas (1225–1274)	
Reformation (1517–1648)	Peter Martyr Vermigli (1500–1562)	John Calvin (1509–1564), Theodore Beza (1519–1605)	Philip Melanchthon (1497–1560), Thomas Cranmer (1489–1556), John Hooper (1555 d.), John Bradford (1510–1555), Hugo Grotius (1583–1645)	Pius IV (1499–1565); Pope: (1559–1565)
Protestant Scholasticism (1648–1700)		John Owen (1616–1683) Francis Turretin (1623–1687) Stephen Charnock (1628–1680)	John Bunyan (1628–1688), Jeremy Taylor (1613–1667), Issac Barrow (1630–1677), Salomon Deyling (1677–1755), John Tillotson (1630–1694)	

Time Period	Metaphor (Anthropomorphism)	Passive Presence	*Vocalis et Realis*	Perpetual Offering (Roman Catholic)
Revival (1700) to Modernity (1914) Enlightenment (1650/1700–1790/1800)		William Symington (1795–1862), Charles Hodge (1797–1878), Thomas Houston (1803–1882), Heinrich Heppe (1820–1879), Henry Barclay Swete (1835–1917), Henry Parr Liddon (1829–1890), Brooke Foss Westcott (1825–1901), William Milligan (1821–1893), Canon Robert Campbell Moberly (1845–1903), Nathaniel Dimock (1825–1909), Moule (1841–1920)	Henry Alford (1810–1871), Heinrich August Wilhelm Meyer (1800–1873), Franz Julius Delitzsch (1813–1890), Frédéric Louis Godet (1812–1900), William Sanday (1843–1920)	
Late Modernity (1914–1950) to Post–Modernity (1950–)	Alexander Nairne (1863–1936)	Arthur J. Tait (1872–1944) Alred Cody (1932 b.) James Kurianal (1959 b.)	Franz Pieper (1852–1931) John Theodore Mueller (1885–1967) Louis Berkhof (1873–1957) Arthur Cayley Headlam (1862–1947) David MacLeod	Pius XI (1857–1939; Pope: 1922–1939)

3

---

3 While the Denzinger documents for Pius XI do not explicitly teach the perpetual offering in the heavenly intercession, they seem to presuppose and imply it. Aquinas, *Super Epistolam B. Pauli ad Romanos lectura* C.8 L.7.719–20 ed. J. Mortensen and E. Alarcón, trans. F. R. Larcher, Under the title *Commentary on the Letter of Saint Paul to the Romans*, Latin/English ed., Biblical Commentaries 37 (The Aquinas Institute, 2012), 239–240; Henry Denzinger, Roy J. Deferrari, and Karl Rahner, ed. *The Sources of Catholic Dogma* (B. Herder Book Co., 1954), 298, 292; Arthur J. Tait, *The Heavenly Session of Our Lord: An Introduction to the History of the Doctrine* (Robert Scott, 1912), 149–176; John Bunyan, *Christ a Complete Saviour or the Intercession of Christ and Who Are Privileged in It* (Works 1:203); Stephen Charnock, *Christ's Intercession* (Works 5:99, 101–102, 109); Heinrich Heppe, *Die Dogmatik der evangelisch-reformierte Kirche: Dargestellt und aus den Quellen belegt*, 2nd ed. (Neukirchener Verlag, Kreis Moers, 1958), 382–383; Charles Hodge, *Systematic Theology* (Logos Research Systems, 1997), 2:593–594; Thomas Houston, *The Intercession of Christ* (James Gemmell, 1882), 47–48; William Symington, *The Atonement and Intercession of Jesus Christ*, rep. ed. (Reformation Heritage Books, 2006), 264–266; Arthur J. Tait, *The*

Appendix 5 Table A 5:
Linguistic and Thematic Connection
of Intercession Passages

	Heb 2:14–18	Heb 4:14–16	Heb 7:23–28	Heb 9:23–28	Rom 8:26–27, 34	1 John 2:1–2	Luke 22: 31–32	John 17:6–26
High priest	ἀρχιερεὺς v. 17	ἀρχιερέα v. 14 ἀρχιερέα v. 15	ἀρχιερεῖς v. 27 ἀρχιερεῖς v. 28	ἀρχιερεὺς v. 25				
Suffer	πέπονθεν v. 18			παθεῖν v. 26			σινιάσαι ὡς τὸν σῖτον v. 31	
Help	ἐπιλαμ-βάνεται v. 16 βοηθῆσαι v. 18	βοήθειαν v. 16z			συναντιλαμ-βάνεται v. 26	παράκ-λητον v. 1	μὴ ἐκλίπῃ ἡ πίστις σου v. 32	τήρησον αὐτοὺς v. 11 ἐτήρουν αὐτοὺς v. 12 τηρήσῃς αὐτοὺς v. 15

Heavenly Session of Our Lord: An Introduction to the History of the Doctrine (Robert Scott, 1912), 19–22, 149–176; Francis Turretin, *Inst.* 14.15.7, 11, 13 (2:425); Not all of the classifications of the scholars are clear cut and readers may move at least some of them into other classes at their discretion. For example, Symington qualifies that he is not taking a view, but his interpretation seems to fall into the passive presence position. Berkhof does not use the phrase *vocalis et realis* and emphasizes presence as part of the Reformed tradition, but he does also stress actual prayer rather than a mere symbol. Kurianal's view is closer to, but not identical with the passive presence view and he seems to deny the *vocalis et realis* view. However, others such as Gregory of Nazianzus, Calvin, and Turretin make their position so explicit that readers move them at their own peril. While the Denzinger documents for Pius XI do not explicitly teach the perpetual offering in the heavenly intercession, they seem to presuppose and imply it. Louis Berkhof, *Systematic Theology* (Eerdmans, 1938), 401–403; Aelred Cody, *Heavenly Sanctuary and Liturgy in the Epistle to the Hebrews: The Achievement of Salvation in the Epistle's Perspective* (Grail Publications, 1960), 198–201; Denzinger, Deferrari, and Rahner, ed. *The Sources of Catholic Dogma*, 610; James Kurianal, *Jesus Our High Priest: Ps 110,4 as the Substructure of Heb 5,1–7,28*, European University Studies, Series 23 (Peter Lang, 2000) 135–136, 218–219; David J MacLeod, "Christ, the Believer's High Priest: An Exposition of Hebrews 7:26–28," *BSac* 162, no. 647 (Jl–S 2005): 335, 338; John Theodore Mueller, *Christian Dogmatics* (Concordia, 1999), 313–314; Alexander Nairne, *The Epistle of Priesthood, Studies in the Epistle to the Hebrews* (T&T Clark, 1913), 183–184, 198–202; Franz Pieper, *Christliche Dogmatik* (Evangelisch-Lutherischen Synode von Missouri und Anderen Staaten, 1946), 422; Arthur J. Tait, *The Heavenly Session of Our Lord: An Introduction to the History of the Doctrine* (Robert Scott, 1912), 19–22, 149–176.

	Heb 2:14–18	Heb 4:14–16	Heb 7:23–28	Heb 9:23–28	Rom 8:26–27, 34	1 John 2:1–2	Luke 22:31–32	John 17:6–26
Temptation	πειρασθείς, πειραζομένοις v. 18	πεπειρασμένον v. 15						
Weakness	ὅσοι φόβῳ θανάτου διὰ παντὸς τοῦ ζῆν ἔνοχοι ἦσαν δουλείας v. 15	ἀσθενείαις ἡμῶν v. 15	ἀνθρώπους ... ἔχοντας ἀσθένειαν v. 28		ἀσθενείᾳ ἡμῶν v. 26	ἁμάρτητε. ... ἁμάρτῃ ... ἁμαρτιῶν v. 1–2		
Sacrifice	διὰ τοῦ θανάτου v. 14 ἱλάσκεσθαι v. 17		ἑαυτὸν ἀνενέγκας v. 27 θυσίας ἀναφέρειν v. 27	θυσίαις v. 23 προσφέρῃ ἑαυτόν v. 25 θυσίας αὐτοῦ v. 26 προσενεχθεὶς v. 28	ὁ ἀποθανών v. 34	ἱλασμός v. 2		
Intercede	τὰ πρὸς τὸν θεὸν v. 17 (cp. Heb 5:1)	διεληλυθότα τοὺς οὐρανούς v. 14	ἐντυγχάνειν v. 25	ἀλλ' εἰς αὐτὸν τὸν οὐρανόν, νῦν ἐμφανισθῆναι τῷ προσώπῳ τοῦ θεοῦ ὑπὲρ ἡμῶν· v. 24	ὑπερεντυγχάνει v. 26 ἐντυγχάνει v. 27 ἐντυγχάνει v. 34	παράκλητον v. 1	ἐδεήθην v. 32	περὶ αὐτῶν ἐρωτῶ ... ἐρωτῶ ἀλλὰ περὶ ὧν δέδωκάς μοι v. 9 ἀλλὰ καὶ περὶ τῶν πιστευόντων V. 20
Exaltation (Right hand of God/ through heavens)		διεληλυθότα τοὺς οὐρανούς v. 14	ὑψηλότερος τῶν οὐρανῶν γενόμενος v. 26	ἀλλ' εἰς αὐτὸν τὸν οὐρανόν, v. 24	ὃς καί ἐστιν ἐν δεξιᾷ τοῦ θεοῦ v. 34	πρὸς τὸν πατέρα v. 1		νῦν δὲ πρὸς σὲ ἔρχομαι v. 13

Appendix 6: The Issue of John 16:26–27 and the Two Intercessions

An interpretative problem with the Spirit's intercession occurs when some commentators claim that the function of the Spirit's intercession of praying for believers is to make the prayers "pleasing" to God or "efficacious." If this is true, then this function seems to contradict John 16:26–27, where Jesus explicitly states that he will not do this. This function also seems to contradict 1 Tim 2:5, where Christ alone and not the Spirit is the one who makes or provides propitiatory intercession, which makes believers pleasing to God.[4] To keep in harmony with John 16:26–27 and 1 Tim 2:5–6, it seems much more prudent to understand the Spirit's intercession as merely testifying to Christ's salvific forensic propitiation and as only providing sanctifying and need-based (vv. 26, 35, 38–39) supplicatory intercession by his initiation of and leading in prayer.

With regard to Jesus' intercession, someone might object that John 16:26–27 means that Jesus will not make intercessory supplication. John 16:26–27 indicates that believers do not need Christ to intercede for them in a supplicatory way in order for their prayers to be effective or for him to "persuade the Father to be gracious" but it does not rule out the possibility that Christ makes requests on their behalf.[5] For example, in Luke 22:31–32, Jesus intercedes for the disciples without them making any request since they are unaware of the need they have. Furthermore, in John 14:16, Jesus explicitly claims that he ἐρωτήσω, "will ask," or intercede for the disciples after his glorification in order to send them the Spirit. Against Morris, who claims that the request in John 14:16 is made during Jesus' earthly ministry, there is no indication that Jesus asks for the Spirit to be sent during his earthly ministry in fulfillment of this promise.[6] Moreover, in John 16:7 since the Spirit is not sent until after Jesus' ascension, then this fact indicates that the request for sending the Spirit will not be made until after Jesus' ascension.[7] Therefore, Luke 22:31–32 and John 14:16 indicate that Jesus has and imply that he continues to intercede for be-

---

4 F. F. Bruce, *Romans*, rev. ed., TNTC 6 (Eerdmans, 1993), 162; Peter T. O'Brien, "Romans 8:26, 27: A Revolutionary Approach to Prayer?" *RTR* 46 (1987): 72; James E. Rosscup, "The Spirit's Intercession," *MSJ* 10, no. 1 (1999): 151.

5 George R. Beasley-Murray, *John*, 2nd ed., WBC (Word, 2002), 287; Leon Morris, *The Gospel According to John*, NICNT (Eerdmans, 1971), 710.

6 Ibid., 710; Murray sees John 14:16 as a possible heavenly intercession of Christ. John Murray, *The Epistle to the Romans*, NICNT (Eerdmans, 1968), 1:329.

7 While John 20:21 may be a partial fulfillment, the passage does not say that Jesus asked for the Spirit to be sent but only that he ἐνεφύσησεν, "breathed." Ibid., 329; Rosscup, "Intercession," 151.

lievers not by making their prayers acceptable to God, but rather by making requests for believers of which they are unaware and so for which they are unable to ask on their own.

Bibliography

Abbots, Francis Ellingwood. *Scientific Theism*. Rep. ed. Kessinger, 2004.
Akin, Daniel L. *1, 2, 3 John*. NAC. B&H, 2001.
———. *Hebrews*. NAC. B&H, 2010.
Alexander, Donald, ed. *Christian Spirituality: Five Views of Sanctification*. InterVarsity, 1988.
Alford, Henry. *Alford's Greek Testament: An Exegetical and Critical Commentary*. Vol. 2. Logos Bible Software, 2010.
Allen, David L. *Hebrews* NAC. B&H, 2010.
Almond, Brenda. "Applied Ethics." Page 42 in *Concise Routledge Encyclopedia of Philosophy*, ed. Edward Craig. Taylor & Francis, 2002.
Alston, William P. "What Metaphysical Realism Is Not." In *Realism and Antirealism*, ed. William P. Alston. Cornell University Press, 2002.
Ambrose. *De Spiritu Sancto*. Edited by Otto Faller. CCSL 79. Hoelder-Pichler-Tempsky, 1964.
Ames, William. *The Marrow of Theology*. Baker, 1997.
Anderson, Ray Sherman. *Historical Transcendence and the Reality of God: A Christological Critique*. 1st American ed. Eerdmans, 1975.
Annas, Julia. "Should Virtue Make You Happy?" *Apeiron* 35, no. 4 (2002): 1–19.
Anscombe, G. E. M. "Modern Moral Philosophy." *Philosophy* 33, no. 124 (1958): 1–16.
Aquinas, Thomas, ed. *Catena Aurea: Commentary on the Four Gospels, Collected out of the Works of the Fathers, Volume 3: St. Luke*. Translated by John Henry Newman. John Henry Parker, 1843.
———. *Opera Omnia Iussu Impensaque, Leonis XIII P.M. Edita*. 16 vols. to date. Ex Typographia Polyglotta S.C. de Propaganda Fide, 1882–2011.
———. *Super Epistolam B. Pauli ad Romanos lectura*. Edited by J. Mortensen and E. Alarcón. Translated by F. R. Larcher. Under the title *Commentary on the Letter of Saint Paul to the Romans*. Latin/English ed. Biblical Commentaries 37. The Aquinas Institute, 2012.
Aristotle. *Aristotelis Opera*, 11 vols., Edited by Immanuel Bekker, Karl Friedrich Neumann and Friedrich Sylburg. e Typographeo academico, 1837.
———. "Magna Moralia." In *The Works of Aristotle*. Vol. 9. Edited by W. D. Ross. Translated by George Stock. Clarendon, 1925.
Athanassoulis, Nafsika. "Virtue Ethics." In *Internet Encyclopedia of Philosophy: A Peer-Reviewed Academic Resource*, ed. James Fieser and Bradley Dowden, 2010. https://www.iep.utm.edu/virtue.
Augustine. *Confessionum*. Edited by Pius Knöll. CSEL 33. Hoelder-Pichler-Tempsky, 1896.
———. *Contra duas epistolas Pelagianorum*. Edited by Carolus F. Vrba and Josephus Zycha. CSEL 60. Hoelder-Pichler-Tempsky, 1913.
———. *De baptismo contra Donatistas*. Edited by M. Petschenig. CSEL 51. Hoelder-Pichler-Tempsky, 1908.
———. *De civitate Dei*. Edited by Emanuel Hoffmann. CSEL 40/1–2. Hoelder-Pichler-Tempsky, 1899–1900.

———. *De diversis quaestionibus octoginta tribus.* Edited by Mutzenbecher. CCSL 44A. Brepols, 1975.

———. *De doctrina christiana.* Edited by Daur. et al. CCSL 32. Brepols, 1962.

———. *De gestis Pelagii.* Edited by C. F. Vrba and J. Zycha. CCSL 42. Hoelder-Pichler-Tempsky, 1902.

———. *De libero arbitrio.* Edited by Green. et al. CCSL 29. Brepols, 1970.

———. *De moribus ecclesiae catholicae.* Edited by J. B. Bauer. CSEL 90. Hoelder-Pichler-Tempsky, 1992.

———. *De spiritu et littera.* Edited by Carolus F. Vrba and Josephus Zycha. CSEL 60. Hoelder-Pichler-Tempsky, 1913.

———. *De trinitate.* Edited by W. J. Mountain. et al. CSEL 50–50A. Brepols, 1968, 2001.

———. *De vera religione.* Edited by Daur. et al. CCSL 32. Brepols, 1962.

———. *Enchiridion.* Edited by M. P. J. van den Hout et al. CCSL 46. Brepols, 1969.

Aulén, Gustaf. *Eucharist and Sacrifice.* Translated by Eric H. Wahlstrom. Muhlenberg, 1958.

Baier, Annette. *Postures of the Mind: Essays on Mind and Morals.* University of Minnesota Press, 1985.

Baillie, John, John T. McNeill, and Henry P. Van Dusen, eds. *Christology of the Later Fathers.* The Library of Christian Classics. Westminster John Knox Press, 2006.

Barnes, Jonathan, ed. *The Cambridge Companion to Aristotle.* Cambridge University Press, 1995.

Barrick, William D. "Sanctification: The Work of the Holy Spirit and Scripture." *MSJ* 21, no. 2 (2010): 179–191.

Brant, Jo-Ann. "The Place of Mimēsis in Paul's Thought." *Studies in Religion/Sciences Religieuses* 22, no. 3 (1993): 285–300.

Basil. *De Spiritu Sancto.* Edited, translated, and annotated by Benoît Pruche. Under the title *Basile De Césarée sur le Saint-Esprit: Introduction, Texte, Traduction et Notes.* Sources Chrétiennes, Vol. 17. 2nd, Rep. ed. Éditions du Cerf, 2002.

Barnabas. *Barnabae epistula 5.* In *Patrum Apostolicorum Opera: Textum ad Fidem Codicum et Graecorum et Latinorum.* Vol. 1. Pt. 2. 5th ed. Edited by Oscar de Gebhardt, Alfred Harnack, and Theodore Zahn. J. C. Hinrichs, 1906.

Barth, Karl. *The Doctrine of the Word of God.* Vol. 1.1 of *Church Dogmatics.* Edited by G. W. Bromiley and T. F. Torrance. Translated by G. W. Bromiley. 2nd ed. T&T Clark, 2004.

———. *The Epistle to the Romans.* Translated by Edwyn C. Hoskyns. Oxford University Press, G. Cumberlege, 1933.

———. *The Theology of Schleiermacher: Lectures at Göttingen, Winter Semester of 1923–24.* Translated by Geoffrey W. Bromiley. Eerdmans, 1982.

Barth, Markus. *Ephesians: Translation and Commentary on Chapters 4–6.* AB 34A. Doubleday 1974.

Bauder, Kevin T., Jr., R. Albert Mohler, Jr., John G. Stackhouse, and Roger E. Olson, eds. *Four Views on the Spectrum of Evangelicalism.* Zondervan Counterpoints Collection. Zondervan, 2011.

Bavinck, Herman. *Reformed Dogmatics*. 4 vols. Edited by John Bolt, Translated by John Vriend. Baker Academic, 2003–2008.
Beasley-Murray, George R. *John*. WBC 36. 2nd ed. Word, 2002.
Bentham, Jeremy. *Deòntology or the Science of Morality*. Vol. 1. Edited by John Bowring. Longman, Rees, Orme, Browne, Green, and Longman; William Tait, 1834.
Berkhof, Louis. *Systematic Theology*. Eerdmans, 1938.
Berkouwer, G. C. *Faith and Sanctification*. Studies in Dogmatics. Eerdmans, 1952.
Bermejo, Luis M. *The Spirit of Life: The Holy Spirit in the Life of the Christian*. Loyola University Press, 1989.
Bernard of Clairvaux. *Ad Clericos de Conversione*. Edited, translated, and annotated by J. Leclercq et al. Under the title *Bernard de Clairvaux: Le Précepte et la Dispense. La Conversion.* SC 457. Éditions du Cerf, 2000.
———. *De Diligendo Deo*. Edited, translated, and annotated by Françoise Callerot et al. Under the title *Bernard de Clairvaux L'amour de Dieu: La Grâce et le Libre Arbitre*. 1st, Rep. ed. SC 393. Éditions du Cerf, 2010.
———. *On Loving God*. Wyatt North, 2012.
———. *Super Cantica Sermo*. Edited, translated, and annotated by J. Leclercq et al. Under the title *Bernard De Clairvaux: Sermons sur le Cantique*. Vol 1. SC 414. Éditions du Cerf, 1996.
Betz, Hans Dieter. *The Sermon on the Mount: A Commentary on the Sermon on the Mount, Including the Sermon on the Plain*. Hermeneia: A Critical and Historical Commentary on the Bible. Edited by Adela Yarbro Collins. Fortress, 1995.
Bloesch, Donald G. *The Christian Life and Salvation*. Eerdmans, 1967.
Blomberg, Craig. *Matthew*. NAC. B&H, 1992.
Bloomfield, Paul. *Moral Reality*. Oxford University Press, 2001.
Bockmuehl, K. "Sanctification." Pages 613–616 in *New Dictionary of Theology*. Edited by Sinclair B. Ferguson and J.I. Packer. InterVarsity, 2000.
Borchert, Gerald L. *John 1–11* NAC. B&H, 1996.
———. *John 12–21*. NAC. B&H, 2002.
Borgman, Brian S. *Feelings and Faith: Cultivating Godly Emotions in the Christian Life*. Crossway, 2009.
Bornkamm, Günther. *Paul*. Translated by D. M. G. Stalker. Harper and Row, 1971.
Bosson, Christopher James. "A Scriptural Appraisal of the Necessary Connection between Progressive Sanctification and Compatibilist Freedom." PhD. diss., The Southern Baptist Theological Seminary, 2010.
Bovon, Francois. *Luke 1: A Commentary on the Gospel of Luke 1:1–9:50*. Hermeneia: A Critical & Historical Commentary on the Bible, Edited by Helmut Koester. Translated by Christine M. Thomas. Fortress, 2002.
Boyd, Gregory A., and Paul R. Eddy. *Across the Spectrum: Understanding Issues in Evangelical Theology*. 2nd ed. Baker Academic, 2009.
Bradshaw, Paul. "God, Christ, and the Holy Spirit in Early Christian Praying." Pages 51–64 in *The Place of Christ in Liturgical Prayer: Trinity, Christology, and Liturgical Theology*. Edited by Bryan D. Spinks. Liturgical, 2008.

Brady, Gary. *What Jesus Is Doing Now*. EP Books, 2012.
Brannan, Rick, ed. *Historic Creeds and Confessions*. Logos Research Systems, 1997.
Bray, G. L. "Trinity." Pages 691–694 in *New Dictionary of Theology*. Edited by Sinclair B. Ferguson and J. I. Packer. InterVarsity, 2000.
Brink, David O. *Moral Realism and the Foundations of Ethics*. Cambridge University Press, 1989.
Broad, C. D. *Five Types of Ethical Theory*. ILPPSM 204. Routledge & Kegan Paul, 1951.
Bromiley, Geoffrey W., ed. *IBSE*. Rev. ed. Eerdmans, 1979–1988.
Brooks, James A. *Mark*. NAC. B&H, 1991.
Bruce, F. F. *1 and 2 Thessalonians*. WBC 45. Word, 1998.
_____. *Romans*. Rev. ed. TNTC 6. Eerdmans, 1993.
_____. *The Epistle to the Hebrews*. Rev. ed. NICNT. Eerdmans, 1990.
_____. *The Epistles to the Colossians, to Philemon, and to the Ephesians*. NICNT. Rev. ed. Eerdmans, 1984.
Brunner, Emil. *Die Mystik und Das Wort: Der Gegensatz zwischen moderner Religionsauffassung und christlichem Glauben dargestellt an der Theologie Schleiermachers*. 2nd stark veränderte ed. J. C. B. Mohr (Paul Siebeck), 1928.
_____. *Erlebnis, Erkenntnis und Glaube*. 4th und 5th ed. Zwingli-Verlag, 1923.
Burkhardt, Helmut. "Regeneration." In *New Dictionary of Theology*. Edited by Sinclair B. Ferguson and J. I. Packer, 574. InterVarsity, 2000.
Calvin, John. *Calvin's Commentaries*, 46 vols. in 19 vols. Logos Bible Software, 2010.
_____. *Ioannis Calvini Opera quae supersunt omnia*. Edited by Wilhelm Baum, Eduard Cunitz, and Eduard Reuss. 59 vols. in 58. Corpus Reformatorum, vols. 29–87. C. A. Schwetschke and Son, 1863–1900; reprint, Johnston Reprint, 1964.
Carney, Frederick S. "The Structure of Augustine's Ethic." Pages 11–37 in *The Ethics of St. Augustine*. Edited by William S. Babcock. JRESR 3. Scholars Press, 1991.
Carson, D. A. and Douglas J. Moo. *An Introduction to the New Testament*. 2nd ed. Zondervan, 2005.
Carson, D. A. *The Gospel According to John*. PNTC. Eerdmans, 1991.
Case, David A., and David W. Holdren. *1–2 Peter, 1–3 John, Jude: A Commentary for Bible Students*. Wesleyan Publishing House, 2006.
Cessario, Romanus. "The Trinitarian Imprint on the Moral Life." Pages 487–492 in *The Oxford Handbook of the Trinity*. Edited by Gilles Emery and Matthew Levering,. Oxford University Press, 2011.
Chafer, Lewis Sperry. *Systematic Theology*, 8 vols. Kregel, 1948.
_____. *He That Is Spiritual: A Classic Study of the Biblical Doctrine of Spirituality*. Kessinger, 2010.
Chambers, Talbot W. *The Book of Zechariah*. Translated by Philip Schaff A Commentary on the Holy Scriptures. Edited by John Peter Lange. Logos Bible Software, 2008.
Chantry, Walter J. "Sanctification: 5. Obedience-Legal or Evangelical? Luke 15:17–32." *Banner of Truth* 512 (May 2006): 1–6.

Charnock, Stephen. *Christ's Intercession*. In *The Complete Works of Stephen Charnock*. Vol. 5. James Nichol, 1864–1866.

Clark, David J. and Howard A. Hatton. *A Handbook on Zechariah*. UBS Handbook Series. United Bible Societies, 2002.

Clement of Alexandria. *Paedagogus* 1. Edited by Otto Stählin. Vol. 1 of *Clemens Alexandrinus: Protrepticus und Paedagogus*. GCS 39. 3rd Rev. ed. Akademie-Verlag, 1972.

———. *Paedagogus* 3. Edited, translated, and annotated by Henri-Irénée Marrou and Marguerite Harl. Under the title *Clément D'alexandrie: Le Pédagogue*. SC 29. Éditions du Cerf, 1970.

Clement of Rome. 1 *Clementis* 30. In *Patrum Apostolicorum Opera: Textum ad Fidem Codicum et Graecorum et Latinorum*. 5th ed. Vol. 1. Pt. 1. Edited by Oscar de Gebhardt, Alfred Harnack, and Theodore Zahn. J. C. Hinrichs, 1906.

Cobb, John B., Jr. "The Relativization of the Trinity." In *Trinity in Process: A Relational Theology of God*. Continuum, 1997.

Coberly, William G. "An Exegetical Argument for the Position-only View of Sanctification." M.T. thesis, The Master's Seminary, 2004.

Cockerill, Garath Lee. *The Epistle to the Hebrews*. NICNT. Eerdmans, 2012.

Cody, Aelred. *Heavenly Sanctuary and Liturgy in the Epistle to the Hebrews: The Achievement of Salvation in the Epistle's Perspective*. Grail, 1960.

Cohen, Jonathan. "XI.—Teleological Explanation." *Proceedings of the Aristotelian Society: New Series* 51 (1950–1951): 255–292.

Cole, Graham A. *Engaging with the Holy Spirit: Real Questions, Practical Answers*. Crossway, 2007.

Collins, John F. *A Primer of Ecclesiastical Latin*. The Catholic University Press, 1985.

Collins, Kenneth. "A Hermeneutical Model for the Wesleyan Ordo Salutis." *Wesleyan Theological Journal* 19, no. 2 (1984): 23–37.

Conzelmann, Hans. *1 Corinthians: A Commentary on the First Epistle to the Corinthians*. Hermeneia: A Critical and Historical Commentary on the Bible. Edited by George W. McRae. Translated by James W. Dunkly. Fortress, 1975.

Cosgrove, Charles H. "Moral Formation." In *Dictionary of Scripture and Ethics*. Edited by Joel B. Green. Baker Academic, 2011.

Cox, D. Michael, and Brad J. Kallenberg. "Character." In *Dictionary of Scripture and Ethics*. Edited by Joel B. Green. Baker Academic, 2011.

Craig, C. T. *The First Epistle to the Corinthians*. Volume 10 of *IB*. Edited by George Arthur Buttrick. Abingdon, 1953.

Craig, Clarence Tucker. "Paradox of Holiness." *Interpretation* 6 (1952): 147–161.

Crisp, Roger. "Ethics." Pages 256–258 in *Concise Routledge Encyclopedia of Philosophy*. Edited by Edward Craig. Taylor & Francis, 2002.

———. "Virtue Ethics." Pages 622–626 in vol. 9 of *Routledge Encyclopedia of Philosophy*. Edited by Edward Craig, Routledge, 1998.

Cross, F. L., and Elizabeth A. Livingstone, eds. *The Oxford Dictionary of the Christian Church*. 3rd Rev. ed. Oxford University Press, 2005.

Crump, David Michael. *Jesus the Intercessor: Prayer and Christology in Luke–Acts.* WUNT 2.49. J. B. C. Mohr, 1992.

Chisholm, Roderick M. *Brentano and Intrinsic Value.* Cambridge University Press, 1986.

Cunningham, David S. *These Three Are One: The Practice of Trinitarian Theology.* Challenges in Contemporary Theology. Blackwell Publishers, 1998.

Cunningham, Lawrence S., ed. *Thomas Merton: Spiritual Master, the Essential Writings.* Paulist, 1992.

Cutler, Gertrude L., ed. *The Whole Word for the Whole World: The Life and Ministry of J. Vernon Mcgee.* Thru the Bible Radio Network, 1991.

Darwall, Stephen, ed. *Virtue Ethics.* Edited by Steven M. Cahn. Blackwell Readings in Philosophy. Blackwell Publishing, 2003.

Davenport, John J. "Towards and Existential Virtue Ethics: Kierkegaard and Macintyre." Pages 265–316 in *Kierkegaard after Macintyre: Essays on Freedom, Narrative, and Virtue.* Edited by John J. Davenport and Anthony Rudd. Open Court, 2001.

Davids, Peter H. *The Letters of 2 Peter and Jude.* PNTC. Eerdmans, 2006.

Davies, Brian. *The Thought of Thomas Aquinas.* Oxford University Press, 1992.

Dawes, Gregory W. *The Body in Question: Metaphor and Meaning in the Interpretation of Ephesians 5:21–33.* BibInt 30. Brill, 1998.

Denzinger, Henry, Roy J. Deferrari, and Karl Rahner, ed. *The Sources of Catholic Dogma.* B. Herder, 1954.

Driver, Julia. *Uneasy Virtue.* Cambridge University Press, 2001.

Downs, David J. "Vices and Virtues, Lists Of." In *Dictionary of Scripture and Ethics.* Edited by Joel B. Green. Baker Academic, 2011.

Dunn, James D. G. *The Epistles to the Colossians and to Philemon: A Commentary on the Greek Text.* NIGTC. Eerdmans, 1996.

———. *Romans 1–8.* WBC 38A. Word, 2002.

———. *Romans 9–16.* WBC 38B. Word, 2002.

Easton, Burton Scott. "New Testament Ethical Lists." *JBL* 51 (1932): 1–12.

Edwards, Jonathan. "A Dissertation Concerning the Nature of True Virtue." Pages 122–142 in vol. 1 of *The Works of Jonathan Edwards.* Logos Bible Software, 2008.

———. "A Treatise Concerning Religious Affections: In Three Parts." Pages 234–343 in vol. 1 of *The Works of Jonathan Edwards.* Logos Bible Software, 2008.

Ellingworth, Paul. *The Epistle to the Hebrews: A Commentary on the Greek Text.* NIGTC. Eerdmans, 1993.

Elliott, Matthew. *Faithful Feelings: Rethinking Emotion in the New Testament.* Kregel, 2006.

Ellis, E. Earl. *The Gospel of Luke.* NCBC. Rev. ed. Eerdmans; 1974.

Emery, Gilles, and Matthew Levering, eds. *The Oxford Handbook of the Trinity.* Oxford University Press, 2011.

Emery, Gilles. *The Trinitarian Theology of Saint Thomas Aquinas.* Oxford University Press, 2007.

———. *Trinity in Aquinas.* Sapientia Press of Ave Maria College, 2003.

Enns, Paul P. *The Moody Handbook of Theology*. Moody, 1989.
Elwell, Walter A., ed. *Baker Encyclopedia of the Bible*. Baker, 1988.
Epictetus. *The Discourses of Epictetus: With the Encheiridion and Fragments*. Translated by George Long. A. L. Burt, 1900.
Erickson, Millard J. *Christian Theology*. 3rd ed. Baker Academic, 2013.
———. "Lordship Theology: The Current Controversy." *SWJT* 33, no. 2 (1991): 5–15.
———. *Making Sense of the Trinity: Three Crucial Questions*. Baker Academic, 2000.
Essex, Keith. "Sanctification: The Biblically Identifiable Fruit." *MSJ* 21, no. 2 (2010): 193–213.
Evans, C. Stephen. *Pocket Dictionary of Apologetics & Philosophy of Religion*. InterVarsity, 2002.
Evans, Craig A. *Matthew*. NCBC. Cambridge University Press, 2012.
Farley, Benjamin W. *In Praise of Virtue: An Exploration of the Biblical Virtues in a Christian Context*. Eerdmans, 1995.
Farstad, Arthur L. "We Believe in Sanctification—Part 1: Introduction." *Journal of the Grace Evangelical Society* 5, no. 2 (1992). http://www.faithalone.org/journal.
———. "We Believe in Sanctification—Part 5: Future Sanctification: Perfect, or Ultimate Sanctification." *Journal of the Grace Evangelical Society* 8, no. 14 (1995). http://www.faithalone.org/journal.
Fee, Gordon. *The First Epistle to the Corinthians*. NICNT. Eerdmans, 1988.
Feenstra, Ronald Jay, and Cornelius Plantinga. "Introduction." Pages 1–20 in *Trinity, Incarnation, and Atonement: Philosophical and Theological Essays*, ed. Ronald Jay Feenstra and Cornelius Plantinga. LRP 1. University of Notre Dame Press, 1989.
Ferguson, Sinclair B. *John Owen on the Christian Life*. Banner of Truth, 1987.
Finney, Charles. *Principles of Sanctification*. Bethany House, 1986.
———. *Systematic Theology*. Original, Unabridged 1851. Holiness, 2011.
———. *The Works of Charles Finney*. Packard Technologies, 2004.
Foot, Philippa. *Natural Goodness*. Oxford University Press, 2001.
Fortman, Edmund J. *The Triune God: A Historical Study of the Doctrine of the Trinity*. Theological Resources. Westminster, 1972.
France, R. T. "The Church and the Kingdom of God: Some Hermeneutical Issues." Pages 27–42 in *Biblical Interpretation and the Church: Text and Context*, ed. D. A. Carson. Paternoster, 2000.
———. *The Gospel of Mark: A Commentary on the Greek Text*. NIGTC. Eerdmans, 2002.
———. *The Gospel of Matthew*. NICNT. Eerdmans, 2007.
Franks, Robert S. *The Work of Christ: A Historical Study of Christian Doctrine*. Edited by H. H. Rowley and C. W. Dugmore. Thomas Nelson and Sons Ltd, 1962.
Frost, R. N. "Sin and Grace." Pages 101–112 in *Trinitarian Soundings in Systematic Theology*. Edited by Paul Louis Metzger. T&T Clark International, 2006.
Furnish, Victor Paul. *Theology and Ethics in Paul*. The New Testament Library. 1968. Reprint, Westminster John Knox, 2009.
Gangel, Kenneth O. *John*. HNTC 4. B&H, 2000.

Garland, David E. *2 Corinthians*. NAC. B&H, 1999.
Garraghan, Gilbert J. *A Guide to Historical Method*. Fordham University Press, 1946.
Garrett, James Leo. *Systematic Theology: Biblical, Historical, and Evangelical*, 2 vols. 2nd ed. Ages Digital Library, 2006.
Geisler, Norman L. and Paul D. Feinberg. *Introduction to Philosophy: A Christian Perspective*. Baker, 1980.
Geisler, Norman L. *Christian Ethics: Contemporary Issues and Options*. 2nd ed. Baker Academic, 1989.
———. *Colossians*. In *The Bible Knowledge Commentary*. Edited by John F. Walvoord and Roy B. Zuck. Victor Books, 1985.
———. *Ethics: Alternatives and Issues*. Zondervan, 1971.
George, Timothy. "Introduction." Pages 9–16 in *God the Holy Trinity: Reflections on Christian Faith and Practice*. Edited by Timothy George. Baker Academic, 2006.
Gerhardsson, B., and J. T. Willis. "Tradition." Pages 883–885 in vol. 4 of *ISBE*. Edited by Geoffrey W. Bromiley. Eerdmans, 1988.
Gill, Christopher. "Cynicism and Stoicism." In *The Oxford Handbook of the History of Ethics*. Edited by Roger Crisp. Oxford University Press, 2013.
Gilligan, Carol. *In a Different Voice: Psychological Theory and Women's Development*. Harvard University Press, 1982.
Green, Joel B. *The Gospel of Luke*. NICNT. Eerdmans, 1997.
Green, Pamela D. "The Function of Romans 6–8 in Four Models of Sanctification: A Critical and Exegetical Analysis." M.A. Th. thesis, Southwestern Baptist Theological Seminary, 2005.
Gregory Nazianzus. *Oratio XXX*. Edited by Paul Gallay. Under the title *Grégoire De Nazianze Discours 27–31*. SC 250. Éditions du Cerf, 1978.
Gregory of Nyssa. *De anima et resurrectione*. In *De anima et resurrectione; Vita Macrinae*. Bibliothek Der Kirchenväter 1. Edited and Translated by Franz Oehler. Wilhem Engelmann, 1858.
———. *Gregorii Nysseni Opera*, 10 vols. to date. Edited by Werner et al. Jaeger. E. J. Brill, 1921–2009.
Grenz, Stanley J. *Rediscovering the Triune God: The Trinity in Contemporary Theology*. Fortress, 2004.
Grudem, Wayne A. *Systematic Theology: An Introduction to Biblical Doctrine*. Zondervan, 2004.
Guelich, Robert A. *Mark 1–8:26*. WBC 34A. Word, 1998.
Gundry, Stanley N., ed. *Five Views on Sanctification*. Zondervan Counterpoints Collection. Zondervan, 1987.
———, ed. *Three Views on the New Testament Use of the Old Testament*. Counterpoints. Zondervan, 2008.
Gunton, Colin E., ed. *The Doctrine of Creation: Essays in Dogmatics, History and Philosophy*. T&T Clark, 1997.
Hagner, Donald A. *Matthew 1–13*. WBC 33A. Word, 1998.
———. *Matthew 14–28*. WBC 33B. Word, 1998.

Hare, John E. *God and Morality: A Philosophical History*. Wiley-Blackwell, 2009.
Harrington, Daniel J., and James F. Keenan. *Jesus and Virtue Ethics: Building Bridges between New Testament Studies and Moral Theology*. Sheed & Ward, 2002.
Harris, Murray. *Prepositions and Theology in the Greek New Testament: An Essential Reference Resource for Exegesis*. Zondervan, 2012.
Harrison, E. F. "Glory." Pages 477–483 in vol. 2 of *IBSE*. Edited by Geoffrey W. Bromiley. Eerdmans, 1988.
———. *Romans*. Vol. 10 of *EBC*, Edited by Frank E. Gaebelein and J. D. Douglas. Zondervan, 1981.
Harrison, R. K., ed. *Encyclopedia of Biblical and Christian Ethics*. Thomas Nelson, 1987.
Hartley, John E. *Leviticus*. WBC 4. Word, 1998.
Hauerwas, Stanley, David B. Burrell, and Richard Bondi. *Truthfulness and Tragedy: Further Investigations in Christian Ethics*. University of Notre Dame Press, 1977.
Hauerwas, Stanley. *Character and the Christian Life: A Study in Theological Ethics*. Trinity University Press, 1975.
———. *A Community of Character: Toward a Constructive Christian Social Ethic*. University of Notre Dame Press, 1981.
———. *Vision and Virtue: Essays in Christian Ethical Reflection*. Fides, 1974.
Hawhee, Debra. *Bodily Arts: Rhetoric and Athletics in Ancient Greece*. University of Texas Press, 2004.
Hay, David M. *Glory at the Right Hand: Psalm 110 in Early Christianity*. SBLMS. Edited by Robert A. Kraft and Leander Keck. Abingdon, 1973.
Heer, Ken. *Luke: A Commentary for Bible Students*. Wesleyan, 2007.
Helmer, Christine. "Between History and Speculation: Christian Trinitarian Thinking after the Reformation." Pages 149–169 in *The Cambridge Companion to the Trinity* ed. Peter C. Phan. Cambridge University Press, 2011.
Hemer, C. J. "Imitate." Page 806 in vol 4 of *ISBE*. Edited by Geoffrey W. Bromiley. Eerdmans, 1988.
Henry, Carl Ferdinand Howard. *God Who Speaks and Shows*. Vol. 1 of *God, Revelation, and Authority*. Crossway, 1999.
Heppe, Heinrich. *Die Dogmatik der evangelisch-reformierte Kirche: Dargestellt und aus den Quellen belegt*. 2nd ed. Neukirchener Verlag, Kreis Moers, 1958.
Herman, Barbara. "Making Room for Character." Pages 36–62 in *Aristotle, Kant, and the Stoics: Rethinking Happiness and Duty*. Edited by Stephen Engstrom and Jennifer Whiting. Cambridge University Press, 1996.
———. *The Practice of Moral Judgment*. Harvard University Press, 1993.
Hermas. *Similitudines*. Edited by Molly Whittaker. Vol. 1 of *Die Apostolischen Väter: Der Hirt des Hermas*. GCS 48. 2nd ed. Akademie-Verlag, 1967.
Hill, Daniel, and Daniel J. Treier. "Philosophy." Pages 591–594 in *Dictionary for Theological Interpretation of the Bible*. Edited by Kevin J. Vanhoozer, Craig G. Bartholomew, Daniel J. Treier and N. T. Wright. Baker Academic, 2005.
Hodge, Charles. *Systematic Theology*, 3 vols. Logos Research Systems, 1997.

Hodgson, Leonard. *The Doctrine of the Trinity: Croall Lectures, 1942–1943*. C. Scribner's Sons, 1944.
Hoehner, Harold W. *Ephesians: An Exegetical Commentary*. Baker Academic, 2002.
Hoekema, Anthony A. "The Reformed Perspective." Pages 59–90 in *Five Views on Sanctification*. Edited by Stanley N. Gundry. Zondervan Counterpoints Collection. Zondervan, 1987.
Holland, Richard L. "The Pastor's Sanctifying Role in the Church." *MSJ* 21, no. 2 (2010): 215–229.
Hollinger, Dennis P. *Choosing the Good: Christian Ethics in a Complex World*. Baker Academic, 2002.
Holmes, Arthur F. *Fact, Value, and God*. Eerdmans, 1997.
Holmes, Stephen R. *The Quest for the Trinity: The Doctrine of God in Scripture, History and Modernity*. IVP Academic, 2012.
Hornsby, Jennifer. "Action." In *Concise Routledge Encyclopaedia of Philosophy*. Edited by Edward Craig, 5. Routledge, 2000.
Horton, Michael. "God." Pages 343–348 in *Evangelical Dictionary of Theology*. Edited by Daniel J. Treier and Walter A. Elwell. Baker Academic, 2017.
Horton, Stanley M. "The Pentecostal Perspective." Pages 103–135 in *Five Views on Sanctification*. Edited by Stanley N. Gundry. Zondervan, 1987.
House, H. Wayne. *Charts of Christian Theology and Doctrine*. Zondervan, 1992.
Houston, James M. "The Nature and Purpose of Spiritual Theology." *Evangelical Review of Theology* 16, no. 1 (1992): 118–142.
Houston, Thomas. *The Intercession of Christ*. James Gemmell, 1882.
Howard, James M. *Paul, the Community, and Progressive Sanctification: An Exploration into Community-Based Transformation within Pauline Theology*. Edited by Hemchand Gossai. StBibLit 90, Peter Lang, 2007.
Hughes, Gerard J. *Routledge Philosophy Guidebook to Aristotle on Ethics*. Routledge Philosophy Guidebooks. Routledge, 2001.
Hughes, Philip Edgcumbe. *A Commentary on the Epistle to the Hebrews*. Rep. ed. Eerdmans, 1977.
Hume, David. *A Treatise of Human Nature*. Edited by L. A. Selby-Bigge. The Clarendon Press, 1888.
Hunt, John. *From the Reformation to the End of the Last Century*. Vol. 2 of *Religious Thought in England: A Contribution to the History of Theology*. AMS Press, 1973.
Hunter, Archibald M. *Paul and His Predecessors*. New Rev. ed. The Westminster Press, 1961.
Hurka, Thomas. "Teleological Ethics." Pages 382–384 in vol. 9 of *Macmillan Encyclopedia of Philosophy*. Edited by Donald M. Borchert. Macmillan, 2006.
———. *Virtue, Vice, and Value*. Oxford University Press, 2001.
Hursthouse, Rosalind. *On Virtue Ethics*. Oxford University Press, 2001.
———. "Virtue Ethics." In *The Stanford Encyclopedia of Philosophy*. Edited by Edward N. Zalta, 2012. http://plato.stanford.edu.

Ignatius Loyola. *The Spiritual Exercises of St. Ignatius Loyola; Spanish and English with a Continuous Commentary.* Edited by Joseph Rickaby. Burns & Oates, 1915.

Irwin, T. H. "Aristotle (384–322 BC)." Pages 50–51 in *Concise Routledge Encyclopedia of Philosophy.* Edited by Edward Craig. Taylor & Francis, 2002.

Jaffa, Harry V. *Thomism and Aristotelianism.* University of Chicago Press, 1952.

Jenney, Timothy P. "The Holy Spirit and Sanctification." In *Systematic Theology: A Pentecostal Perspective.* Edited by Stanley M. Horton. Gospel, 2012.

Jenson, Robert W. *Systematic Theology,* 2 vols. Oxford University Press, 1997, 1999.

Jobes, Karen H. *1 Peter.* BECNT. Baker Academic, 2005.

John of the Cross. *Dark Night of the Soul.* Neeland Media, 2010.

Johnson, Eric L. "Rewording the Justification/Sanctification Relation with Some Help from Speech Act Theory." *JETS* 54, no. 4 (2011): 767–785.

Johnston, Mark G. "Sanctification: 4. Alone, but Never Alone!" *Banner of Truth* 511 (2006): 7–13.

Jones, Hywel R. "Sanctification: 6. And Then—to Rest Forever." *Banner of Truth* 512 (2006): 7–13.

Jones, L. Gregory. *Transformed Judgment: Toward a Trinitarian Account of the Moral Life.* University of Notre Dame Press, 1990.

Jost, Lawrence J. "Virtue and Vice." Pages 678–682 in vol. 9 of *Macmillan Encyclopedia of Philosophy.* Edited by Donald M. Borchert. Macmillan, 2006.

Just, Arthur A., Jr., ed. *Luke.* Ancient Christian Commentary. InterVarsity Press, 2003.

Justin Martyr. *Apologie.* Edited, translated, and annotated by Charles Munier. Under the title *Justin Apologie pour les Chrétiens: Introduction, Texte Critique, Traduction et Notes.* SC 507. Éditsions du Cerf, 2006.

Kant, Immanuel. "The Conflict of the Faculties." Pages 233–293 in *Religion and Rational Theology.* Edited by Allen W. Wood and George Di Giovanni. The Cambridge Edition of the Works of Immanuel Kant. Cambridge University Press, 1996.

———. *Kant's Werke,* 29 vols. to date. *Kant's Gesammelte Schriften,* Edited by Wilhelm Dilthey. Georg Reimer, 1900–.

Kapic, Kelly M. "*Simul Iustus et Peccator.*" *Tabletalk Magazine* 34, no. 5 (May 2010): 10–13.

Kärkkäinen, Veli-Matti. *Christology: A Global Introduction.* Baker Academic, 2003.

———. *The Trinity: Global Perspectives.* Westminster John Knox Press, 2007.

Keathley, Kenneth. "The Work of God: Salvation." In *A Theology for the Church.* Edited by Daniel L. Akin. B&H, 2007.

Keenan, James F. "Moral Theological Reflections." Pages 1–8 in *Jesus and Virtue Ethics: Building Bridges between New Testament Studies and Moral Theology.* MD: Sheed & Ward, 2002.

Keener, Craig S. *The Gospel of Matthew: A Socio-Rhetorical Commentary.* Eerdmans, 2009.

———. *The IVP Bible Background Commentary: New Testament.* InterVarsity, 1993.

Keil, Carl Friedrich, and Franz Delitzsch. *Commentary on the Old Testament.* 10 vols. Rev. ed. Hendrickson, 1996.

Kelly, J. N. D. *The Epistles of Peter and of Jude*. BNTC. Continuum, 1969.
Kettenring, Keith A. "A Conceptual Integration of Human Participation within Sanctification Using Ford's Personal Agency Beliefs." PhD. thesis, Biola, 2005.
Kilby, Karen. "Aquinas, the Trinity and the Limits of Understanding." *International Journal of Systematic Theology* 7, no. 4 (2005): 414–427.
King, Peter. "Emotions." Pages 209–226 in *The Oxford Handbook of Aquinas*. Edited by Brian Davies and Eleanore Stump. Oxford University Press, 2012.
Klein, George L. *Zechariah*. NAC. B&H, 2008.
Knuuttila, Simo and Robert F. Brown. "Nominalism." Pages 766–68 in vol. 3 of *EC*. Edited by Erwin Fahlbusch and Geoffrey William Bromiley. Eerdmans; Brill, 2003.
Korsgaard, Christine. "From Duty and for the Sake of the Noble: Kant and Aristotle on Morally Good Action." Pages 203–236 in *Aristotle, Kant, and the Stoics: Rethinking Happiness and Duty*. Edited by Stephen Engstrom and Jennifer Whiting. Cambridge University Press, 1996.
_____. "Teleological Ethics." Pages 294–295 in vol. 9 of *Routledge Encyclopedia of Philosophy*. Edited by Edward Craig, Routledge, 1998.
Kotva, Joseph J. *The Christian Case for Virtue Ethics*. Georgetown University Press, 1996.
Kraut, Richard, ed. *Cambridge Companion to Plato*. Cambridge University Press, 1999.
Kruse, Colin G. *The Letters of John*. PNTC. Eerdmans, 2000.
_____. "Virtues and Vices." Pages 962–963 in *Dictionary of Paul and His Letters*. Edited by Gerald F. Hawthorne, Ralph P. Martin and Daniel G. Reid. InterVarsity, 1993.
Kurianal, James. *Jesus Our High Priest: Ps 110,4 as the Substructure of Heb 5,1–7,28* European University Studies, Series 23. Peter Lang, 2000.
Kuyper, Abraham. *The Work of the Holy Spirit*. Translated by Henri de Vries. Funk & Wagnalls, 1900.
Kwon, Ae-Hoe. "Sanctification and the Christian Life: An Integrated Approach of Theory and Practice." PhD. diss., Fuller Theological Seminary, 2002.
LaCugna, Catherine Mowry. *God for Us: The Trinity and Christian Life*. HarperSanFrancisco, 1991.
Lage, Dietmar. *Martin Luther's Christology and Ethics*. TSR 45. Edwin Mellen Press, 1990.
Lane, William L. *Hebrews 1–8*. WBC 47A. Word, 2002.
_____. *Hebrews 9–13*. WBC 47B. Word, 2002.
Lang, Friedrich. *Die Briefe an die Korinther*. 16th ed., NTD 7 Vandenhoeck and Ruprecht, 1986.
Lea, Thomas D. *Hebrews, James*. HNTC 10. B&H, 1999.
Lea, Thomas D., and Hayne P. Griffin. *1, 2 Timothy, Titus*. NAC. B&H, 1992.
Lee, A. Elizabeth. "Made in the Images of God: Towards a Trinitarian Virtue Ethics." Ph. D. diss., Graduate Theological Union, 2010.
Lemos, Noah M. *Intrinsic Value: Concept and Warrant*. Cambridge University Press, 1994.

Lenski, R. C. H. *The Interpretation of St. Paul's Epistle to the Romans.* Lutheran Book Concern, 1936.

Letham, Robert. *The Holy Trinity: In Scripture, History, Theology, and Worship.* P&R, 2004.

Levering, Matthew. *Scripture and Metaphysics: Aquinas and the Renewal of Trinitarian Theology.* Blackwell, 2004.

Lincoln, Andrew T. *Ephesians.* WBC 42. Word, 1990.

———. *The Gospel According to Saint John.* BNTC. Continuum, 2005.

Lindsey, F. Duane. *Zechariah.* In *The Bible Knowledge Commentary.* Edited by John F. Walvoord and Roy B. Zuck. Victor, 1985.

Link, H. G., and A. Ringwald. "Virtue, Blameless." Pages 923–928 in vol. 3 of *NIDNTT.* Edited by Colin Brown. Zondervan, 1986.

Loader, William R. G. *Sohn und Hoherpriester: eine traditionsgeschichtliche Untersuchung zur Christologie des Hebräerbriefes.* WMANT 53. Neukirchener Verlag, 1981.

Lombard, Peter. *The Sentences,* 4 vols. MST 42, 43, 45, 48, Edited by Joseph Goering and Giulio Silano. Translated by Giulio Silano. Pontifical Institute of Mediaeval Studies, 2007–2010.

Louden, Robert B. "Kant's Virtue Ethics." *Philosophy* 61, no. 238 (1986): 473–489.

———. "On Some Vices of Virtue Ethics." *American Philosophical Quarterly* 21, no. 3 (1984): 227–236.

———. "Virtue Ethics." Pages 687–689 in vol. 9 of *Macmillan Encyclopedia of Philosophy.* Edited by Donald M. Borchert. New York: Macmillan, 2006.

Loux, Michael J. "Nominalism." Pages 17–23 in vol. 9 of *Routledge Encyclopedia of Philosophy.* Edited by Edward Craig. Routledge, 1998.

Lowry, Charles W. *The Trinity and Christian Devotion.* Eyre and Spottiswoode, 1946.

Lukaszewski, Albert L., Mark Dubis, and J. Ted Blakley, eds. *The Lexham Syntactic Greek New Testament.* SBL ed. Logos Research Systems, 2011.

Luther, Martin. *D. Martin Luthers Werke: Kritische Gesamtausgabe.* 73 vols. to date. Hermarur Böhlaus Nachfolger, 1883–.

———. *Luther's Works.* Edited by Jeroslav Pelikan (vols. 1–30) and Helmut T. Lehmann (vols. 31–55). Fortress, 1955–1986.

Luz, Ulrich. *Matthew 1–7.* Hermeneia: A Critical & Historical Commentary on the Bible. Edited by Helmut Koester. Translated by James E. Crouch. Fortress, 2007.

———. *Matthew 8–20.* Hermeneia: A Critical & Historical Commentary on the Bible. Edited by Helmut Koester. Translated by James E. Crouch. Fortress, 2001.

Macarius the Egyptian. *Makarios/Symeon Reden und Briefe: Die Sammlung I des Vaticanus Graecus 694 B,* Vol. 2. GCS (Unnumbered). Edited by Heinz Berthold. Akademie-Verlag, 1973.

MacArthur, John F., Jr. *Ephesians.* Macarthur New Testament Commentary. Moody, 1986.

Maccovius, Johannes. *Loci Communes Theologici.* Ludovicum & Danielem Elzevirios, 1667.

MacIntyre, Alasdair. "Preface." In *Metaphysical Beliefs: Three Essays*, 9. of The Library of Philosophy and Theology. SCM, 1957.

———. *After Virtue: A Study in Moral Theory.* 2nd ed. University of Notre Dame Press, 1984.

———. *Whose Justice? Which Rationality?* University of Notre Dame Press, 1988.

Mackintosh, H. R. *Types of Modern Theology: Schleiermacher to Barth.* Nisbet and Co., 1937.

MacLeod, David J. "Christ, the Believer's High Priest: An Exposition of Hebrews 7:26–28." *BSac* 162, no. 647 (2005): 331–343.

MacRae, George. "A Note on Romans 8:26–27." *HTR* 73 (1980): 227–230.

Mahan, Asa. *Out of Darkness into Light.* Amazon Digital Services, 2010.

———. *Christian Perfection.* Amazon Digital Services, 2012.

Margerie, Bertrand de. *The Christian Trinity in History*, SHT 1. Translated by Edmund J. Fortman. St. Bede's Publications, 1982.

Marshall, Bruce D. "Philosophy and Theology." Pages 195–199 in vol. 4 of *EC*. Edited by Erwin Fahlbusch and Geoffrey William Bromiley. Eerdmans; Brill, 2005.

———. "Trinity." Pages 183–203 in *The Blackwell Companion to Modern Theology*. Edited by Gareth Jones. Blackwell Companions to Religion. Blackwell, 2004.

Marshall, I. Howard. *1 Peter*. IVPNTC. InterVarsity, 1991.

———. *The Gospel of Luke: A Commentary on the Greek Text.* NIGTC. Paternoster, 1978.

Marshall, Walter. *The Gospel-Mystery of Sanctification.* Southwick and Peluse, 1811.

Martin, John A. "Luke." In *The Bible Knowledge Commentary*. Edited by John F. Walvoord and Roy B. Zuck. Victor Books, 1985.

Martin, Ralph P. "Virtue, Haustafeln." Pages 928–932 in vol. 3 of *NIDNTT*. Edited by Colin Brown. Zondervan, 1986.

———. *2 Corinthians.* WBC 40. Word, 1998.

Mathews, K. A. *Genesis 1–11:26.* NAC. B&H, 1996.

Mauchline, John. "Jesus Christ as Intercessor." *Expository Times* 64, no. 12 (1953): 355–360.

Mayhue, Richard L. "Sanctification: The Biblical Basics." *MSJ* 21, no. 2 (2010): 143–157.

McDowell, John. "Deliberation and Moral Development in Aristotle's Ethics." Pages 19–35 in *Aristotle, Kant, and the Stoics: Rethinking Happiness and Duty*. Edited by Stephen Engstrom and Jennifer Whiting. Cambridge University Press, 1996.

McGrath, Alister E. *Historical Theology: An Introduction to the History of Christian Thought.* 2nd ed. Wiley-Blackwell, 2013.

———. *Iustitia Dei: A History of the Christian Doctrine of Justification.* 3rd ed. Cambridge University Press, 2005.

———. *The Intellectual Origins of the European Reformation.* 2nd ed. Blackwell, 2004.

McNaughton, David. "Deontological Ethics." Pages 890–892 in vol. 2 of *Routledge Encyclopedia of Philosophy*. Edited by Edward Craig. Routledge, 1998.

McNicole, Allen James. "The Relationship of the Image of the Highest Angel to the High Priest Concept in Hebrews." PhD. diss., Vanderbilt University, 1974.
McQuilkin, J. Robertson. "The Keswick Perspective." Pages 151–183 in *Five Views on Sanctification*. Edited by Stanley N. Gundry. Zondervan, 1987.
Meilaender, Gilbert C. *The Theory and Practice of Virtue*. University of Notre Dame Press, 1984.
Melanchthon, Philip. *Melanchthons Werke in Auswahl*. Edited by Robert Stupperich. 7 vols. in 9. C. Bertelsmann Verlag, 1951–1975.
_____. *Philippi Melanthonis Opera quae supersunt omnia*. Edited by Henricus Ernestus Bindseil. 59 vols. in 58. Corpus Reformatorum, vols. 1–28. C. A. Schwetschke and Son, 1863–1900; reprint, Johnston, 1964.
Michaels, J. Ramsey. *1 Peter*. WBC 49. Word, 2002.
Miley, John. *Systematic Theology*. Vol. 2. Hunt & Eaton, 1893.
Mill, John Stuart. *Collected Works of John Stuart Mill*, 33 vols. Edited by J. M. Robson. University of Toronto Press, 1963–1991.
Mitchell, Craig. "Overview of Ethical Theory." Classroom lecture notes, Ethic 7624-A—Metaethics, Fall 2009. Electronic PowerPoint Presentation.
Moo, Douglas J. *The Epistle to the Romans*. NICNT. Eerdmans, 1996.
_____. *The Letters to the Colossians and to Philemon*. PNTC. Eerdmans, 2008.
Moore, G. E. *Principia Ethica*, Edited by Thomas Baldwin. Rev. ed. Cambridge University Press, 1993.
Moreland, J. P. *Universals*. Central Problems of Philosophy. Edited by John Shand. McGill-Queen's University Press, 2001.
Morris, Leon. *The Epistle to the Romans*. PNTC. InterVarsity, 1988.
_____. *The Gospel According to John*. NICNT. Eerdmans, 1971.
_____. *The Gospel According to Matthew*. PNTC. Eerdmans, 1992.
Mostert, Christiaan. *God and the Future: Wolfhart Pannenberg's Eschatological Doctrine of God*. T&T Clark, 2002.
Mounce, Robert A. *Romans*. NAC. B&H, 1995.
Mounce, William D. *Pastoral Epistles*. WBC 46. Word, 2000.
Muddiman, John. *The Epistle to the Ephesians*. BNTC. Continuum, 2001.
Mueller, John Theodore. *Christian Dogmatics*. Concordia Publishing House, 1999.
Muller, R. A. "Sanctification." Pages 321–331 in 4 of *ISBE*. Edited by Geoffrey W. Bromiley. Eerdmans, 1988.
_____. *The Triunity of God*. Vol. 4 of *Post-Reformation Reformed Dogmatics: The Rise and Development of Reformed Orthodoxy*, Ca. 1520 to Ca. 1725. Baker Academic, 2003.
Mulligan, Kevin. "Predication." In *Concise Routledge Encyclopedia of Philosophy*. Edited by Edward Craig, 708. Taylor & Francis, 2002.
Murray, John J. "Sanctification: 3. Through the Power of the Spirit." *Banner of Truth* 511 (2006): 1–6.
Murray, John. "Definitive Sanctification." *CTJ* 2, no. 1 (1967): 5–21.
_____. *The Epistle to the Romans*. NICNT. Combined ed. Eerdmans, 1968.

_____. "The Heavenly, Priestly Activity of Christ." Pages 44–58 in *The Claims of Truth*. Vol. 1 of *Collected Writings of John Murray: Professor of Systematic Theology, Westminster Theological Seminary, Philadelphia, Pennsylvania, 1937–1966*. Banner of Truth Trust, 1976.

_____. *Redemption: Accomplished and Applied*. Eerdmans, 1954.

Nadelhoffer, Thomas, Eddy Nahmias, and Shaun Nichols. "Introduction." Pages 1–3 in *Moral Psychology: Historical and Contemporary Readings*. Edited by Thomas Nadelhoffer, Eddy Nahmias and Shaun Nichols. Blackwell, 2010.

Nairne, Alexander. *The Epistle of Priesthood, Studies in the Epistle to the Hebrews*. T&T Clark, 1913.

Niebuhr, Richard R. *Schleiermacher on Christ and Religion, a New Introduction*. Scribner, 1964.

Niemelä, John H. "Where in the World Is the Old Man?: Old-Man and New-Man in Paul." Paper presented at the annual meeting of the Grace Evangelical Society, Fort Worth, TX, 24 April 2013.

Noddings, Nel. *Caring: A Feminist Approach to Ethics and Moral Education*. University of California Press, 2003.

Nolland, John. *The Gospel of Matthew: A Commentary on the Greek Text*. NIGTC. Eerdmans, 2005.

_____. *Luke 1:1–9:20*. WBC 35A. Word, 2002.

_____. *Luke 9:21–18:34*. WBC 35B. Word, 1998.

Norris, Robert M. "Preaching Grace." *Tabletalk Magazine* 34, no. 5 (May 2010): 24–25.

Nussbaum, Martha C. *The Fragility of Goodness: Luck and Ethics in Greek Tragedy and Philosophy*. 2nd ed. Cambridge University Press, 2001.

_____. *Upheavals of Thought: The Intelligence of Emotions*. Cambridge University Press, 2001.

Obeng, E. A. "The Origins of the Spirit Intercession Motif in Romans 8:26." *NTS* 32, no. 4 (1986): 621–632.

O'Brien Wicker, Kathleen, ed. *Porphyry the Philosopher to Marcella: Text and Translation with Introduction and Notes*. SBLTT 28/SBLGRRS 10. Scholars, 1987.

_____. *The Letter to the Hebrews*. PNTC. Eerdmans, 2010.

_____. "Romans 8:26, 27: A Revolutionary Approach to Prayer?" *Reformed Theological Review* 46 (1987): 65–73.

O'Donovan, Oliver. *Resurrection and Moral Order: An Outline for Evangelical Ethics*. Eerdmans, 1994.

O'Neill, Onora. "Kant's Virtues." Pages 77–98 in *How Should One Live? Essays on the Virtues*. Edited by Roger Crisp. Clarendon, 1996.

Oden, Thomas C. *Systematic Theology*, 3 vols. HarperSanFrancisco, 1992.

Ogletree, Thomas W. "Love, Love Command." In *Dictionary of Scripture and Ethics*. Edited by Joel B. Green. Baker Academic, 2011.

Olshausen, Hermann. *The Epistle of St Paul to the Romans*. Biblical Commentary on the New Testament: Adapted Especially for Preachers and Students. Translated by n. t. T&T Clark, 1849.

Origen. *Contra Celesum.* In *Origenes contra Celesum Libri VIII.* Edited by J. Den Boeft, et al. Supplements to Vigiliae Christianae 54. Brill, 2001.

———. *De principiis.* Edited by P. Koetschau. Vol. 5 of *Origenes Werke.* GCS 22. J. C. Hinrichs, 1913.

Owen, John. *Of Communion with God the Father, Son, and Holy Ghost.* Vol. 2 of *The Works of John Owen.* Edited by William H. Goold. T&T Clark, 1862.

———. Vol. 5 of *An Exposition of the Epistle to the Hebrews.* Vol. 22. of *The Works of John Owen.* Edited by William H. Goold. Johnstone and Hunter, 1855.

———. *Πνευματολογια· or, a Discourse Concerning the Holy Spirit.* Vol. 3 of *The Works of John Owen.* Edited by William H. Goold. T&T Clark, 1862.

Owens, Will L. "The Doctrine of Sanctification with Respect to Its Role in Eternal Salvation." PhD. diss., Southeastern Baptist Theological Seminary, 2008.

Packer, J. I. *Keep in Step with the Spirit.* F. H. Revell, 1984.

———. "Regeneration." Pages 1000–1001 in *Evangelical Dictionary of Theology.* Edited by Walter A. Elwell. Baker Reference Library. Baker, 2001.

Parsons, Burk. "Coram Deo // Living before the Face of God: Set Apart to Die and to Live." *Tabletalk Magazine* 34, no. 5 (2010): 2.

Peirce, Charles Sanders. *Principles of Philosophy and Elements of Logic (Volumes 1 and 2).* Vol. 1 of *Collected Papers.* Edited by Charles Hartshorne and Paul Weiss. Rep. ed. Belknap Press of Harvard University Press, 1958.

Pelikan, Jaroslav. *Historical Theology: Continuity and Change in Christian Doctrine.* Theological Resources. Westminster, 1971.

Perez, J. du. "'Sperma Auto' in 1 John 3:9." *Neotestamentica* 9 (1975): 105–110.

Perry, Ben Edwin, ed. *Aesopica: A Series of Texts Relating to Aesop or Ascribed to Him or Closely Connected with the Literary Tradition That Bears His Name.* Vol. 1. University of Illinois Press, 1952.

Peterson, David G. *Hebrews and Perfection: An Examination of the Concept of Perfection in the "Epistle to the Hebrews."* SNTSMS 47. Edited by R. McL. Wilson. Cambridge University Press, 1982.

Peterson, D. G. "Holiness." Pages 544–550 in *New Dictionary of Biblical Theology.* Edited by T. Desmond Alexander and Brian S. Rosner. InterVarsity, 2000.

———. *Possessed by God: A New Testament Theology of Sanctification and Holiness.* NSBT 1. InterVarsity, 1995.

Phillips, Edward. "Prayer in the First Four Centuries A.D." Pages 31–58 in *A History of Prayer: The First to the Fifteenth Century.* Edited by Roy Hammerling. Brill's Companions to the Christian Tradition 13. Brill, 2008.

Pieper, Franz. *Christliche Dogmatik.* Evangelisch-Lutherischen Synode von Missouri und Anderen Staaten, 1946.

Pinckaers, Servais. *The Sources of Christian Ethics.* Translated by Mary Thomas Noble. Catholic University of America Press, 1995.

———. "The Sources of the Ethics of St. Thomas Aquinas." Pages 17–29 in *The Ethics of Aquinas.* Moral Traditions Series. Georgetown University Press, 2002.

Pincoffs, Edmund L. *Quandaries and Virtues: Against Reductivism in Ethics.* University Press of Kansas 1986.

Pink, Arthur Walkington. *The Doctrine of Sanctification.* Logos Research Systems, 2005.

Politis, Vasilis. *Routledge Philosophy Guidebook to Aristotle and the Metaphysics.* Routledge, 2004.

Pope, Stephen J. "Natural Law and Christian Ethics." Pages 67–86 in *The Cambridge Companion to Christian Ethics.* Edited by Robin Gill. Cambridge Companions to Religion. Cambridge University Press, 2012.

_____. "Overview of the Ethics of Thomas Aquinas." Pages 30–53 in *The Ethics of Aquinas.* Moral Traditions Series. Georgetown University Press, 2002.

Porter, Stanley E. *Verbal Aspect in the Greek of the New Testament: With Reference to Tense and Mood.* SBG 1. Edited by D. A. Carson. P. Lang, 1989.

Porter, Steven L. "On the Renewal of Interest in the Doctrine of Sanctification: A Methodological Reminder." *JETS* 45, no. 3 (2002): 415–426.

Powell, Samuel M. "Nineteenth-Century Protestant Doctrines of the Trinity." Pages 267–280 in *The Oxford Handbook of the Trinity.* Edited by Gilles Emery and Matthew Levering. Oxford University Press, 2011.

_____. *The Trinity in German Thought.* Cambridge University Press, 2001.

Pratt, Jonathan R. "The Relationship between Justification and Sanctification in Romans 5–8." PhD. diss., Dallas Theological Seminary, 1999.

Prenter, Regin. *Spiritus Creator.* Translated by John M. Jenson. Wipf and Stock, 1946.

Quine, W.V.O. "The Two Dogmas of Empiricism." *The Journal of Symbolic Logic* 17, no. 4 (1952): 20–43.

Rahner, Karl. *The Trinity.* Translated by Joseph Donceel. Crossroad, 1970.

Railton, Peter. "Analytic Ethics." Pages 28–29 in *Concise Routledge Encyclopedia of Philosophy.* Edited by Edward Craig. Taylor & Francis, 2002.

Rankin, W. Duncan. "Being and Becoming." *Tabletalk Magazine* 34, no. 5 (May 2010): 20–23.

Raymer, Roger M. *1 Peter.* In *The Bible Knowledge Commentary.* Edited by John F. and Roy B. Zuck Walvoord. Victor Books, 1985.

Redditt, Paul L. "Source Criticism." Pages 761–763 in *Dictionary for Theological Interpretation of the Bible.* Edited by Kevin J. Vanhoozer, Craig G. Bartholomew, Daniel J. Treier and N. T. Wright. Baker Academic, 2005.

Reeder, Jesse A. "Definitive Sanctification: A Needed Component in Resolving the Johannine Perfectionism Puzzle of 1 John." PhD. diss., Mid-America Baptist Theological Seminary, 2009.

Reiling, J., and J. L. Swellengrebel. *A Handbook on the Gospel of Luke.* UBS Handbook Series. United Bible Societies, 1993.

Reinders, Johannes S. "The Meaning of Sanctification: Stanley Hauerwas on Christian Identity and Moral Judgment." Pages 141–167 in *Does Religion Matter Morally?: The Critical Reappraisal of the Thesis of Morality's Independence from Religion* ed. Bert Musschenga. MML 2. Kok Pharos, 1995.

Reitzenstein, Richard. *Historia monachorum und Historia lausiaca.* FRLANTNF 7. Vandenhoeck und Ruprecht, 1916.

Richardson, Henry S. "Deontological Ethics." Pages 712–715 in vol. 2 of *Macmillan Encyclopedia of Philosophy.* Edited by Donald M. Borchert. Macmillan, 2006.

Rist, John. "Faith and Reason." Pages 474–709 in *The Cambridge Companion to Augustine.* Edited by Eleonore Stump and Norman Kretzmann. Cambridge University Press, 2001.

Roberts, Mostyn. "Sanctification: 1. Sin Shall Not Be Your Master." *Banner of Truth* 509 (Feb 2006): 1–7.

Roberts, Robert C. "Aristotle on Virtues and Emotions." *Philosophical Studies* 56, no. 3 (1989): 293–306.

———. *Emotions: An Essay in Aid of Moral Psychology.* Cambridge University Press, 2003.

———. *Spiritual Emotions: A Psychology of Christian Virtues.* Eerdmans, 2007.

Robertson, A.T. *Word Pictures in the New Testament.* Broadman Press, 1933.

Rohls, Jan and Robert Kolb. "Predestination." Pages 340–344 in vol. 4 of *EC.* Edited by Erwin Fahlbusch and Geoffrey William Bromiley. Eerdmans, 2005.

Rooker, Mark F. *Leviticus.* NAC. B&H, 2000.

Rosscup, James E. "The Spirit's Intercession." *MSJ* 10, no. 1 (Spr 1999): 139–162.

Rothenberg, Ronald M. "A Biblically Consistent Metaethic: The Consistency of Moral Realism with the Bible." Paper presented at the regional meeting of the Evangelical Theological Society, New Orleans, LA, 27 February 2010.

Rupp, Gordon. "The Finished Work of Christ in Word and Sacrament." Pages 175–192 in *The Finality of Christ.* Edited by Dow Kirkpatrick. Abingdon, 1966.

Russell, Helene Tallon. *Irigaray and Kierkegaard: On the Construction of the Self.* Mercer University Press, 2009.

Ryle, J. C. *Holiness: Its Nature, Hindrances, Difficulties and Roots.* William Hunt and Company, 1889

Sailhamer, John H. *Genesis.* Vol. 2 of *EBC.* Edited by Frank E. Gaebelein and J. D. Douglas. Zondervan, 1981.

Sanders, Fred. "The State of the Doctrine of the Trinity in Evangelical Theology." *SWJT* 47, no. 2 (Spr 2005): 153–175.

———. "Trinity." Pages 35–53 in *The Oxford Handbook of Systematic Theology.* Edited by J. B. Webster, Kathryn Tanner and Iain R. Torrance. Oxford Handbooks. Oxford University Press, 2007.

———. *The Deep Things of God: How the Trinity Changes Everything.* Crossway Books, 2010.

Santas, Gerasimos X. "Does Aristotle Have a Virtue Ethics?" Pages 260–285 in *Virtue Ethics.* Edited by Daniel Statman. Georgetown University Press, 1997.

Sartelle, John P. "No Ordinary Mercy." *Tabletalk Magazine* 34, no. 5 (2010): 14–17.

Sauer, James B. *Faithful Ethics According to John Calvin: The Teachability of the Heart.* TST 74. Mellen Press, 1997.

Schaff, Philip and David Schley Schaff. *History of the Christian Church*. 3rd Revised and Electronic ed. Charles Scribner's Sons, 1910.

Schleiermacher, Friedrich. *The Christian Faith*. Edited by H. R. Mackintosh and J. S. Steward. Paperback ed. T&T Clark, 1999.

Schnackenburg, Rudolf. *Ephesians: A Commentary*. Translated by Helen Heron. T&T Clark, 1991.

———. *The Gospel According to St. John*. NTSR 3. Crossroad, 1982.

Schreiner, Thomas R. *1, 2 Peter, Jude*. NAC. B&H, 2003.

Schroeder, D. "Lists, Ethical." Pages 546–547 in *Supplementary Volume*. Vol. 5 of *IDB*. Edited by Keith Crim. Abingdon, 1962.

Schwöbel, Christoph. "Introduction." Pages 1–30 in *Trinitarian Theology Today: Essays on Divine Being and Act*. Edited by Christoph Schwöbel. T&T Clark, 1995.

Scott, John. "Sanctification: 2. The Continuing Warfare with Sin." *Banner of Truth* 509 (2006): 8–14.

Seneca. *Seneca ad Lucilium epistulae morales*. Vol. 2. LCL 76. Translated by Richard M. Gummere. Harvard University Press, 1962.

Septuaginta: With Morphology. Deutsche Bibelgesellschaft, 1996.

Sexton, Jason S. "The State of the Evangelical Trinitarian Resurgance." *JETS* 54, no. 4 (2001): 787–807.

———. "Stanley Grenz's Relatedness and Relevancy to British Evangelicalism." *Scottish Bulletin of Evangelical Theology* 28, no. 1 (2010): 62–79.

Shafer-Landau, Russ. *Moral Realism: A Defence*. Oxford University Press, 2003.

Shedd, William Greenough Thayer. *Dogmatic Theology*, Edited by Alan W. Gomes. 3rd ed. P&R, 2003.

Sidgwick, Henry. *Outlines of the History of Ethics*. Macmillan, 1886.

Simonetti, Manlio, ed. *Matthew 1–13*. Ancient Christian Commentary. InterVarsity, 2003.

Slote, Michael A. "Agent-Based Virtue Ethics." Pages 83–101 in *Moral Concepts*. Edited by Peter A. French, Theodore Edward Uehling and Howard K. Wettstein. MSP 20. University of Notre Dame Press, 1995.

———. *From Morality to Virtue*. Oxford University Press, 1992.

———. *Morals from Motives*. Oxford University Press, 2003.

———. "Moral Psychology." In *Concise Routledge Encyclopedia of Philosophy*. Edited by Edward Craig, 596. Taylor & Francis, 2002.

———. "Virtue Ethics and Democratic Values." *Journal of Social Philosophy* 24, no. 2 (1993): 5–37.

Smalley, Stephen S. *1, 2, 3 John*. WBC 51. Word, 1989.

Smeaton, George. *The Doctrine of the Atonement as Taught by Christ Himself*. 2nd ed. T&T Clark, 1871.

Smith, Geoffrey. "The Function of 'Likewise' (Osautos) in Romans 8:26." *TynBul* 49, no. 1 (1998): 29–38.

Smith, Ralph L. *Micah-Malachi*. WBC. Word, 1998.

Smith, R. Scott. *Virtue Ethics and Moral Knowledge: Philosophy of Language after Macintyre and Hauerwas*. Ashgate New Critical Thinking in Philosophy. Ashgate, 2003.

Snider, Andrew V. "Sanctification and Justification: A Unity of Distinctions." *MSJ* 21, no. 2 (2010): 159–178.

Solomon, Robert C. *Not Passion's Slave: Emotions and Choice. The Passionate Life*. Oxford University Press, 2003.

Songer, Harold S. "A Superior Priesthood: Hebrews 4:14–7:27." *RevExp* 82, no. 3 (1985): 345–359.

Sorley, W. R. "The Beginnings of English Philosophy." Pages 268–294 in vol. 4 of *The Cambridge History of English and American Literature*. Edited by W. A. Ward and A. R. Waller. Cambridge University Press, 1909.

Spohn, William. "The Return of Virtue Ethics." *TS* 53 (1992): 60–75.

Sprigge, T.L.S. "Idealism." Pages 379–380 in *Concise Routledge Encyclopedia of Philosophy*. Edited by Edward Craig. Taylor & Francis, 2002.

Sproul, R. C. "Molehills out of Mountains." *Tabletalk Magazine* 34, no. 5 (2010): 4–7.

Stackhouse, John J., ed. *Evangelical Futures: A Conversation on Theological Method*. Baker, 2000.

Stassen, Glen H. and David P. Gushee. *Kingdom Ethics: Following Jesus in Contemporary Context*. InterVarsity, 2003.

Statman, Daniel "Introduction to Virtue Ethics." Pages 1–41 in *Virtue Ethics*. Edited by Daniel Statman. Georgetown University Press, 1997.

Stein, Robert H. *Luke*. NAC. B&H, 1992.

Stiver, Dan R. *Theology after Ricoeur: New Directions in Hermeneutical Theology*. 1st ed. Westminster John Knox, 2001.

Stohr, Karen, and Christopher Heath Wellman. "Recent Work on Virtue Ethics." *American Philosophical Quarterly* 39, no. 1 (2002): 49–72.

Stott, John R. W. *The Message of Ephesians*. BST. InterVarity, 1979.

Strong, Augustus Hopkins. *Systematic Theology*, 3 vols. American Baptist Publication Society, 1907.

Sturgeon, Nicholas L. "Natualism in Ethics." Pages 615–616 in *Concise Routledge Encyclopedia of Philosophy*. Edited by Edward Craig. Taylor & Francis, 2002.

Swanson, Dennis M. "Bibliography of Works on Biblical Sanctification." *MSJ* 21, no. 2 (2010): 231–236.

Swete, Henry Barclay. *The Ascended Christ: A Study in the Earliest Christian Teaching*. Macmillan, 1910.

Symington, William. *The Atonement and Intercession of Jesus Christ*. Rep. ed. Reformation Heritage Books, 2006.

Tait, Arthur J. *The Heavenly Session of Our Lord: An Introduction to the History of the Doctrine*. Robert Scott, 1912.

Talbert, Charles H. *Ephesians and Colossians*. Paideia Commentaries on the New Testament. Baker Academic, 2007.

Tertullian. *Adversus Praxean.* Edited by E. Kroymann. CSEL 47. Hoelder-Pichler-Tempsky, 1906.

———. *De baptismo.* Edited by Augusti Reifferscheid and George Wissowa. CSEL 20. Hoelder-Pichler-Tempsky, 1890.

———. *De carnis resurrectione.* Edited by Aemilii Kroymann. CSEL 47. Hoelder-Pichler-Tempsky, 1906.

Thielman, Frank. *Ephesians.* BECNT. Baker Academic, 2010.

Thiselton, Anthony C. *The First Epistle to the Corinthians: A Commentary on the Greek Text.* NIGTC. Eerdmans, 2000.

Thompson, James W. *Hebrews.* Paideia Commentaries on the New Testament. Baker Academic, 2008.

Toon, Peter. *Justification and Sanctification.* Foundations for Faith. Crossway, 1983.

Topel, L. John. *Children of a Compassionate God: A Theological Exegesis of Luke 6:20–49.* Liturgical, 2001.

Torrance, James B. *Worship, Community, and the Triune God of Grace.* InterVarsity, 1996.

Torrance, Thomas F. *The Christian Doctrine of God: One Being Three Persons.* T&T Clark, 1996.

Torrell, Jean-Pierre. *The Person and His Work.* Vol. 1 of *Saint Thomas Aquinas.* Translated by Robert Royal. Rev. ed. Catholic University of America Press, 2005.

Tousley, Nikki Coffey, and Brad J. Kallenberg. "Virtue Ethics." In *Dictionary of Scripture and Ethics.* Edited by Joel B. Green. Baker Academic, 2011.

Towner, Philip H. "Mind/Reason." Pages 527–530 in *EDBT.* Edited by Walter A. Elwell. Baker, 1996.

Traill, Robert. "Sermon VI: 1 Peter 1:2." Pages 70–80 in vol. 4 of *Works of the Late Reverend Robert Traill.* J. Ogle, 1810.

Treier, Daniel J., and David Lauber. "Introduction." In *Trinitarian Theology for the Church: Scripture, Community, Worship.* IVP Academic, 2009.

Trianosky, Gregory Velazco y. "What Is Virtue Ethics All About?" *American Philosophical Quarterly* 27 (1990): 335–344.

Trueman, Carl. "A Man More Sinned Against Than Sinning? The Portrait of Martin Luther in Contemporary New Testament Scholarship: Some Casual Observations of a Mere Historian." http://www.crcchico.com.

Turner, David L. *Matthew.* BECNT. Baker Academic, 2008.

Turretin, Francis. *Instutio Theologiae Elencticae.* Vol. 1. Francisci Turrettini Opera. John D. Lowe, 1847.

Turretin, Francis. *Instutio Theologiae Elencticae.* Vol. 2. Robert Carter, 1847.

Vanhoozer, Kevin J., Craig G. Bartholomew, Daniel J. Treier, and N. T. Wright, eds. *Dictionary for Theological Interpretation of the Bible.* Baker Academic, 2005.

Vinson, Richard B. *Luke.* Smyth & Helwys Bible Commentary. Smyth & Helwys, 2008.

Voltaire. "*Foi ou Foy.*" Pages 505–506 in *Dictionnaire philosophique.* Cosse et Gaultier-Laguionie, 1838.

Wainwright, Arthur William. *The Trinity in the New Testament.* S.P.C.K., 1962.

Wainwright, Geoffrey. *Doxology: The Praise of God in Worship, Doctrine, and Life: A Systematic Theology*. Oxford University Press, 1980.

Walker, William O. *Interpolations in the Pauline Letters*. JSNT Sup 213. Sheffield Academic Press, 2001.

Wallace, Daniel B. *Greek Grammar Beyond the Basics: Exegetical Syntax of the New Testament*. Zondervan, 1999.

Walter, Steven E. "Mortification as an Expression of Regeneration." PhD. thesis, Mid-America Baptist Theological Seminary, 2009.

Wanamaker, Charles A. *The Epistles to the Thessalonians: A Commentary on the Greek Text*. NIGTC. Eerdmans, 1990.

Waltke, Bruce K. "Heart." Pages 331–332 in *EDBT*. Edited by Walter A. Elwell. Baker, 1996.

Walvoord, John F. *The Holy Spirit: A Comprehensive Study of the Person and Work of the Holy Spirit*. Zondervan, 2010.

Wannenwetsch, Bernd. "Luther's Moral Theology." Pages 120–135 in *The Cambridge Companion to Martin Luther*. Edited by Donald K. McKim. Cambridge Companions to Religion. Cambridge University Press, 2003.

Ware, Bruce A. *Father, Son, and Holy Spirit: Relationships, Roles, and Relevance*. Crossway, 2005.

Watson, Francis. *Text, Church and World: Biblical Interpretation in Theological Perspective*. Eerdmans, 1994.

Weaver, Jason G. "Paul's Call to Imitation: The Rhetorical Function of the Theme of Imitation in Its Epistolary Context." PhD. diss., The Catholic University of America, 2013.

Webster, John. *Holiness*. Eerdmans, 2003.

―――. "Theologies of Retrieval." Pages 583–599 in *The Oxford Handbook of Systematic Theology*. Edited by Kathryn Tanner, John Webster, and Iain Torrance. Oxford University Press, 2007.

Weiss, Johannes. *Der erste Korintherbrief*. Rep. ed. Vandenhoeck & Ruprecht, 1977.

Welch, Claude. *In This Name: The Doctrine of the Trinity in Contemporary Theology*. Scribner, 1952.

Wenham, Gordon J. *Genesis 1–15*. WBC 1. Word, 1998.

Wesley, John. "A Plain Account of Christian Perfection." Pages 158–250 in vol. 11 of *The Works of John Wesley*. Edited by Thomas Jackson. Wesleyan Methodist Book Room, 1872.

Whitacre, Rodney A. *John*. IVPNTC. InterVarsity, 1999.

Wilckens, Ulrich. *Der Brief an die Römer*. EKKNT 6. Neukirchener Verlag, 1978.

Wilkin, Robert N. "We Believe In: Sanctification: Part 2: Past Sanctification." *Journal of the Grace Evangelical Society* 6, no. 10 (1993). http://www.faithalone.org/journal.

―――. "We Believe In: Sanctification: Part 3: Present Sanctification: God's Role in Present Sanctification." *Journal of the Grace Evangelical Society* 7, no. 12 (1994). http://www.faithalone.org/journal.

_____. "We Believe In: Sanctification: Part 4: Man's Role in Present Sanctification." *Journal of the Grace Evangelical Society* 7, no. 13 (1994). http://www.faithalone.org/journal.

Wilkin, Robert N. to Ronald M. Rothenberg. "Question about Sanctification Articles." 26 June 2012, e-mail.

Williams, Bernard. "Moral Luck." *Aristotelian Society: Supplementary Volume* 50 (1976): 115–136.

Williams, Robert R. *Schleiermacher the Theologian: The Construction of the Doctrine of God*. Fortress, 1978.

Williams, Stephen. "The Theological Task and the Theological Method." Pages 159–177 in *Evangelical Futures: A Conversation on Theological Method*, ed. John J. Stackhouse. Baker, 2000.

Wilson, Jonathan R. *Gospel Virtues: Practicing Faith, Hope & Love in Uncertain Times*. InterVarsity, 1998.

_____. "Virtue(s)." In *Dictionary of Scripture and Ethics*, ed. Joel B. Green. Baker Academic, 2011.

Wilson, Scott Sparling. "Trinity and Sanctification: A Proposal for Understanding the Doctrine of Sanctification According to a Triune Ordering." PhD. diss., Southeastern Baptist Theological Seminary, 2009.

Winward, Stephen F. *Fruit of the Spirit*. Eerdmans, 1981.

Witmar, John A. *Romans*. In *The Bible Knowledge Commentary*. Edited by John F. Walvoord and Roy B. Zuck. Victor Books, 1985.

Wittgenstein, Ludwig. *Philosophische Untersuchungen*. 2nd ed. Blackwell, 1958.

Wolff, Christian. *Philosophia rationalis, sive Logica: methodo scientifica pertractata et as usum sicentiarum atque vitae aptata*. 3rd ed. Ex Typographia Dionysii Ramanzini, 1935.

Wood, Allen W. *Kant's Ethical Thought*. Cambridge University Press, 1999.

Woodill, Joseph. *The Fellowship of Life: Virtue Ethics and Orthodox Christianity*. Georgetown Universiy Press, 1998.

Wright, Christopher J. H. *Old Testament Ethics for the People of God*. InterVarsity, 2004.

Wright, John W., ed. *Postliberal Theology and the Church Catholic: Conversations with George Lindbeck, David Burrell, and Stanley Hauerwas*. Baker Academic, 2012.

Yarnell, Malcolm B., III. *The Formation of Christian Doctrine*. B&H Academic, 2007.

Yearly, Lee H. "Recent Work on Virtue." *Religious Studies Review* 16 (Jan 1990): 1–9.

Zizioulas, John. "The Doctrine of God the Trinity Today: Suggestions for an Ecumenical Study." Pages 19–32 in *A Selection of Papers Presented to the BCC Study Commission on Trinitarian Doctrine Today*. Edited by Alasdair I. C. Heron. The Forgotten Trinity 3. BCC/CCBI Inter-Church House, 1991.

Zwingli, Ulrich. *Huldreich Zwinglis sämtliche Werke: einzig vollständige Ausgabe der Werke Zwinglis*. Edited by Emil Egli, et al. 14 vols. Corpus Reformatorum, vols. 88–101. C. A. Schuetachke and Son, 1905–1956; reprint, Theologischer Verlag, 1982.

www.ingramcontent.com/pod-product-compliance
Lightning Source LLC
Chambersburg PA
CBHW072006110526
44592CB00012B/1220